AF564771

READING SKILLS FOR COLLEGE STUDIES

READING SKILLS FOR COLLEGE STUDIES

By

Dr. D.B. Rao

M.Sc., M.A., M.A., M.Ed., Ph.D. (Education)
Reader & Research Director
R.V.R. College of Education
Guntur – 52 006 (A.P.)
(India)

DISCOVERY PUBLISHING HOUSE PVT. LTD.
NEW DELHI-110002

First Published-2009

ISBN: 978-81-8356-431-1

Published by:

DISCOVERY PUBLISHING HOUSE PVT. LTD.
4831/24, Ansari Road, Prahlad Street
Darya Ganj, New Delhi-110 002 (India)
E-mail: dphtemp@indiatimes.com
dphbooks@rediffmail.com
Website: www.discoverypublishinghouse.com

Printed at:
Arora Enterprises
Laxmi Nagar, Delhi–110 092

Contents

Preface

Reading is one of the basic elements of language learning. It can be acquired both independently of and along with some other skills, like listening, speaking and of course comprehension. Generally, the skill of reading is developed in societies with a literary taste, because it can lead to develop comprehension and enrich vocabulary.

There is an adage, "Practice makes a man perfect." The proverb also holds true to the skill of reading. Regular reading, either, loudly or silently leads to the development of reading. An immediate effect of reading is increase in vocabulary, which helps gradually in acquisition of writing skill, which in turn is one of the most significant constituent of language learning. The more one reads, the more one writes.

For more proficient reading, there are certain other factors, which have to be taken into account. For instance, awareness of phonetics, vocabulary, comprehension and fluency. Phonetics deals with sounds of letters and their proper combination in a word, stress on certain letters of a word and voiced or unvoiced parts of the words. Similarly, vocabulary deals with meaning of words, which are directly related to comprehension. The richer the vocabulary, the better the reading.

In this area, much has been written by different educationists and linguists. But, they have dealt with some specific aspects of reading skill. Therefore, the need arose for a work, encompassing various aspects, within a single cover. Present work, namely, *Reading Skill for College Studies*, is an humble attempt in the same direction, which is expected to fill the bill.

Readers' enlightened feedback is always solicited

Preface

Skills for Reading

Reading is a significant part of educational process. Reading is the receptive skill in the written mode. It can develop independently of listening and speaking skills, but often develops along with them, especially in societies with a highly-developed literary tradition. Reading can help build vocabulary that helps listening comprehension at the later stages, particularly.

Here are some of the micro-skills involved in reading. The reader has to:

- decipher the script. In an alphabetic system or a syllabary, this means establishing a relationship between sounds and symbols. In a pictograph system, it means associating the meaning of the words with written symbols;
- recognise vocabulary;
- pick out key words, such as those identifying topics and main ideas;
- figure out the meaning of the words, including unfamiliar vocabulary, from the (written) context;
- recognise grammatical word classes: noun, adjective, etc.;
- detect sentence constituents, such as subject, verb, object, prepositions, etc.;

- recognise basic syntactic patterns;
- reconstruct and infer situations, goals and participants;
- use both knowledge of the world and lexical and grammatical cohesive devices to make the foregoing inferences, predict outcomes, and infer links and connections among the parts of the text;
- get the main point or the most important information;
- distinguish the main idea from supporting details;
- adjust reading strategies to different reading purposes, such as skimming for main ideas or studying in-depth.

Reading and Study Skill System

SURVEY – Gather the Information Necessary to Focus and Formulate Goals

1. Read the title – help your mind prepare to receive the subject at hand.
2. Read the introduction and/or summary – orient yourself to how this chapter fits the author's purposes, and focus on the author's statement of most important points.
3. Notice each boldface heading and subheading – organise your mind before you begin to read – build a structure for the thoughts and details to come.
4. Notice any graphics – charts, maps, diagrams, etc. are there to make a point – don't miss them.
5. Notice reading aids – italics, bold face print, chapter objective, end-of-chapter questions are all included to help you sort, comprehend, and remember.

QUESTION – Help Your Mind Engage and Concentrate

One section at a time, turn the boldface heading into as many questions as you think will be answered in that section. The better the questions, the better your comprehension is likely to be. You may always add further questions as you proceed. When your mind is actively searching for answers to questions it becomes engaged in learning.

READ – Fill in the Information Around the Mental Structures You've been Building

Read each section (one at a time) with your questions in mind. Look for the answers, and notice if you need to make up some new questions.

RECITE – Retrain Your Mind to Concentrate and Learn as it Reads

After each section stop, recall your questions, and see if you can answer them from memory. If not, look back again (as often as necessary) but don't go on to the next section until you can recite.

REVIEW – Refine Your Mental Organisation and Begin Building Memory

Once you've finished the entire chapter using the preceding steps, go back over all the questions from all the headings. See if you can still answer them. If not, look back and refresh your memory, then continue.

Reading Skill Acquisition

Reading skills acquisition is the process of acquiring the basic skills necessary for learning to read; that is, the ability to acquire meaning from print.

According to the report by the US National Reading Panel (NRP) in 2000, the skills required for proficient reading are phonological awareness, phonics (sound-symbol correspondence), fluency, vocabulary, and text comprehension.

Skills Required for Proficient Reading

According to the National Reading Panel, the ability to read requires proficiency in a number of language domains: phonemic awareness, phonics (sound-symbol correspondence), fluency, vocabulary, and text comprehension.

- *Phonemic Awareness:* The ability to distinguish and manipulate the individual sounds of language. The broader term, phonological awareness, also includes rhymes, syllables, and onsets and rimes.

- *Phonics:* Method that stresses the acquisition of letter-sound correspondences and their use in reading and spelling. This helps beginning readers understand how letters are linked to sounds (phonemes), patterns of letter-sound correspondences and spelling in English, and how to apply this knowledge when they read.
- *Fluency:* The ability to read orally with speed, accuracy, and vocal expression. The ability to read fluently is one of several critical factors necessary for reading comprehension. If a reader is not fluent, it may be difficult to remember what has been read and to relate the ideas expressed in the text to his or her background knowledge. This accuracy and automaticity of reading serves as a bridge between decoding and comprehension.
- *Vocabulary:* A critical aspect of reading comprehension is vocabulary development. When a reader encounters an unfamiliar word in print and decodes it to derive its spoken pronunciation, the reader understands the word if it is in the reader's spoken vocabulary. Otherwise, the reader must derive the meaning of the word using another strategy, such as context.
- *Reading Comprehension:* The NRP describes comprehension as a complex cognitive process in which a reader intentionally and interactively engages with the text. Reading comprehension is heavily dependent on skilled word recognition and decoding, oral reading fluency, a well-developed vocabulary and active engagement with the text.

Chall's Stages of Reading Development

Jeanne Chall's model of the stages of reading acquisition is well known. In Chall's model, each stage builds on skills mastered in earlier stages; lack of mastery at any level can halt the progress beyond that level.

Stage 0 – Pre-reading: The learner gains familiarity with the language and its sounds. A person in this stage becomes aware of sound similarities between words, learns to predict the next part in a familiar story, and may start to recognise a few familiar written words. Chall's Stage 0 is considered comparable to what is often called "reading readiness." Typically developing readers achieve this stage about the age of 6.

Stage 1 – Initial Reading Stage, or Decoding Stage: The learner becomes aware of the relationship between sounds and letters and begins applying the knowledge to text. This demonstrates the reader has achieved understanding of the critical concept of the alphabetic principle and is learning sound-symbol correspondences, the alphabetic code. Typically developing readers usually reach this stage by the age of 6 or 7.

Stage 2 – Confirmation: This stage involves confirming the knowledge acquired in the previous two stages and gaining fluency in those skills. Decoding skills continue to improve, and they begin to develop speed in addition to accuracy in word recognition. At this point, the reader should be able to give attention both to meaning and to the print, using them interactively to build their skills and fluency. This stage is critical for the beginning reader. If the developing reader stops making progress during this stage, the individual remains, in Chall's words, "glued to the print." Typically developing readers usually reach this stage around the age of 8.

Stage 3 – Reading to Learn: At this stage, the motivation for reading changes. The reader has enough reading skill to begin to read text in order to gain information. Readers' vocabulary development accelerates at this point resulting from increased exposure to the written word. Typically developing children usually achieve this stage in 4th grade, around the age of 9.

Stage 4 – Multiple Viewpoints: The reader at this stage begins to be able to analyse what they read, understand different points of view, and react critically to what they read. Typical readers are developing this skill set during the high school years, around ages 14 to 19.

Stage 5 – Construction and Judgement: At this stage, readers have learned to read selectively and form their own opinions about what they read; they construct their knowledge from that of others. This highest level of reading development is not usually reached until college age, or later, and may in fact be achieved only by those who have an intellectual inclination.

Reading Speed

Speed reading can help you to read and understand written information much more quickly. This makes it an essential skill in any environment where you have to master large volumes of information quickly, as is the norm in fast-moving professional environments. What's more, it's a key technique to learn if you suffer from "information overload", because it helps you to become much more discriminating about the information that you consume.

The Key Insight

The most important trick about speed reading is to know what information you want from a document before you start reading it. If you only want an outline of the issue that the document discusses, then you can skim the document quickly and extract only the essential facts. If you need to understand the real detail of the document, then you need to read it slowly enough to gain the full understanding you need.

You will get the greatest time savings from speed reading by learning to skim excessively detailed documents, although the techniques you'll learn will help you to improve the speed of all the reading you do.

Technical Issues

Even when you know how to ignore irrelevant detail, there are other technical improvements you can make to your reading style which will increase your reading speed.

Most people learn to read the way young children read – either letter-by-letter, or word-by-word. As an adult, this is probably not the way you read now: Just think about how your eye muscles are moving as you read this. You will probably find that you are fixing your eyes on one block of words, then moving your eyes to the next block of words, and so on. You are reading blocks of words at a time, not individual words one-by-one. You may also notice that you do not always go from one block to the next: sometimes you may move back to a previous block if you are unsure about something.

A skilled reader will read many words in each block. He or she will only dwell on each block for an instant, and will then move on. Only rarely will the reader's eyes skip back to a previous block of words. This reduces the amount of work that the reader's eyes have to do. It also increases the volume of information that can be assimilated in a given period of time.

A poor reader will become bogged down, spending a lot of time reading small blocks of words. He or she will skip back often, losing the flow and structure of the text, and confusing his or her overall understanding of the subject. This irregular eye movement makes reading tiring. Poor readers tend to dislike reading, and they may find it harder to concentrate, and understand written information.

How to Use Tool

Speed reading aims to improve reading skills by:

- increasing the number of words read in each block;
- reducing the length of time spent reading each block;
- reducing the number of times your eyes skip back to a previous sentence.

These are explained below:

- *Increasing the Number of Words in Each Block:* This needs a conscious effort. Try to expand the number of words that you read at a time: With practice, you'll find you read faster. You may also find that you can increase the number of words in each block by holding the text a little further from your eyes. The more words you can read in each block, the faster you will read!
- *Reducing Fixation Time:* The minimum length of time needed to read each block is probably only a quarter of a second. By pushing yourself to reduce the time you take, you will get better at picking up information quickly. Again, this is a matter of practice and confidence.
- *Reducing Skip-back:* To reduce the number of times that your eyes skip back to a previous sentence, run a pointer along the line as you read. This could be a finger, or a pen or pencil. Your eyes will follow the tip of your pointer, smoothing the flow of your reading. The speed at which you read using this

method will largely depend on the speed at which you move the pointer.

You will be able to increase your reading speed a certain amount on your own by applying these speed reading techniques.

What you don't get out of self-study is the use of specialist reading machines and the confidence gained from successful speed-reading – this is where a good one-day course can revolutionise your reading skills.

Key Points

By speed reading you can read information more quickly. You may also get a better understanding of it, as you will hold more of it in short term memory.

To improve the speed of your reading, read more words in each block and reduce the length of time spent reading each block. Use a pointer to smooth the way your eyes move and reduce skip-back.

Reading Strategies

Good reading strategies help you to read in a very efficient way. Using them, you aim to get the maximum benefit from your reading with the minimum effort. The six different strategies to read intelligently are giving below.

Strategy 1: Knowing What You Want to Know

The first thing to ask yourself is: Why you are reading the text? Are you reading with a purpose or just for pleasure? What do you want to know after reading it?

Once you know this, you can examine the text to see whether it is going to move you towards this goal.

An easy way of doing this is to look at the introduction and the chapter headings. The introduction should let you know whom the book is targeted at, and what it seeks to achieve. Chapter headings will give you an overall view of the structure of the subject.

Ask yourself whether the book meets your needs. Ask yourself if it assumes too much or too little knowledge. If the book isn't ideal, would it be better to find a better one?

Strategy 2: Knowing How Deeply to Study the Material

Where you only need the shallowest knowledge of the subject, you can skim material. Here you read only chapter headings, introductions and summaries.

If you need a moderate level of information on a subject, then you can scan the text. Here you read the chapter introductions and summaries in detail. You may then speed read the contents of the chapters, picking out and understanding key words and concepts. At this level of looking at the document it is worth paying attention to diagrams and graphs.

Only when you need detailed knowledge of a subject is it worth studying the text. Here it is best to skim the material first to get an overview of the subject. This gives you an understanding of its structure, into which you can fit the detail gained from a full, receptive reading of the material.

Strategy 3: Active Reading

When you are reading a document in detail, it often helps if you highlight, underline and annotate it as you go on. This emphasises information in your mind, and helps you to review important points later.

Doing this also helps to keep your mind focused on the material and stops it wandering.

This is obviously only something to do if you own the document! If you own the book and find that active reading helps, then it may be worth photocopying information in more expensive texts. You can then read and mark the photocopies.

If you are worried about destroying the material, ask yourself how much your investment of time is worth. If the benefit you get by active reading reasonably exceeds the value of the book, then the book is disposable.

Strategy 4: How to Study Different Sorts of Material

Different sorts of documents hold information in different places and in different ways. They have different depths and breadths of coverage. By understanding the layout of the material you are reading, you can extract useful information much more efficiently.

Reading Magazines and Newspapers: These tend to give a very fragmented coverage of an area. They will typically only concentrate on the most interesting and glamorous parts of a topic – this helps them to sell copies! They will often ignore less interesting information that may be essential to a full understanding of a subject. Typically areas of useful information are padded out with large amounts of irrelevant waffle or with advertising.

The most effective way of getting information from magazines is to scan the contents tables or indexes and turn directly to interesting articles. If you find an article useful, then cut it out and file it in a folder specifically covering that sort of information. In this way you will build up sets of related articles that may begin to explain the subject.

Newspapers tend to be arranged in sections. If you read a paper often, you can learn quickly which sections are useful and which ones you can skip altogether.

Reading Individual Articles: Articles within newspapers and magazines tend to be in three main types:

- *News Articles:* Here the most important information is presented first, with information being less and less useful as the article progresses. News articles are designed to explain the key points first, and then flesh them out with detail.
- *Opinion Articles:* Opinion articles present a point of view. Here the most important information is contained in the introduction and the summary, with the middle of the article containing supporting arguments.
- *Feature Articles:* These are written to provide entertainment or background on a subject. Typically the most important information is in the body of the text.

If you know what you want from an article, and recognise its type, you can extract information from it quickly and efficiently.

Strategy 5: Reading 'Whole Subject' Documents

When you are reading an important document, it is easy to accept the writer's structure of thought. This can mean that you may not notice that important information has been omitted or that irrelevant detail has been included. A good way of recognising this is to compile your own table of contents before you open the document. You can then use this table of contents to read the document in the order that you want. You will be able to spot omissions quickly.

Strategy 6: Using Glossaries with Technical Documents

If you are reading large amounts of difficult technical material, it may be useful to photocopy or compile a glossary. Keep this beside you as you read. It will probably also be useful to note down the key concepts in your own words, and refer to them when necessary.

Usually it is best to make notes as you go. Effective way of doing this include creating Concept Maps or using the Cornell Note Taking System.

Key Points

This section shows six different strategies and techniques that you can use to read more effectively.

These are:

- Knowing what you need to know, and reading appropriately.
- Knowing how deeply to read the document: skimming, scanning or studying.
- Using active reading techniques to pick out key points and keep your mind focused on the material.
- Using the table of contents for reading magazines and newspapers, and clipping useful articles.
- Understanding how to extract information from different article types.
- Creating your own table of contents for reviewing material.
- Using indexes, tables of contents, and glossaries to help you assimilate technical information.

Centrality of Word: Knowledge

The brain holds much insight into how children and adults learn to read words and develop reading skills. In particular, word knowledge is important in how the brain reads, according to

Charles Perfetti, associate director of the learning research and development centre at the University of Pittsburgh.

Perfetti shared his research at the third annual Jeanne Chall Lecture, "Beyond Decoding: The Centrality of Word Knowledge to Reading Skill,". Chall was a professor at HGSE and a leading expert in her field. Her seminal work on reading research and instruction influenced scholarship on the teaching of reading in schools and universities throughout the country. "As someone who's a researcher on science and only occasionally on education and reading, I'm an admirer of Chall," Perfetti said. "It's a privilege to be here."

Learning to read is difficult. To date, educators have used a variety of methods like teaching phonics, word meanings, balanced instruction in phonics and word meaning, and whole word study, in teaching children to read. Perfetti's research focuses on the context of words and how neuroscience can add another dimension to understanding how one learns to read. When children or adults learn to read words, Perfetti studies the brain's response or, rather the "reading network." Most notably the brain's reading network responds to training, he said, which supports a Chall article from the 1970s in which she wrote that learning to read isn't a right or left-brain activity, but rather something entirely dependent upon good instruction.

Perfetti tests many common aspects of learning to read – like reading words in context, learned definitions, phonics, and rare words – in the brains of both skilled and low-skilled readers. The results demonstrate that skilled and low-skilled readers often have different efficiency levels based on learning methods and reaction times. For example, when a child sees an unfamiliar word, the brain shows a negative shift within 400 milliseconds, Perfetti said. But if that same unfamiliar word is put into some type of context or paraphrased, skilled readers respond better whereas less-skilled readers have a more "sluggish" response when integrating words in text. Perfetti suspects this has to do with the reader's knowledge of the word.

"Word meaning is the link between decoding and comprehension," Perfetti said. This is even true of adults, who during one study were trained on the meaning of some rare words like "gloaming" and "tiglon." Perfetti then tested the adults on trained and untrained word meaning recognition while charting the brain response. Perfetti noticed that when both skilled and low-skilled readers saw the familiar or trained words, they would attempt to recall the meaning. However, the skilled readers were more successful, which may indicate that word meaning can affect ability to learn to read words efficiently.

"This (brain) provides timing information on the unfolding of cognitive events in reading and learning," Perfetti said.

While this timing may have implications for educational practice, Perfetti also cautioned that educators shouldn't throw out what they already know about teaching word form and meaning either.

"We have a lot of technology that is helpful in practice," he said, pointing out that a larger problem in the field is the failure to identify a child's motivation in seeking to read on their own.

Improving a Child's Reading Skill

We love to hear our children reading for the first time, it gives us a sense of accomplishment. For many children reading has become a chore and it shouldn't be this way. Over the past years children have struggled with reading and often fall behind in school. One way to help your child to keep up with the rest of his class is through continuous reading.

It's very necessary to talk about something that many parents do when they begin to teach their child to read. It is an instinct in many of us to correct our child while they are reading and we shouldn't. Correcting your child doesn't help them learn it only shows them that they made a mistake. Instead of correcting your child when they first begin to read, you should allow them time to correct themselves.

Read to Your Child at a Fast Pace

When you first begin to read to your child you should do it like you normally would so that they can try to keep up. Your child will more than likely not understand or know the words that you are reading but in time they will know where you are at in the paragraph by seeing you constantly read and through memorisation. The idea here is to teach them to follow along. If you don't think that they can follow along as you read in the beginning then use your finger as a guide until you have read the book a few times.

Beginning Reading

Teaching your child to read should begin with books that are below their grade level and work your way up. If you start your child on a book that is on their grade level and yet they don't seem to know the words then it will be much harder for them to read it. If you start out with books that are below their grade level and they seem to catch onto it fast then it might be time to move up a level.

Correcting the Child's Mistakes

As said before; correcting a child's mistakes comes natural to most parents. We try to shield our children and sometimes we can go too far. After you have read a book a few times and decide that it is time for your child to take over, allow them to make mistakes while reading without correcting them. Most children will realise that they have made a mistake when they notice that the word that they have said sounds different from the way that you said it. I usually read a book to my child, read it together by taking turns, and then allow them to read it by themselves.

Reading should be fun and not something that your child feels is a chore. Many professionals such as paediatricians have been explaining the benefits of reading at a young age to many parents. The idea behind reading to children is that they will develop a love for it and want to do it.

Personal Reading Improvement

1. The Basic Programme
   a. Two or three times a day, read something you enjoy for 15 to 20 minutes without stopping. Time yourself to within 30 seconds.
   b. Record your reading rate and chart your progress. Recording and charting are essential if you wish to make real progress.

2. Speed – push yourself gently as you read. If your mind wanders, get it back on track.
3. Vocabulary – Wait until you've finished reading to look up unfamiliar words. (If you stop, you'll reduce your level of comprehension).
4. Comprehension – to improve comprehension, recite the chapter after closing the book. See how many specific details you can recall. The more you interact with your text, the more you'll recall. Recollection and comprehension require a vigorous approach.
5. Practice – twice a week for an hour, use Speed Reader II. This excellent computer reading programme will boost your rate, eventually resulting in skill transfer.
6. Rate Goals – set reading rate goals for yourself. A 10 per cent increase in your reading rate over the previous record is a good rule of thumb.
7. Skimming and Scanning – find an interesting newspaper column or magazine article. Rapidly read the article, sampling just the first sentence or two of each paragraph and a few key words. Jot down all the facts you can remember. Then reread the article slowly, giving yourself a point for every item you can recall.

Calculating Words Per Minute

Example Problem

Using the information below, determine your reading speed (WPM):

1. Multiply the number of pages by the number of words per page.
2. Multiply the number of lines by the number of words per line.
3. Add the products of steps 1 and 2.
4. Divide the total number of words by the reading time.

Reading Skills for Teens

Reading is often discussed at the elementary levels. But what does a parent do to help reluctant readers in their teens? Or how about a college-bound high schooler getting ready for those tough entrance exams?

Three skills can help both groups reach their potential as readers. As a bonus, all of their schoolwork, even maths, will benefit from their efforts:

Skim to Find Themes

Choose a newspaper article that appeals to your teen (sports or fashion will work just fine). Tell him to use his index finger to pull his eyes through the article as quickly as possible. Then ask what he thinks the article was about.

Show him how to use the headline as his first clue, the opening sentence as the second, and how to select key words with his eyes for the third.

Next, have her read another article using her regular reading strategies. Then reread the same passage, repeating the first step (placing her finger on the page to pull her eyes through the text). Was this method faster? Did she learn even more?

This skill works with any printed material. The technique works best when readers need to know general content, not details, or when they are reviewing material they have already read in preparation for a test.

Scan to Find Facts

An even faster method, scanning helps find specific facts that are buried in pages of more general information.

Using a passage you have read, instruct your teens to find one fact that you have already discovered in the text. This could be a statistic, a name, an important date, or the name of the town where someone was born.

Tell them what to look for. Remind them they do not need to know what the text says; they just need to find the fact. Use a 3 by 5 card to help them scan, and see how quickly they can locate the fact. This works best if you use specific words the first time you do this, and then become more general as you practice.

Search to Gather Resources

Much of the work done at the high school level requires research. For students who struggle to read, the amount of information that technology allows us to compile can be overwhelming. Use this exercise to teach students to gather the most relevant information.

Take a subject your teen loves and help him/her discover the many ways to find information on it (e.g. internet search, online databases, wikipaedia, google scholar, card catalogues, magazine searches). He does not need to write about or read any of what he finds – the exercise is simply to see how much he can find.

Help him/her narrow the topic he/she chooses or she will be overwhelmed with information. Does he/she love baseball? Encourage him/her to choose her favourite player or to limit the search to one season, and then begin. Has he/she chosen to research rock stars? Choose one artist and one year, then begin.

When searching for books in the card catalogue or library database, choose a subject keyword that the catalogue recognises such as music or popular music. Ask your local librarian for assistance with this. After locating the books in the library, help your teen use the table of contents and the index to find the information they want. Once they have spotted it, they're done!

With magazines and the internet, encourage your student to identify specific titles that contain the required information. Again, encourage your student to save the reading until later. The key now is to learn how much information is available and how to conduct a search. This skill will put them light years ahead of their classmates when a research project is assigned.

Improving Reading Skills

Ask yourself this question: Do I read every word in my own language when I am reading a schedule, summary, or other outlining document? The answer is most definitely: No! Reading in English is like reading in your native language. This means that it is not always necessary to read and understand each and every word in English. Remember that reading skills in your native language and English are basically the same.

Here is a quick overview of the four types of reading skills used in every language:

Skimming

Skimming is used to quickly gather the most important information, or 'gist'. Run your eyes over the text, noting important information. Use skimming to quickly get-up to speed on a current business situation. It's not essential to understand each word when skimming.

Examples of Skimming:

- The Newspaper (quickly to get the general news of the day).
- Magazines (quickly to discover which articles you would like to read in more detail).
- Business and Travel Brochures (quickly to get informed).

Scanning

Scanning is used to find a particular piece of information. Run your eyes over the text looking for the specific piece of information you need. Use scanning on schedules, meeting plans, etc. in order to find the specific details you require. If you see words or phrases that you don't understand, don't worry when scanning.

Examples of Scanning

- The "What's on TV" section of your newspaper.
- A train/airplane schedule.
- A conference guide.

Extensive Reading

Extensive reading is used to obtain a general understanding of a subject and includes reading longer texts for pleasure, as well as business books. Use extensive reading skills to improve your general knowledge of business procedures. Do not worry if you understand each word.

Examples of Extensive Reading

- The latest marketing strategy book.
- A novel you read before going to bed.
- Magazine articles that interest you.

Intensive Reading

Intensive reading is used on shorter texts in order to extract specific information. It includes very close accurate reading for detail. Use intensive reading skills to grasp the details of a specific situation. In this case, it is important that you understand each word, number or fact.

Examples of Intensive Reading

- A bookkeeping report.
- An insurance claim.
- A contract.

Now that you've reviewed the four reading skills, take this reading skills quiz to help you improve reading skills through understanding of these basic reading types.

Important Reading Skills

High school teachers are less likely to teach important reading skills to classes of students they view as "non-college bound" than to classes of students they feel are headed for college, according to results from ACT's recently completed National Curriculum Survey. The results indicate that teachers are particularly less likely to teach certain higher level reading skills to classes made up primarily of students who they assume aren't going to college.

"These results are troubling, particularly since we don't really know what criteria schools are using to categorise students as 'non-college bound,'" said Cynthia Schmeiser, ACT's senior vice president of research and development. "If students are unfairly labelled as non-college bound in middle school or high school, the negative consequences can affect them for the rest of their lives."

The US Department of Labour reports that all of the job categories projected to have faster-than-average employment growth in the next decade require at least a post-secondary vocational or academic certificate, and many require two or four-year college degrees.

"More and more jobs are requiring at least some type of education beyond high school," said Schmeiser. "As a result, the large majority of students will, in fact, end up going on to post-secondary education, and they will need strong reading skills to do well."

The need for strong reading skills, however, is not limited to jobs that require a college degree. Results from ACT's WorkKeys programme, an assessment system of foundational skills necessary for success in the workplace, indicate that a person would need a reading skill level of at least 5 – comparable to what is needed by an entering college freshman – to be prepared for 80 per cent of the jobs that pay more than minimum wage but that don't demand a four-year degree.

"A lot of jobs that don't require a four-year college degree – from assemblers to clerk-typists to sales representatives – demand good critical reading and comprehension skills," said Thomas Saterfiel, ACT's senior vice president of corporate development.

In addition, some educators argue that students' plans after high school should have no impact on the type of education they receive.

"In a standards-based system – which is what 49 states have committed to – there should be no differences between college bound and non-college bound in terms of basic reading instruction," said Carol Jago, a high school English teacher, author, and co-director of UCLA's California Reading and Literature Project. "All students are expected and deserve to be taught to read with comprehension. Important reading skills should be absolutes."

ACT conducts its National Curriculum Survey every three to four years to determine what specific knowledge and skills are being taught in America's secondary schools and expected of incoming college freshmen. The survey is completed by high school and junior high teachers and instructors of first-year college courses in the areas of maths, science, English, and reading across the country. The results are used to guide the development of ACT's curriculum-based assessment programmes.

The curriculum survey results show a high level of agreement between secondary school teachers and college instructors on what reading skills are most important for students to learn and know. Among these skills are:

- Making inferences from the text concerning the main idea(s).
- Recognising and recalling main ideas by summarising.
- Drawing conclusions from information given.

- Making inferences from the text concerning details that support the main idea(s).
- Recognising and recalling specific details.

Secondary teachers' responses indicate that a large majority—around three-fourths—of the reading skills in the survey are taught with greater frequency in high school courses composed primarily of college bound students than in courses composed primarily of non-college bound students. Some of the greatest disparities in this regard are in higher-order reading skills such as:

- Analysing a text to identify an author's unstated assumptions.
- Evaluating information in a text for completeness.
- Recognising and understanding the use of satire.
- Analysing a text to identify confusing, ambiguous, or vague language.

Although these critical reading skills are ranked below more functional skills in terms of overall importance by both high school and college instructors, all of the reading skills in the survey are deemed by teachers as important for students to learn and know.

"The distinction isn't in what teachers think is important; it's in what they are actually teaching," said Schmeiser.

The findings of the survey are based on the responses of 297 college instructors, 495 high school teachers, and 249 junior high/middle school teachers from across the nation. College instructors rated each of 64 reading skills according to its importance as a prerequisite for students' success with the reading required by their classes. Secondary English/language arts teachers indicated whether each skill was or was not taught in a particular course they teach and the importance placed on each skill in that course.

Trauma Risk

Good reading skills may not only earn children better grades in school but may keep them safer too.

Difficult kids lead difficult lives, depressed kids lead psychologically vulnerable lives, but good readers have a better chance of avoiding trouble and its aftermath, according to a 15-

year prospective study connecting childhood personality and behaviour to later trauma exposure.

Researchers from Johns Hopkins University and Michigan State University studied 2,311 children who entered first grade in the mid-1980s in a large mid-Atlantic city and followed them until young adulthood. About 67 per cent were members of minority groups, 52 per cent received subsidised or free lunches (an indicator of poverty status), and there was about an equal number of boys and girls.

When they entered school, the students were evaluated by reading-readiness tests, depression and anxiety self-reports and by their teachers for aggressive or disruptive behaviours, concentration problems, and low social interaction or shyness. When the students were between the ages of 20 and 23, the 1,698 available for follow-up (about 75 per cent of the original group) were interviewed about traumatic events in their lives and PTSD symptoms. Traumatic events included assaultive violence (such as being raped, beaten, or shot) and other experiences such as serious accidents, natural disasters, or hearing of a close friend's or relative's injury or unexpected death.

An estimated 82.5 per cent of these children experienced one or more *DSM-IV* qualifying traumatic events in their lives. Among that group, 47.2 per cent experienced assaultive violence.

"We found that the occurrence of traumatic events up to age 6-7 was less than 1 per cent, and that age-specific occurrence rose markedly after age 15, with the highest rate observed between 16 and 18 years of age," said Carla Storr, Sc. D., and Nicholas Ialongo, Ph.D., of Johns Hopkins University and James Anthony, Ph.D., and Naomi Breslau, Ph.D., of Michigan State University. Their findings appear in the January *American Journal of Psychiatry*. Grants from the National Institute of Mental Health and National Institute on Drug Abuse funded the study.

Teacher ratings in the first grade of aggressive or disruptive behaviour that fell into the highest two quartiles pointed to nearly double the risk of exposure to an assaultive event, but not to other traumatic events in the absence of assaultive violence.

Children in the highest quartile of concentration problems were also at higher risk for exposure to assaultive violence, but not other kinds of trauma. Those with the highest reading-readiness scores were less likely to experience assaultive violence than were children scoring in the lowest quartile.

About 8.8 per cent of children who experienced a traumatic event developed post-traumatic stress disorder (PTSD). There was an association between risk of PTSD and first-grade levels of anxious or depressive mood, but it was not statistically significant.

"The results suggest potential risk factors for PTSD that can be identified early in life and might be amenable to interventions," the researchers noted.

In a separate long-term study, Breslau, Victoria Lucia, Ph.D., and German Alvarado, M.D., M.P.H., all from the Department of Epidemiology at Michigan State University, examined the relationship of IQ measurements to trauma and PTSD. That study appeared in the November 2006 *Archives of General Psychiatry.* It included children randomly selected from 1983-1985 discharge lists of one urban and one suburban hospital in southeast Michigan and was originally designed to look at the sequelae of low birth weights in the communities served by the hospitals. Of the 823 children enrolled in the study, 713 were followed until age 17. Breslau and her colleagues adjusted their results to account for a disproportionately high percentage of children born at less than normal weight.

The most common traumatic event in this cohort was learning of the sudden, unexpected death of a close friend or relative. Traumatic events occurred more often among boys than girls and more often among urban than suburban youth.

The researchers found that children who had an IQ of at least 115 at age 6 were at lower risk for exposure to traumatic events or assaultive trauma or to have PTSD by age 17.

Exposure to traumatic events and PTSD was determined at age 17 through a computerised version of the National Institute of Mental Health Diagnostic Interview Schedule. After all lifetime *DSM-IV*-qualifying traumatic events were identified, respondents selected the worst event they had experienced. *DSM-IV* algorithms were then applied to diagnose PTSD. Above-normal ratings of externalising problems for 6-year-olds indicated increased risk of exposure to assaultive violence.

The researchers did note that while high IQ – at least one standard deviation above the population mean – appeared protective against PTSD, lower than normal IQ did not increase risk.

At present, Breslau told *Psychiatric News,* she can only speculate about the mechanisms by which reading or higher IQ (which are related) are protective. For instance, people with higher IQs may become better educated and take greater care to avoid potentially traumatic events. Or they may be able to cope better after experiencing trauma.

"If exposed to a difficult situation, they face a cognitive challenge to their views of themselves and their world, but they may tell themselves, I've solved problems before, I'm capable, I can handle this situation,'" she said.

Children with behavioural problems may choose more dangerous peers or take more risks, making them more likely to become victims of crime or accidents.

This IQ-PTSD link applies to both urban and suburban youth, she noted.

Breslau, a sociologist and psychiatric epidemiologist, is continuing to analyse study data to track the interaction of cognitive abilities, conduct problems, and emotional problems through the elementary-school years. Conceivably, better understanding of predisposing factors for trauma and PTSD may allow early interventions that could lessen their risk as the child passes through life.

Critical Reading towards Critical Writing

Critical writing depends on critical reading. Most of the papers you write will involve reflection on written texts – the thinking and research that has already been done on your subject. In order to write your own analysis of this subject, you will need to do careful critical reading of sources and to use them critically to make your own argument. The judgements and interpretations you make of the texts you read are the first steps towards formulating your own approach.

Critical Reading: What is It?

To read critically is to make judgements about how a text is argued. This is a highly reflective skill requiring you to "stand back" and gain some distance from the text you are reading. (You might have to read a text through once to get a basic grasp of content before you launch into an intensive critical reading.) The key is this:

- Don't read looking only or primarily for information.
- Do read looking for ways of thinking about the subject matter.

When you are reading, highlighting, or taking notes, avoid extracting and compiling lists of evidence, lists of facts and examples. Avoid approaching a text by asking "What information can I get out of it?" Rather ask "How does this text work? How is it argued? How is the evidence (the facts, examples, etc.) used and interpreted? How does the text reach its conclusions?

How Do I Read Looking for Ways of Thinking?

1. First determine the central claims or purpose of the text (its thesis). A critical reading attempts to assess how these central claims are developed or argued.
2. Begin to make some judgements about context. What audience is the text written for? Who is it in dialogue with? (This will probably be other scholars or authors with differing viewpoints.) In what historical context is it written? All these matters of context can contribute to your assessment of what is going on in a text.
3. Distinguish the kinds of reasoning the text employs. What concepts are defined and used? Does the text appeal to a theory or theories? Is any specific methodology laid out? If there is an appeal to a particular concept, theory, or method, how is that concept, theory, or method then used to organise and interpret the data? You might also examine how the text is organised: how has the author analysed (broken down) the material? Be aware that different disciplines (i.e. history, sociology, philosophy, biology) will have different ways of arguing.

4. Examine the evidence (the supporting facts, examples, etc.) the text employs. Supporting evidence is indispensable to an argument. Having worked through Steps 1-3, you are now in a position to grasp how the evidence is used to develop the argument and its controlling claims and concepts. Steps 1-3 allow you to see evidence in its context. Consider the kinds of evidence that are used. What counts as evidence in this argument? Is the evidence statistical, literary or historical, etc.? From what sources is the evidence taken? Are these sources primary or secondary?
5. Critical reading may involve evaluation. Your reading of a text is already critical if it accounts for and makes a series of judgements about how a text is argued. However, some essays may also require you to assess the strengths and weaknesses of an argument. If the argument is strong, why? Could it be better or differently supported? Are there gaps, leaps, or inconsistencies in the argument? Is the method of analysis problematic? Could the evidence be interpreted differently? Are the conclusions warranted by the evidence presented? What are the unargued assumptions? Are they problematic? What might an opposing argument be?

Some Practical Tips

1. Critical reading occurs after some preliminary processes of reading. Begin by skimming research materials, especially introductions and conclusions, in order to strategically choose where to focus your critical efforts.
2. When highlighting a text or taking notes from it, teach yourself to highlight argument: those places in a text where an author explains her analytical moves, the concepts she uses, how she uses them, how she arrives at conclusions. Don't let yourself foreground and isolate facts and examples, no matter how interesting they may be. First, look for the large patterns that give purpose, order, and meaning to those examples. The opening sentences of paragraphs can be important to this task.
3. When you begin to think about how you might use a portion of a text in the argument you are forging in your own paper,

try to remain aware of how this portion fits into the whole argument from which it is taken. Paying attention to context is a fundamental critical move.

4. When you quote directly from a source, use the quotation critically. This means that you should not substitute the quotation for your own articulation of a point. Rather, introduce the quotation by laying out the judgements you are making about it, and the reasons why you are using it. Often a quotation is followed by some further analysis.
5. Critical reading skills are also critical listening skills. In your lectures, listen not only for information but also for ways of thinking. Your instructor will often explicate and model ways of thinking appropriate to a discipline.

Methods of Reading

The Behaviour

Psychology is concerned with the study of the behaviour of all living organisms. The various methods it adopts for such study can be named as below:

1. Introspection Method.
2. Observation Method.
3. Psycho-analytic Method.
4. Experimental Method.
5. Differential Method.
6. Survey Method.
7. Clinical Method.
8. Questionnaire Method.
9. Interview Method.
10. Rating Method.
11. Case Study Method.
12. Sociometric Method.
13. Projective Methods.

All these above methods have their own merits and limitations with regard to their use in the study of behaviour. Therefore, decision of using a particular method or methods in a particular situation for studying the behaviour of particular subject depends upon so many factors like whose behaviour is to be studied, what is the purpose of this study, what facilities, resources and equipments are available for the study, etc.

Keeping all these things in view the task of the behaviour investigation requires proper knowledge, understanding and skill of the various methods mentioned above. However, for the purpose of this text we are hereby concentrating our attention on a few important methods like observation, experimental, Interview, Survey and Case study only.

Reading Methods

Definition of Experimental Method: In experimental method due emphasis is laid on the experiments and their subsequent observed results. The word experiment comes from a Latin word meaning "to try", "put to the test". Therefore, in experimentation we try or put to the test the material or phenomenon, the characteristics or consequences of which we wish to ascertain. In sciences, while doing such experiments in an indoor or outdoor laboratory in natural environment, we may be interested to learn the effect of friction on motion, the effect of sunlight on the growth of the plants, etc.

In psychology also, we perform such experiments in our psychological laboratory or outside laboratory in the physical or social settings to study the cause and effect relationship regarding the nature of human behaviour, *i.e.* the effect of anxiety, drugs or stresses on the human behaviour, effect of intelligence or the participation in co-curricular activities on the academic performance of the students. In performing all such experiments we try to establish certain cause and effect relationship through the objective observations of the actions performed and the subsequent changes produced under prearranged or rigidly controlled conditions. From these observations certain conclusions are drawn and theories or principles are formulated.

Features and Characteristics: Main features and characteristics of the experimental method may be summarised as below:

- Psychological experiments performed in this method essentially require two persons, the experimenter and the subject or the person whose behaviour is to be observed.
- Psychological experiments are always conducted on living organisms in contrast to experiments in physical sciences which are generally conducted on inorganic or dead subjects.
- The key factor in this method is the controlling of the conditions or variables. By this control we can eliminate irrelevant conditions or variables and isolate relevant ones. In this way, we become able to observe the casual relationship between two phenomena keeping all other conditions almost constant.

Let us illustrate this feature of experimental method with the help of an example.

Suppose under an experimental study of the behaviour, we want to study the effect of intelligence on academic achievement. Then we will definitely need to discover the causative relation between the two phenomena (variables)– intelligence and academic achievement. One of these variables, the effect of which we want to study, will be called independent variable and the other as dependent variable. Thus, independent variable stands for the cause and dependent variable is characterised as the effect of that cause. The other conditions like study habits, sex, socio-economic conditions, parental education, home environment, health, past learning, memory, etc., which exercise desirable impact upon one's achievement besides his intelligence are termed as intervening variables. In experimentation all such intervening variables are to be controlled, *i.e.* made constant or equalised and the effect of only one independent variable, is studied on the dependent variable. Here in the present case intelligence is the independent variable whose effect on academic achievement, the dependent variable we want to study. For experimental study now we will try to change and vary the independent variable (intelligence) for observing the concomitant changes in the dependent variable (academic achievement).

The further task concerns with the objective observation and measurement of these changes and their drawing of the relevant conclusions about the relationship of intelligence with academic achievement.

Experimental Designs: For exercising control over the intervening variables and studying the exclusive effect of the independent variable on dependent variable, the following experimental designs or techniques can be adopted by an investigator.

The Control Test Method: In this method or technique we try to differentiate by observing the performance under different conditions. First we observe under normal conditions and then again with one condition changed. In this experimental design, there is no need of having two different groups of subjects for the experiment. Only the measures can be taken several times under different conditions.

Example. Suppose we want to know whether students can do better on an intelligence test under the influence of a specific drug (like benzedrine sulphate, caffeine or Brahmi).

For its finding we will take only one group of some students preferably of the same age, sex, health conditions, etc. The process of experimentation, then will run in the following steps:

1. These students can be given sugar capsules. After giving the capsules they can be tested on some intelligence test. This will make the initial testing under normal conditions.
2. Sometimes later, they can be given drug capsules and tested on the same intelligence test. This will make a test under changed conditions.
3. The I.Q. scores under these two situations are noted down and the difference is calculated. If any significant difference is found, it is attributed to the influence of the drug.

Control-Group Method: Control-test method possesses a serious drawback known as positive practice effect. In control-group method we can minimise the practice effect. Here two separate groups, known as experimental group and control group — are taken. They are equated or matched on various traits like age, sex, intelligence and other personality characteristics. There is one to one correspondence in the two equated groups.

Now the one group – control group – is given sugar capsules and tested on some intelligence test. At the same time the experimental group is given drug capsules and tested on the same intelligence test. Then the differences in the intelligence scores of groups are calculated. In case we find some significant differences, they are attributed to the effect of the drug.

Rotation Method: This method consists in presenting two or more stimulating situations to the experimental subjects in as many sequences as necessary to control the serial effects of fatigue or practice.

For example if we want to determine the relative influence of two specified conditions A and B (say praise and blame) on a group of subjects we will not measure all the subjects under condition A and then under condition B. Condition A might so fatigue or train the subjects that the measures under condition B would not be independent of the fatigue or training effects. Here two alternatives can be adopted:

1. We may obtain half the measures for condition A, all the measures for condition B and then the other half of the measures for condition A. This technique is sometimes called the ABBA order.
2. Another alternative is to separate the subjects into two equated groups, one of which receives treatment A and then B, whereas the other group receives treatment B and then A. Both sets of A results and both sets of B results may then be combined and the difference between these calculated.

The Limitations:

1. Experimental method advocates the study of behaviour under completely controlled rigid conditions. These conditions demand the creation of artificial situation or environment and the behaviour studied under these conditions may be or is usually different from spontaneous or natural behaviour. Therefore, experimental method fails to study the behaviour in naturalistic conditions as otherwise may be studied through naturalistic observation.
2. The second limitation or difficulty lies in exercising actual control or handling of the independent variable and the

intervening variables. It is quite difficult to know and control all the intervening variables. Similarly we cannot, always, control the independent variable. Therefore, it is not always possible to create conditions in the laboratory as we would like to and consequently in the absence of the desired controlled conditions, the success of this method becomes quite unpredictable.

3. In the experimental method we often make use of animals or birds as subjects for the experimentation. It is also debatable whether experimental results obtained from such sources are applicable to human beings or not.
4. The experimental method has a limited scope. All problems of psychology cannot be studied by this method as we cannot perform experiments for all the problems that may be raised in the heterogeneous subject matter of psychology.
5. The dynamic nature of human behaviour does not always allow the independent variable leading to the change in the dependent variable. Human behaviour is not like a machine-like behaviour. The anger or fear producing stimuli or variables may or may not yield the required responses as desired under experiment and hence it is not possible to get the uniform responses or changes in the dependent variables on account of the concomitant changes in the independent variable.
6. The experimental method is a costly and time-consuming method. Moreover, handling of this method demands specialised knowledge and skill. In the absence of such expertise this method is not functionable.

Reading Techniques

Observation method may be regarded as one of the most convenient and appropriate methods for the study of human behaviour. We can get valuable information about the behaviour and personality traits of an individual by a systematic and careful observation of his behavioural activities related to his day to day life. In some cases, we may create the situations or conditions for the occurrence of a particular type of behaviour so that necessary inferences may be drawn by its observation.

For example to draw inferences about the trait of honesty, we can leave or drop some cash or valuable for observing the reactions or responses of an individual to such artificially created situation. In this way the situations, whether natural or artificially created, may be utilised for the observation of one's behaviour and the data collected from the observation may be utilised for drawing interferences about one's behaviour or personality characteristics.

Definition of Observation Method: Observation, as we know it in sciences, means knowing the environment through sense organs. In the field of Psychology it concerns with the perception of an individual's behaviour by the other individuals and the interpretation and analysis of this perceived behaviour by them. By this method we can infer the mental processes of other persons through the observation of their external behaviour. In fact, it is an indirect approach for the study of the mental processes. If someone frowns, howls, grinds his teeth, closes his fists, by observing external signs of his behaviour we can say that he is angry. In this way as a result of observation – purposive perception – of human conduct we can know a lot about his mental processes and personality. This observation stands as one of the important methods of studying the human behaviour.

Styles and Ways: Observations may be carried out in many ways, forms and styles. Here we are describing a few of such forms and styles.

1. *Formal Observation:* In such a type or style of observation, it is carried out in quite a formal way by observing the necessary formalities like (i) providing the information to the individual or individuals about the nature and purpose of the observation (ii) the date, timings and place of observation (iii) the names and introduction of the observers (iv) the necessary preparation needed on the part of the subjects for such an observation just as showing of any maintained record or preparing them or their environment for such inspection, etc. However, such a type of observation cannot prove more fruitful in terms of drawing some reliable and valid conclusions about one's behaviour or personality. For example, if we announce to the inmates of a hostel that we

are going to have an inspection of their rooms regarding their habit of cleanliness on a particular date and time, such type of a formally announced observation will surely fail in its objective of knowing about the habit of cleanlines among the hostlers. The prior information, will automatically make them quite alert. Thus, the cleanliness behaviour shown at the time of such formal observation will not be a true representation of their real behaviour. It will have an artificial mask with the aim of turning the results of the observation in their favour. The similar thing may happen at the time of the school's formal inspection or inspection of the house of a bride or groom for the matrimonial purpose simply because on account of prior information, everything or behaviour under observation is covered with the artificial mask. Hence no real picture or conclusion about one's behaviour can ever be drawn through the method of formal observation.

2. *Informal Observation:* Contrary to the formal observation, informal observation is carried out in a quite informal, spontaneous and natural way. Here no prior information about the nature, purpose, timings and place of the observation is given to the individual or individuals. They are thus caught unaware, engaging in their behavioural activities in a quite usual and natural way. In such naturalistic observational situations we may have a relatively and true picture of the things and events, traits and characteristics of one's behaviour.
3. *Participant Observation:* In this type of observation, the observer tries to observe the behaviour of an individual or individuals by joining them as an associate or participant in any of their individual or group activities. For example, he may join them in their play activities or accompany them on tour and excursion activities for having a close observation of them. Such a type of observation may provide good opportunity for the observation of the behaviour of the individuals. However, it suffers from a serious limitation as the presence of an observer may obstruct the natural and spontaneous flow of the behavioural activities of those individuals.

4. *Non-participant Observation:* This type of observation tries to do away with the above cited defect or limitation of the participant observation. Here the observer observes the behaviour of the individuals in such a way that they may not have any idea about the observation of their behaviour in any way by one or the other observer. For this purpose as observer he may take his position on such a place in such a way, that while the individuals under observation may not see him but he can clearly watch and hear if possible all about their behaviour in action. There may be a screen or a curtain of such a nature as can help for real observation while hiding his presence.

The use of some modern equipments like secret cameras, video recording, audio recording, etc. may also serve such purposes. While sitting at quite a far distance, he may also take the help of a telescope for a clear secret observation. Whatever means and methods may be employed by the observer, his motive in such an observation always remains to come into contact with the natural and spontaneous behaviour of the subject without making him aware of his presence.

Observation Method in Use: The use of the observation method for the investigation of behaviour generally requires the following four systematic steps.

1. *Planning and Preparation for Observation:* The success of an observation depends much on its proper planning and preparation. This initial task requires proper attention on the following aspects.
   a. What type of behavioural activities or personality traits are to be assessed through observation?
   b. How the observation work is to be carried out, what type of methods or resources will be used for such observation ?
   c. What type of situation or environment is to be maintained for carrying out the observation work?
   d. What type of difficulties or adverse situations may occur during the observation work and how can these be overcome for carrying out effective observation?

e. How can the observation results may be made more reliable, informative, objective and valid?

2. *Observation of the Behaviour:* This second step is related with the actual observation work done by the observer as per planning and preparations made in the first step. Here as far as possible the best methods and techniques should be used for the observation of the behaviour depending upon the purpose of observation and availability of the resources and environmental situations at the time of observation. In this concern for obtaining better results, the following things should always be kept in mind.

   a. The subject should not have any idea that his behaviour is under observation. As far as possible his behaviour is to be observed in a quite naturalistic condition for deriving the sample of his most natural and spontaneous behaviour.

   b. The observation work must be carried out properly in a quite effective way. The eyes have to play a key role in such an observation. If possible, one should also try to hear about the behavioural activities in action.

   c. It is always better to make use of a telescope for viewing the activities of individuals specially while sitting at a far off place.

   d. There must be an adequate arrangement for using the modem observation equipments like cameras, video and audio recording. The use of these appliances not only helps in proper observation of the behavioural activities but prove an automatic recording device for the proper analysis and interpretation of the behaviour.

   e. It is not proper to rely over the results of a single observation of the subject's behaviour for taking decision about his one or the other behavioural or personality trait. For a desirable objectivity, reliability and validity, such observation work must be repeated by the same observer for a desirable number of times or it should be carried out by a number of different observers at one or a number of times.

f. The recording about the nature of the behavioural or personality traits should always be done side by side by the observer while making observation of his behaviour. The failure to do so prove quite costly as the observer may forget or miss some or the other important things or links regarding the observed behaviour. It is always better to prepare a check list for tallying or marking the things to be observed in one's behaviour during the observation.

3. *Analysis and Interpretation of the Observed Facts:* In this third step, what is observed and recorded in terms of the behavioural or personality traits during the observations of one's behaviour is subjected to a close analysis for deriving the necessary interpretation about his behaviour and personality.
4. *Generalisation of the Results:* The interpretation made and results arrived at are then used for establishing generalised opinion, facts or principles about the occurrence of behaviour and existence of similar personality characteristics among the similar individuals in the similar situations. It can help us to have prediction of the behaviour in similar circumstances, search for the roots of a particular type of behaviour and study the effects of some remedial or treatment measure in the correction of a maladaptive behaviour.

Merits of Observation Method: For the investigation of behaviour the observation method is said to possess the following points on its credit side.

1. Observation method makes possible to study the behaviour in its quite natural and original form, the way it occurs or performed spontaneously by the subject concerned.
2. Observation and experimentation are said to be the only reliable and valid measures and methods for carrying out any systematic and scientific study. However, it is neither practicable nor feasible to have valid experimentation (observations in the laboratory like controlled situations) for the study of human behaviour. We may have such experiments for the study of the behaviour of animals like

cats, rats, pigeons, chimpanzee, etc., but in the case of the human behaviour, observation is the only reliable and valid measure that can be properly adopted for the investigation of behaviour.

3. The observation method needs to study the behaviour of an individual in its present form or state. It makes possible to draw inferences about one's behaviour on the basis of the observation of his present behaviour. One does not need to care about his past behaviour or previous history for the investigation of his behaviour as happens with the methods like psycho-analysis and case study. In this way the fatigue occurred and the difficulties faced in digging out the past is almost saved through the use of observation method.
4. There is greater scope for the proper verification of the derived results and conclusion reached through observation method. We can have repeated observation of the behaviour for taking decision regarding a particular behavioural characteristic and this observation work can be done by a single observer at different times or a team of observers at a single or number of times.
5. It is quite an economical method in terms of time, money and labour. We can collect huge information about the behaviour of a single subject or a number of subjects at a time within the limited time and resources. We need neither any special type of laboratory facilities or controlled environment, nor the services of any professionally trained or special psychologists or researcher for the investigation of behaviour by the observation method.
6. It is possible to study the behaviour of any living organisms like plants, animals, insects, birds besides the human being through the application of observation method. In this way observation method has provided a wide scope and application to the study of psychology in our day to day life.
7. Observation method proves helpful in carrying out the investigation of the various behavioural characteristics of so many individuals at a particular time and occasion.

8. It can be quite helpful in collecting not only the qualitative data but also the quantitative data. The quantification of the observed behavioural traits thus may help in the maintenance of the required objectivity, reliability and validity in the assessment and measurement of one's behaviour and personality.

Limitations and Defects: Observation method is found to suffer from a number of limitations and shortcomings discussed as below:

1. *Difficulty in Getting Properly Trained Observers:* Observation method rests on the quality of a good observation. Such good observation requires the services of some relatively competent and skilled person as observers. In the absence of such competent observers, observation work is bound to suffer and that may ultimately lead to the failure of the observation method in its objective.
2. *Disadvantage due to the Factor of Subjectivity:* Subjectivity factors on the part of the investigator as well as the process of observation also affect the results of observation. There may arise distortions of observable facts depending on the degree of care in observation. His interest, values, bias and prejudices may also distort the contents and results of observation. One may lay overemphasis on some particular part of one's behaviour and may altogether neglect some very important aspect. The interpretations of the recorded events may also be sufficiently coloured. One may read one's own thoughts, feelings and tendencies in the minds of others.
3. *Partial and Revengeful Attitude of the Observer:* Not only his subjectivity but also the partial and revengeful attitude maintained by the observer towards the subject of observation may colour and distort the results of observation. As a result the favourable and dear ones are always assessed and estimated on quite a higher footing whereas the unfavourable, disliked and thorny ones are looked down upon on one point or the other.
4. *Lack of Reliability and Validity:* The observation method suffers from the lack of reliability and validity on account of its

complete dependability on the observation of the external observable behaviour of the subject. Here it is impossible for observer to know what is going on in the minds of the subjects. He is supposed to observe it through external signs of behaviour. It is quite a difficult task. There is every chance that the subject under observation may play hide and seek and use his all expertise to hide his feelings, emotions and inner personality. A crooked person thus may be able to disguise his evil nature in the garb of artificial sobriety. Similarly, we may be mistaken to consider a person otherwise after observing his discipline and rough attitude, cool temperament and unmixable indifferent behaviour. In this way, overdependence upon the external signs of behaviour may make this method a failure in the investigation of the true nature of the individual concerned.

5. *Difficulty in the Occurrence and Reoccurrence of the Events*: Another serious limitation of the observation method lies in the fact that the behaviour observed is dependent on the particular time and place and on the particular individual or groups of individuals involved. It lacks repeatability as each natural situation can occur only once.
6. *Can't help in the Establishment of Cause and Effect Relationship*: Another important limitation of the observation method lies in its inability to establish a proper cause and effect relationship. In case we observe that two phenomena, say poverty and delinquency behaviour, invariably occur together, we cannot infer from this that poverty is the sufficient and necessary cause of delinquent behaviour or vice verse.
7. *Not helpful in the Study of One's Total Behaviour*: Observation method takes into account only the observation of the external or observable behaviour of the subject. The external behaviour is a quite an incomplete portrait of one's personality. The internal aspects of one's behaviour or inner mechanism of one's personality remain totally unexplorable through the use of observation method. We can't reach the unconscious or even subconscious layers of ones mind through the observation of his observable behaviour. In this way,

observation method fails in the objective of the investigation of one's total behaviour and aspects of personality.

8. *Difficulty in Recording the Observation Data:* The other limitation of observation method lies with the proper timely recording of the observed events or data regarding the occurrence of behaviour. As an observer one has to observe one or the many things occurring at the same time in the behaviour of the subject. All his attention, concentration and energy is then directed to gather information about the ongoing behavioural activities. The task of simultaneous recording at this time becomes an extra burden. Both the tasks are serious and at best can be done properly by taking them one by one. Now if one does not record the observed phenomena side by side, one is to miss a few things or important links afterwards. In case he records them side by side, it may affect the process of proper observation. The subject may become overconscious that his behaviour is being noted down. Even in the case when the observer takes the help of recording devices like camera, video and audio recording, etc., the behaviour of the subject cannot remain spontaneous or natural. As a subject one is quite intelligent to guess the arrangement of such a nature and then one may also like to cover up one's true nature and behaviour under artificial showism and sobriety.

In this way, we can observe that the observation method suffers from a few serious limitations and drawbacks, casting serious doubts about its objectivity, reliability and validity. However, these deficiencies in the application of the observation method cannot be termed as unrepairable. Much depends upon the sincerity, seriousness, abilities and skills of the observer. If he is determined he can find ways and means for the proper investigation of the behaviour of a subject within the limited resources at his disposal.

How to Conduct a Case Study?

Definition of the Term: The term 'case' is used in a number of ways conveying different meanings in our day to day life. A lawyer helps his client by arguing his case in a court of law. A doctor attending a case diagnoses the disease of his patient and prescribes appropriate medicines. A Judge decrees after hearing and studying the case file of an offender. An officer disposes of a number of cases put up by his subordinate clerks.

In all such situations, the term 'case' is used for a person or matter put to examination, observation or investigation for the purpose of helping the concerned individual in deciding or solving the problem related to him. In the subject psychology, the term, case is also used almost in the similar sense. Here the individual who is confronted with an educational, vocational or socio psychological personal problem is termed as a 'case' and is subjected to proper study, investigation, diagnosis and remedial or treatment measures on the similar lines as happens with the cases of the doctors or lawyers.

Such investigation and study of one's behaviour related with the task of finding a solution of his problem is termed as 'Case Study' in the subject of psychology. This investigation or study is quite comprehensive as to cover one's past history related to the problem, the present status of the problem and the future possibilities of dealing with the problem.

Thinking on these lines a workable definition of the term 'Case Study Method' for the investigation of human behaviour can be adopted as under. The case study method is that method of behaviour investigation in which we try to study the behaviour of an individual in all the essential aspects by analysing the past record, present position and future possibilities regarding his felt problem or otherwise guidance functions.

The Objectives: Case study is carried out mainly to serve the following two purposes.

1. *Diagnosis and Treatment of the Behavioural Problems:* Some individuals may suffer from one or the other behavioural problems on account of their lack of adjustment to their self or the environment. For example, the children may have emotional or social maladjustment or may be lagging behind in their studies or normal mental functioning. Such type of problem children, backward, slow learners, delinquents or anti-social personality, need quite a careful attention and it

is paid here through studying them as an individual and unique case in themselves. The case study method thus aims at going into the depth of the nature of the problem, search for the probable cause of the eruption of this behaviour and then suggests the possible remedial or treatment measures for helping the sufferer from getting rid of the problem.

2. *To Provide Better Guidance and Counselling:* The case study methods and techniques are quite helpful to the guidance personnel and counsellors in the task of exercising their responsibilities in an effective way. Whether it may be the field of educational guidance or vocational and personal guidance, the assistance to the guidance seeker is given by treating him as a case, study him in relation to his environment and his problem and then provide development. In this way whatever guidance or counselling is given to a guidance seeker or counsellee depends to a great extent upon the results of his case study. Much in the same way as a doctor has to carry out the proper diagnosis of his patient's problem before subscribing any medicines for the treatment.

The Subjects: With the ongoing discussion, it must be quite clear up till now that whosoever needs any type of difficulty and problem in his adjustment, development or progress or by one reason or the other if we as investigators are interested in the investigation or study of one's behaviour then such individual may be treated as a case for carrying out his study in a quite professional and technical way. In this way all individuals, whether normal or abnormal, average, above average or below average in the possession of the abilities or capacities related to their growth and development, personality traits or adjustment may be taken as a subject for the case study.

However, in general, the case study is more particularly needed for the needy ones who are in search of any assistance or help for solving their felt problems or for those whose behaviour we want to study to bring desirable modification in their behaviour for their necessary adjustment, development and progress. It is why the case studies of the following types of children or individuals are more commonly carried out in the field of education and psychology: i) Creative person; ii) Gifted or Genius; iii) Backward or Slow learners; iv) Delinquents or Criminals; v) Persons suffering from emotional, social phychological and educational problems or maladjustment; vi) Addicted individuals and vii) Anti-social personality.

Case Study Method in Use: In the case study method, any individual who is under study is treated as a unique or individual case in himself. The beginning in the study of his behaviour, thus is made by giving due recognition and respect to his individuality. The next task is concerned with the establishment of a good rapport with him. He must be taken in confidence by winning over his trust and faith in the investigation. Then all attempts are made to know him in relation to his personal identity, past history particularly regarding his felt problem of development adjustment, all relevant information about the present status, circumstances and situations concerning his behaviour, development and adjustment, etc.

Truly speaking, case study aims to study the past and present of the subject thoroughly in all its aspects of behavioural or personality dimensions in relation to his environment. In this way, this study goes quite deep in the investigation of all the essential things related to the subject's case in a very comprehensive way. Technically it is quite proper to use a pre-prepared format for such study. It may provide more objectivity, reliability and validity to the case study work. The use of such a format may be illustrated through the case study of a problem adolescent.

Merits and Demerits:

Merits: Case study method may be credited with some of the following merit points.

1. It provides quite a deep, intensive and overall investigation of the behaviour of the individual in relation to his past and the present. Here he is studied as a complete case in relation to his environmental surroundings, developmental characteristics and adjustment difficulties. Such thorough study and investigation of his behaviour is only possible through this method. As a result, the method has unique advantage of reaching the root causes of a special behaviour and problem of the subject under study.

2. The method can play an effective role in the proper identification, diagnosis and subsequent remedial work, adjustment and rehabilitation of the problem children, maladjusted or maladaptive personalities, emotionally or socially disturbed individuals, delinquents, criminals or anti-social persons by studying them thoroughly as individual cases.
3. In this method of behaviour study the scope and range of study is quite wide and comprehensive. The information and data are collected from various persons and information sources. The behavioural data is subjected to repeated observation. All such efforts make the results of the investigation or study more objective, reliable and valid.
4. This method provides opportunity for collecting data on personal basis, by seeking personal interview, going close to the original source of information, etc. The rapport established and the closeness received may help the investigator to reach and search for the most secret and unconscious seated behaviour of the subject. In this way the information received through the case study may prove more effective in the solution of the felt problems or rendering proper educational, vocational and personal guidance.

The case study method suffers from some of the following limitations and defects.

1. The case study work is quite a technical and professional work. It can't be entrusted to the classroom subject teachers. There is a need of specially trained teacher or professional for carrying out studies.
2. There is a need of collecting so much of the information regarding a case from a number of persons or sources. The work is quite extensive and comprehensive. There are a lot of difficulties and utilisation of individual resources in terms of time, labour and money causing a serious handicap to the collection of the required information for such study.
3. There is no guarantee for the objectivity, reliability and validity of the information or data collected from the variety

of sources for the analysis and investigation of the behaviour of the subject.

4. The field of application of this method is quite narrow and limited. It can only be used properly for the investigation of the behaviour of the problem children or anti-social or deviant personalities.
5. There is no provision of studying the behaviour in a properly controlled laboratory like situations. In this way, we can't expect the required objectivity, reliability and validity in the results of the study carried out through the case study method like in the experimental or other scientific observations.
6. The task of the proper analysis and interpretation of the collected information, drawing conclusions and then having its proper generalisation is quite difficult and technical. There are plenty of chances of drawing erroneous conclusion about the causes and possible remedial work related to the problems and needed assistance to the subject.

The case study method in this way may be seen to be affected with a few drawbacks and limitations. However, keeping in view the advantages of this method we must provide it a due place in the task of investigating human behaviour. Since it is the only method which strives hard for the thorough investigation of one's behaviour in all its sorts, forms and dimensions by using one's past and present record for the future possibilities of one's better adjustment, development and progress in the interest of self and society.

Process of Survey

Survey method is also often utilised in social science studies including psychology mainly to collect information about what exists by studying and analysing important aspects of a pattern of a particular behaviour, quality or characteristic related to a existing group. We can study the interests, aptitudes, attitudes, habits and many other temperamental and personality characteristics of a group with the help of survey method. For example, a researcher can very well study the attitude of the young marriagable Indian Boys and Girls towards dowry system prevalent in our society.

For this study he has to make contact with the group of the youths (included in the appropriately chosen representative sample) for knowing their opinions, views, stereotypes and feelings, etc., related to the dowry system. Such contact with a wide variety of people in a group for arriving at a proper conclusion concerned with the objectives of psychological study can only be possible through survey method.

As a result we can consider and define survey method as a method of extensive study involving all the members of a population or its representative sample to derive the desired specific information for the realisation of the objectives of the study.

As a matter of collecting information from the required population or its representative sample in the survey method, there are two main modes that may be employed by the researchers. These are:

1. Use of Questionnaires technique
2. Use of Interview technique.

Let us discuss these modes one by one.

Use of Questionnaires: Questionnaire, in general is referred to a device or instrument consisting of some systematically planned questions in the shape of a form which the respondents fill in themselves for providing answers to the questions asked. In this way questionnaires are usually paper and pencil instruments (forms) that are filled up by the respondents of a given population or its representative sample for providing desired information.

Types of Surveys:

1. *Mail Survey:* When most people think of questionnaires, they think of the mail survey. All of us have, at one time or another, received a questionnaire in the mail. There are many advantages to mail surveys. They are relatively inexpensive to administer. You can send the exact same instrument to a wide number of people. They allow the respondent to fill it out at their own convenience. But there are some disadvantages as well. Response rates from mail surveys are often very low. And, mail questionnaires are not the best vehicles for asking for detailed written responses.

2. *Group Administered Survey:* A second type is the group administered survey. Here a sample of respondents is brought together and asked to respond to a structured sequence of questions. Traditionally, questionnaires were administered in group settings for convenience. The researcher could give the questionnaire to those who were present and be fairly sure that there would be a high response rate. If the respondents were unclear about the meaning of a question they could ask for clarification. And, there were often organisational settings where it was relatively easy to assemble the group (in a school or club or temple, etc.).
3. *Door to Door Survey:* A less familiar type of survey made with the help of questionnaires is the Door to Door survey. In this approach, a researcher goes to the respondent's home or work place and hands the respondent the instrument. In some cases, the respondent is asked to mail it back or the researcher returns to pick it up. This approach attempts to blend the advantages of the mail survey and the group administered survey. Like the mail survey, the respondent can work on the instrument in private, when it is convenient. Like the group administered survey, the researcher makes personal contact with the respondent. And, the respondent can ask questions about the study and get clarification on what is to be done. Generally, this would be expected to increase the percentage of people who are willing to respond.

Administration of Questionnaires: The success one gets in getting desired information depends upon mainly two things (i) the quality of the questionnaire used as instrument for getting information and (ii) the cooperation of the respondents in providing answers to the questions asked. The former is by all means in the complete control of the researcher. He must pay due attention towards; the proper construction and administration of the questionnaire instrument. The following things may help him for this purpose.

- Frame the questions by keeping in view the objectives of the survey study.
- Keep in mind the educational level and language of the respondents.

- Try to frame the questions as properly as possible for avoiding any confusion or incorrect interpretations. The wording should be quite straight, simple and clear having no difficult or ambiguous terminology. There should be nothing objectionable that may hurt the feelings of the individual or the segments of the society.
- Keep the length of the questionnaire as short as possible.
- Only include what is absolutely necessary.
- Try to observe necessary formalities and courtesy while planning for the format of your questionnaire, such as making the objectives of your study clear, thanking the respondent at the beginning and in the end for responding to the questionnaire, assuring him about maintaining secrecy of his responses, be sensitive to the needs, difficulties, interests and attitudes of the respondents and lastly assuring him that you will inform him about the result of your study.
- Try to pay due attention towards the construction of the proper response format for collecting the desired responses from the respondents.

There must be clear cut directions for filling up the response columns related to the various items/questions of the questionnaire. In general, there may be two types of questions (closed and open ended forms) requiring structured and unstructured responses.

Reading for Mental Development

Aspects in Reading and Learning

Mentally Retarded children have many characteristics in common with the normal children. Some authorities have described the characteristics according to the severity of retardation some other experts have mentioned the characteristics not according to the degree of disability but in terms of there educatability. Thus the characteristics of mentally retarded children are classified in two categories: 1) General characteristics, and 2) Specified characteristics.

General Characteristics: The following are some important features of mentally retarded children:

1. Mentally retarded child has low intelligence but his development is not adequate according his mental level:
2. Mentally retarded children are of two type: a) Educable mentally retarded, and b) Trainable mentally I.Q. (55-50) trainable retarded. I.Q. (50-75) educable.
3. Mentally retarded child differs with regard to learning emotions, adjustment and physical development from normal children.

4. Mentally retarded children has poor adjustment due to several reasons – lack of motivation, feeling of insecurity.
5. Identification is difficult of such children. They lack in abstract thinking concept formation and process of generalisation.
6. Some specific features of Mr. children are:
   a. slow reaction,
   b. absence of clarity,
   c. inability to learn fast,
   d. in-ability to understand quickly,
   e. inability to decide,
   f. lack of concentration,
   g. short temper,
   h. inability to remember,
   i. lack of coordination, and
   j. delay in development.

Specific Characteristics: Some features of MR children are classified into three categories:

1. Educable Mentally Retarded (EMR).
2. Trainable Mentally Retarded (TMAR).
3. Custodial Mentally Retarded (CMR).

Educable Mentally Retarded (EMR): The EMR children have I.Q 50 to 75. They have normal appearance and remain unidentified until late teens. They function at an intellectual level generally limited to learning the most basic school subjects, skills such as reading, spelling, writing and numerical calculation. They are expected to learn up to the seventh standard. They can communicate effectively in everyday conversation, enjoy friendship and group social activities. They can travel with case in their home town or locality. During adulthood, they are able to live independently, marry or have children. They can hold are able to live independently marry or have children. They can hold skilled or semi-skilled jobs. But at times they may need assistance in doing their job. They can be educated in regular classrooms.

Trainable Mentally Retarded (TMR): The TMR children have IQ 25 to 50. They are expected to have physical or sensory impairments and many tend to look different in terms of facial features and physical characteristics. They function at a level where formal academic learning is quite limited.

They can learn to feed, toilet and dress self adequately. They can carry on rudimentary conversation, and do simple house hold work. But they need training in self-care activities, language development and rudimentary academic skills. They are usually placed in special classes or special schools.

Custodial Mentally Retarded (CHR): The CMR have IQ below 25. They are so much retarded in intellectual functioning and adaptive behaviour that they remain totally dependent on others for their existence. It is because of their severe retardation that they are institutionalised early in life. Their speech and toilet habits remain at a primitive level. Behaviour modification and environmental stimulation techniques are usually recommended for their training.

The Reasons: It has been mentioned that mental retardation is due to both type of factors: 1) Heredity-Endo-genous factors and 2) Environment-Exogenous factors.

Heredity Endogenous Factors: may be of the following types:

Development defects: before birth, skull deformities and endocrine disorders.

Metabolic defects: skin diseases, infantile juvenile.

Neuromotor defects: motor skills defects, motor paralysis.

Psychological disorder: Sensory defects, psychic defects.

Environment Exogenous Factors: these may be of the following types:

1. Developments after the birth of the child.
2. Anti-measures used by mother in pregnancy.
3. Post-natal conditions-direct injury, disease, etc.

4. Process of Growth and development: 1) Developmental defects, 2) Metabolic defects, 3) Neuromotor defects, and 4) Psychological disorder.

Kirk has enumerated the causes of retardation into three categories: 1) Organic or biological, 2) Genetic or heredity and 3) Cultural or environmental factors. The empirical research studies have yielded that three types of factors are responsible for the mental retardation of children.

Mentally retarded children are identified by using both observation of their behaviours and administering intelligence test to ascertain their level of intelligence.

Mental Retardation occurs due to genetic and environmental factors which come into play at pre-natal, perinatal and post-natal stages of development.

Heredity-Endogenous Causes of Mr.: One of the most visible conditions associated with mental retardation of Down's Syndrome. Down in 1865, was the first to use the term mongolian idiocy to name a particular form of mental retardation now referred to as mongolism or Down's Syndrome. Down's Syndrome contains the non-sex determining chromosome. Chromosomal anomaly, explains many forms of mental disorders.

In non-dysfunction Down's Syndrome, one pair of genes failed to separate at conception, resulting in an extra or 47th chromosome after forty-six known as Tirsomy-21. The face of the child has palpebral fissures that are oblique and narrow laterally, specked iris, flatness of the nose bridge, enlarged tongue, small ears, and short and broad neck. Other common anomalies are flattening of the occiput, broad hands with the little finger curved, short broad feet with a wide space between the first and second toes, pelvic anomalies, and congenital heart anomalies in almost 25 of patients. Intellectual development is impaired (IQ 25-69).

There is clear cut association between Mental Age and Trisomy-21

Down's Syndrome	Below 20	20-24	25-29	30-34	35-39	40+
Incidence per 1000	0.46	0.65	0.88	1.26	3.92	17.00

Whatever the IQ value, it seems safe to say that Trisomy-21 children will not be able to enjoy an independent life, even if some of them reach borderline intelligence. Mongolism or Down's Syndrome is due to the presence of three types of chromosomal anomalies.

Three main cytonetic forms are known: with 47 chromosome and a standard trisomy-21 (95 per cent of 111 case); with normal mosaics, with 46 chromosomes/trisomy-21 (two three per cent), and with translocations (two to three per cent). Although it is not known that the causes are a close association between maternal age and trisomy 21 has been repeatedly demonstrated.

These children need extra care. Parental support is a vital need to ensure that infant stimulation programmes emphasising self-help skills, language acquisition, feeding, toilet training, and positive socialisation, are provided. Down's syndrome individuals are educable and should have exposure to their non-handicapped peers from their early years.

In the past, professionals advised parents to place their Down's syndrome child in 24 hour institutional care based on the false assumption that the Down's syndrome individual would be severely or profoundly retarded. Custodial care is seldom warranted unless severe medical, psychological or social problems occur.

The greatest general development is found in Down's Syndrome individuals who are reared at home and well stimulated. Optimum programme occurs when facilities are positive and training begins early and comprehensive.

Translocation is common. It occurs because of faulty cell division in which one chromosome is attached to another. In Mosaicism, the cell receives an extra twenty first chromosomes, but there are few abnormalities in this form of Down's Syndrome.

A combination of genetic and environmental actors is responsible for familial type of mental retardation. Early emotional deprivation and disturbed parent-child relationships are some of the potent factors associated with mental retardation of this type.

Emotionally disturbed children are considered to be oversensitive to psychological stress and vitamin deficiency is likely to causes over susceptibility to infection.

Several small-scale surveys report that the familial type of retarded children are found in low socio-economic families. In all these cases, the parents' intellectual and educational levels are low. Heber (1970) Pointed out that the latter factor is responsible for mental retardation. These kinds of mental retardates have a family background characterised by poverty with no facilities for gratification of physiological needs.

In addition to these, the parents' intellectual level is low. As a result, lack of social, emotional and motivational support for the child is found. Study of Benda *et. al,* (1963) has revealed that by eradicating or reducing poverty, the incidence of mental retardation can be considerable reduced.

Certain behavioural signs given an indication of the presence of mental retardation among children. These can be observed by teachers and parents.

1. General academic retardation characterised by slow rate of learning, poor problem solving skills, slow reaction to environmental demands.
2. Poor memory. Inability to retain things mentally for long periods.
3. Difficulty in developing concepts, especially abstract concepts. Absence of clarity.
4. Inability to arrive at generalisations and see common elements among different objects or events.
5. Slow language development-usually the language is limited in terms of vocabulary and variety.
6. Below average in imagination and creative thinking.
7. Inability to delay gratification and satisfaction by immediate reward.
8. Short attention span and intolerance of frustration.
9. Limited play and social interests.

10. Lack of concentration, heightened destructibility and incapacity for comprehension.
11. Lack of coordination in self-help skills (sucking, chewing, eating, use of hands, legs, fingers, etc.).
12. Some have physical features like a small or large head, small eyes, straight hair, fissured tongue, low set ears, and short stature, physical deformities and paralysis of one or more limbs.
13. In case of school going children there are repeated failures and inability to cope with the lessons.

The Recognition: For the mentally retarded, assessment includes basically intelligence and adaptive behaviour along with developmental material supplied by parents, teachers, social workers and professionals. The two most widely used intelligence tests are the Stanford Binet, and the Weschler Intelligence Scale for Children. These individual tests along with functional assessment tests developed by the national institute for mentally handicapped can be used.

Adaptive behaviour is assessed using adaptive behaviour scales. In these scales, assessment is made on the basis of maturational and developmental skills in the areas of communication, motor ability and self help in early childhood. In adolescence, social and vocational adjustments are emphasised. AAMD adaptive behaviour scale and the Vineland Social Maturity Scale are quite well known test of measuring adaptive behaviour.

Educational assessment of the mentally retarded needs to be more functional than verbal. School readiness measures developed by Muralidharan, the Harison reading readiness profile and Furrel analysis of reading difficulty can be given to Mr. children as high as up to the sixth grade. The Illinois test of psycholinguistic abilities form of adoption available in our country can be used for diagnosis and related language processes.

There are tests which can be profitably used; the Peabody Picture Vocabulary Test (PPVT), Auditor, discrimination test, verbal language development scale. The crux of the issue lies in developing systematic testing methods, devising certain norms, modifying them in terms of progress achieved, adapting them to the regional languages and variations.

Different Approach: The approach so far has been the use of psychometric tests even though adaptive behaviour assessment has formed a basic component in testing for screening, placing and making any intervention. Although AAMD Adaptive Behaviour Scale, Vineland Social Maturity Scale and a few others have been adopted in our country, there have been wide shortcomings in their use. There are culturally a typical children, hyperactive children to whom such tests can be administered with lots of difficulties. Their motivation and attitude are different.

The apprehension of parents about testing because of bias of apprehension of stigma, use of tests for identification by Psuedo-professionals, Para-professionals as a measure of social welfare activities attached to such identification have further posed problems.

Various Categories: Children with mental retardation show no physical problem but may be slow in following instructions. Their performance in class is affected by their delayed development. The observable behaviours that will help the teacher in identifying such children are given in the checklist given below:

1. Displays poor academic achievements constantly.
2. Relies too much on presentation of concrete objects.
3. Has short attention span?
4. Displays short term memory.
5. Has a poor self-image?
6. Lacks self-confidence.
7. Has restricted communication?
8. Seeks repetition and practices.
9. Does not take any initiative in group activities?
10. Often inattentive and distracted.
11. Needs immediate reward.

12. Display fear of failure.
13. Has poor muscular coordination?
14. Faces difficulty in doing things for himself.
15. Has a problem in understanding instructions?
16. Some children have problems in speech and are hyperactive.

Severe cases of metal retardation have more speech problems. These children may face multiple problems. They are hyperactive and are unable to sit in one place for more than few minutes, and exhibit restless activities like tapping, pulling, and so on.

There are different methods of classification of mental retardation. The medical classification is based on the cause, the psychological classification on the level of intelligence, and the educational classification on the current level of functioning of the mentally retarded person/child. The proportion of children who fall under the various categories of mental retardation are depicted below:

(1) Mild Retarded	(89%)
(2) Moderate Retarded	(67%)
(3) Severe Retarded	(35%)
(4) Profound Retarded	(15%)

The classification of mentally retarded children has been given in the following table with reference to Medical, Educational and Psychological.

Clinical Classification: There are six categories of clinical type of MR children:

1. Simple types.
2. Mongolism (Down's Syndrome).
3. Microcephaly.
4. Hydrocephaly.
5. Travmatic Amentia.
6. Cretinism (Thyroid Deficiency).

Generally 60 to 70 per cent of mental defective display no distinguishing physical characteristics. No doubt, they are undersised and have a large number of physical defects. Their brain studies reveal no specific abnormalities. Among them two-thirds are morons and the remainder are mainly imbeciles.

Classification of Mental Retardation Children

Medical	*Educational*	*Psychological Wechsler*	*Standard Binet*
1. Infections and Intoxication	1. Educable-IQ 60-85	1. Mild IQ 55-69	IQ-52-67
2. Trauma or physical agent	2. Trainable-IQ 30-59	2. Moderate IQ 40-54	IQ-36-51
3. Metabolism or Nutrition	3. Custodial-IQ Below 30	3. Severe IQ 25-39	IQ-20-35
4. Grossbrain disease (Post natal)		4. Profound IQ Below 25	IQ-20-35
5. Unknown prenatal influence			
6. Chromosomal anomaly			
7. Gestational disorder			
8. Environmental influence			

The various classifications provide an understanding of the level at which the mentally retarded person functions with respect to his education, appropriate behaviour and the degree of the independence. The characteristics of mentally retarded persons very depending upon the level of retardation, country, age, culture, etc. The terms currently used to describe the various degrees of mental retardation are mild, moderate, severe and profound.

Adaptive Behaviours of MR Children

Swaxeuoruib Terminology	*School Age Children Training and Education*
Mildy retarded	Can learn minimal academic skills by late teens; needs special education, particularly at secondary age school age school age levels.
Moderately retarded	Can learn academic skills by late teens if given special education, although still functionally illiterate.

Severely retarded	Can talk or learn to communicate; can be trained in elemental health habits; cannot learn functionally academic skills; profits from systematic habit training.
Profoundly retarded	Some slow motor development; remains bed bound; cannot profit from training in social help, needs total care.

Different Problems: Generally, there is no significant difference between normal children and mentally retarded children with regard to their psychical health, but special psychological difficulties for retardates are found in day-to-day life. These are as follows:

1. Mild depression, feeling of worthlessness and helplessness are experienced.
2. As a retardate grows older, becomes lonely and unable to adjust in society. Evidence points towards the frustration of psychological and social needs which predispose some retardates to feel angry and rebellious.
3. Parents of such children develop a guilt complex, Parental overprotection is a glaring example. Sometimes they do not encourage self-help; rather they continue to dress and feed the child up to an advanced age. As a result, this type of behaviour encourages a dependent style of interaction in the child. Mainly overprotection and denial of the parents invite adjustment difficulties of such type of children.

The mentally retarded children have usually the following type problem:

1. Physiological and mental development problems.
2. Adjustment problems in home, school and society
3. Emotional problems in family, school and society.

Generally the parents have high expectation from his child. Mentally retarded children are unable to come to their expectations because they lack in mental deficiency or low intelligence. The parents get-disappointment from the child. They begin to scold him. The child feel humiliation due to his unabilities. More or less similar situation is the school and classroom. They can not pace with class and teacher can not make them learn any thing through his normal teaching. The child wants to avoid the classroom and become truant. Such children are deprived from the affection sympathing of their parents and their teacher. Thus the problem of adjustment areas in family, school and society.

Programme for Treatment: The treatment and prevention have been discussed in educational programmes of backward and delinquent children. Preventive measures of mental retardation – The intelligence tests should be administered at the time of admission in the school. A check list may be given to the parents to know above his behaviours and activities. The parents should be educated in this context.

Treatment of mental retardation – The special educational programmes should be used for such students. These programmes have been discussed under heading of education of mentally retarded children.

The are three provisions remedial programme:

1. Prevention
2. Special Education
3. Parent Counselling

Prevention: Generally compensatory education aims at preventing developmental defect that interfere with educational progress in the disadvantaged pre-school child. In Western countries like USA, many institutions of this type are found. "Project head Start" is this type of institution which started in Milwaukee, USA. This project was proved successful in USA.

Mainly it demonstrates the effectiveness of early and comprehensive intervention in the prevention of cultural familial retardation. The above project aims at selecting children of mentally retarded parents with and I.Q. of 70. This gives the children some structured programme of sensory and language stimulation that emphasises achievement motivation, problem-solving skills and interpersonal relations, which is imparted to the children daily, and the mothers of these children receive training in the understanding and managing of the retarded children in their homes.

Special Education: We known that a retardate learns at a slow pace. So structured curricular materials and techniques are necessary for educating retarded children. Recently individual centred programmes have been tried out at the Institute of Defectology in Moscow, USSR. At this centre, the retarded child is identified within six months after its birth. From the 6th month till the onset of puberty, individual programmes from multi-disciplinary points of view are devised and implement for children. If given a healing touch to the children with the onset of puberty.

It is true that such kind of individual-based programmes are not found in India and neither does it appear possible in the near future. But an attempt can be made to work out programmes involving small groups.

Parent Counselling: In our society, the parents of mentally retarded children face some special problems. They bother about their children's physical and emotional problems. Also social adjustments of these children place heavy demands in the society. As the children grow older, problems regarding physical health, schooling and placement crop up. Keeping all these problems in the forefront, psychologists suggest parent counselling services. Homer training services with community – sponsored educational training programmes must be provided to the mentally retarded children who live at home.

Day Care Centre: When the children are too young or too retarded to be included in other community programmes, their needs can be met by "Day care centres".

Sheltered Workshop: As its name for mentally retarded persons to develop their opportunity for mentally retarded persons to develop their work skills to a point where they can get a job. In developed countries like USA or USSR, many sheltered workshops are found. In our country, the Department of Social Welfare provides grants to the states to improve services for vocational rehabilitation of the mentally retarded. Many private organisation avail themselves of this opportunity. Still they are all inadequate to meet the needs of the society.

After medical and psychological assessment, the MR child should be placed in a suitable environment/institution for proper care and training. Usually the following kinds of placement are recommended for MR children. The appropriate placement depends upon the degree of retardation.

1. Placement in Regular Classes.
2. Placement in Resource Room.
3. Placement in Special Classes.
4. Placement in Special Schools.
5. Placement in Residential Institutions.
6. Placement in Group Home.
7. Placement in Activity Centres.

Mildly retarded children are to be placed in the regular classes and resource room in IED schools. Moderately retarded children are usually placed in special classes; sheltered workshops for older individuals are also common in various countries. At the pre-school level, moderately retarded children are sometimes placed in special day schools. Placement in residential institution is sometime recommended for moderately retarded children when other types of handicap such as deafness are present and are severe and when community placement is not available or when the family situation is undesirable. Severely and profoundly retarded children are usually placed in residential institutions.

A placement programme growing in popularity is the group home. In group home arrangement many formerly institutionalised individuals are placed in relatively small groups (three to ten people) in houses under the direction of employed house parents.

The level of retardation of individuals in these homes range form mild to severe. Group homes accommodate children, adolescents or adults. But every group home focuses upon a specific age range. Placement in group home can either be a permanent arrangement or a temporary living arrangement depending upon the level of retardation and the training required. For many parents of retarded individuals, the group home provides a positive and less stigmatised alternative to institutional placement.

Another type of arrangement that is becoming more popular is the activity centre suitable for severely and profoundly retarded individuals. The activity centre is a place where parents can take their children for a portion of the day for a variety of activities related to recreation and crafts. The basic purpose is socialisation and not formal training.

Educational Process: The mentally retarded children require special education. The following principles should be followed in the education:

1. Physical, emotional, intellectual and social maturity should be encouraged by employing appropriate measures.
2. They require the sympathetic behaviour from teacher to avoid fear, anxiety and frustration. They should be assigned simple task or easy work.
3. They should be encouraged even on their future, proper recognition, praise, affection and freedom of learning should be provided.
4. The special classes and special school may be established according to their needs and requirements.

There should be the facilities of guidance, counselling and psychological therapy services in the schools. The curriculum should provide the training in manual work, wood craft, house craft and laundry work, etc.

It is true that the mentally retarded child fails to make progress at school. But it is difficult to know why they fail to do so. Researchers put all mentally retarded children in four groups: (i) the slow learner, (ii) the educable mentally retarded, (iii) the trainable mentally retarded, and (iv) totally dependent mentally retarded. Very often, the slow learner and the educable mentally retarded remain undetected in the classroom. Here we will discuss only the provisions for educable mentally retarded and trainable mentally retarded.

We have evidential proof that educable mentally retarded children tend to fail in an ordinary school. However they are capable of making progress in normal schools. So the schools must provide such curriculum and methodology of teaching that will enable them to overcome their difficulties easily. The teacher must give priority in helping the mentally retarded child to become self-sufficient and an accepted adult member of the community in which he lives. The special methods which are generally adopted in teaching the educable mentally retarded are as follows:

Individualisation: While we consider the special methods for educating the educable mentally retarded, obviously the dominant theme which comes to mind is the "individualisation of education". This term does not mean that the children receive individual instructions with small classes, but it implies that each child is allowed to proceed at his own pace of learning according to his own unique growth pattern. Of course, these children need opportunities for group participation, so that correct social attitudes may be developed.

Learning by Doing: For educating the educable mentally retarded children, the implication of the "principle of learning by doing" cannot be ignored. Here the basic principle of special education is that the children should learn by doing. Top priority is given to activity methods which lay emphasis on learning through experience. Generally the defect of the mentally handicapped child lies in the area of relational and abstract thought. So he faces difficulties in learning where the method of communication is largely verbal. These children learn better through such materials which appeal most to their senses.

Need for Learning Readiness: The concepts of maturation and willingness to learn should be given due importance while introducing academic work to the mentally handicapped. These children have the ability to learn to read, but they should be prepared through appropriate readiness programmes. It is advisable to wait until the child is intellectually and psychologically ready to accept the challenge.

Graded Curriculums: It is true that these children learn more slowly than average children. So that necessity of careful gradation of these subjects becomes a must. Here the teachers face difficulties for gradation of students and for preparing the study materials for slow learners. No doubt it is a tough task for teachers, still, not impossible to accomplish.

Repetition: Mentally handicapped children have a poor memory. For them, reaching method must provide for a considerable amount of repetition if learned material is to be retained. However, there is no justification for rote learning. The children should understand the materials clearly before facing any retention test. The memory span of these children can be increased by making them interested and motivated. Research has shown that the memory span of these children increases, if the learning materials have meaningful associations.

Periods of Short Duration: Mentally retarded children have limited power of concentration. For this reason, formal teaching periods should be kept fairly short. It is of importance to note as to how long a child can concentrate when the subject is stimulating.

Projects: "Introduction of Projects" or "Centres of Interest" is a significant approach for teaching mentally retarded children. Research is on to known, how this can be done without serious disruption of the basic subject programme. The teachers should not introduce the topics around which centres of interest grow and develop. But it should arise naturally out of classroom situations where the manifestation of further information is clear.

Here the point of origin maybe a short story, a poem, a song, a film or a picture in a magazine or newspaper. Undue importance should not be given to the source, but the teacher must know how to present it through careful planning and guidance.

Mainstream Education

1. EMR children should receive education in common with others in general schools. Educational programme for the EMR children should aim at development of:
   a. Academic skills,
   b. Social competence,
   c. Personal adjustment, and
   d. Occupational adequacy.
2. Depending upon the nature of retardation they may be educated in the regular classroom or regular classroom with part time instruction in the resource room or special class in the regular school.

3. The curriculum at the primary stage should be an extension of that of pre-school education. The curriculum for EMR children should be oriented towards providing readiness skills, language development, concept formation, socially adaptive behaviours and teaching basic of reading, mathematics and hand-writing. Teaching of tool subjects such as reading, arithmetic, handwriting, oral language should be very simple and interesting and of the standard expected of normal kindergarten-age children.
4. If some retarded children are in need of special class instruction the following principles should be followed.
   a. The younger the children, the smaller the class.
   b. The more heterogeneous the group, the smaller the class.
   c. Special class should always be organised within the regular primary school.
   d. Special class instruction should be given by the resource teacher or the itinerant teacher only.
   e. Àdequate diagnosis should be made before they are placed in the special class.
   f. The resource teacher should have considerable freedom in adapting the curriculum to the needs of individual children.
5. Whether the retarded child is educated in the regular classroom or resources room, instruction should be systematic and sequential in nature.
6. As the child makes progress in the class less and less emphasis should be placed on readiness skills and more and more emphasis should be given on academic skills and the basic tool subjects such as reading, writing and arithmetic.
7. Emphasis should be gradually placed on work-habits, vocational training, and family life education as the child makes progress from primary education to the secondary education, This should be particularly emphasised for older retarded students.

Vocational Training should actually pass through five phases, such as vocational exploration, vocational evaluation, vocational training, vocational placement and follow up. In the phase of vocational exploration, the MER student is familiarised with the nature of various occupations and their skills requirements. In the second phase the retarded student is exposed to experiences with different job skills in order to determine the vocational abilities and preferences of the student. In the third phase emphasis is given on developing job skills and on preparing the student for a range or occupations. The fourth stage consists of locating a job for the student and placing him in the job. The last stage entails counselling and further training or replacement.

Teacher's Role: A large number of mildly and some moderately retarded children do enter the regular primary schools. They remain unidentified and unnoticed for some years until their problems become so serious that they experience failure and frustration and later drop-out from the school. This calls for early identification, diagnosis and assessment and making instruction systematic and sensitive. The regular classroom teacher has to play a significant role in teaching such children in the regular classroom.

1. The regular teacher should be familiar with the behavioural characteristics of Mr. children for purpose of identifying and referring them to the psychologist for assessment.
2. He should develop a positive and optimistic view about the educability of such children.
3. He should avoid as far as possible labelling the child, passing on damaging, remarks and also see that the non-retarded peers behave in a positive way with the child.
4. He should create favourable conditions in his class and the schools for social and academic integration of EMR children.
5. He should constantly attempt to sequence learning tasks. Relatively complex units should be broken down into a hierarchy of sub-units and attempt should be made to teach one sub-unit at a time, help children to learn the sub unit, and then to proceed to the next sub-unit.

6. The teacher should encourage retarded children to make use of verbal mediation in learning the tool subjects. The retarded child should rehearse verbally what he is to learn and remember. Verbal mediation is a very useful learning strategy for learning concepts and problem-solving.
7. Retarded children do not know how to learn different subjects. Learning to learn is a useful technique for retarded children. The retarded child should be told verbally and exposed to models and tutoring by non-disabled peers for learning how to learn.
8. Many retarded children learn best by drill and repetition. Thus the teacher should give emphasis on drill and repetition in teaching language items and arithmetic skills.
9. Retarded children learn bets through concrete experiences, play way method, audio-visual aids and action-oriented teaching, etc. The regular teacher should, therefore make use of concrete objects, storytelling, dramatisation, music, dance, play situations, multisensory approach coloured pictures, picture cards, word cards and toy materials in the teaching-learning situations.
10. Many retarded individuals may be lacking in motivation. The regular teacher should look for ways to increase the motivation of such children. Interesting pictures and stories and novelty can increase motivation. However, progress should be from known to unknown, familiar to new experiences.
11. The retarded child should be given success experiences in learning tool subjects and social behaviours. Each experience of a retarded child should be followed by a consistent programme of reinforcement and feedback. Praise, recognition, reward, positive remarks, love and affection can have stimulating effect on the child in learning various skills.
12. The retarded child should be given opportunity to participate in classroom activities and co-curricular activities in the school. Such children can participate in drawing, painting, games and sports, music, songs and drama, gardening,

beautification of school campus, celebrations and observations, etc.

13. Continuous assessment should be made by the regular teacher about the child's level of functioning. This assessment may be either formal or informal.
14. The regular teacher should seek the advice of the resource teacher whenever he has difficulty with the child's learning and behaviour. The resource teacher who is a consultant in the methodology of teaching the retarded children can help the regular teacher in teaching and behaviour modification techniques.

Organisation of the Class: In order to make the mainstreaming programme effective for the mildly mentally retarded, certain organisational activities are necessary. These would include: scheduling time (catch up time in the few minutes before closure of the school each day, using paraprofessionals, hiring and itinerant teacher) to meet individual needs; providing for mastery learning (combining mastery of basic, most essentially skills, given extra time, ensuring assistance, study, practice, self test-recycle and retest); using small group instruction (proceeding slowly, assigning clear, discrete short term tasks, extending the group work from two or three pupils to more in a group); per tutoring developing resource units; organising learning activities (mathematics, reading, science, etc.) for active participation, using programmed instruction; using micro computers (wherever feasible).

Teacher have to ensure and understand the individualised instruction does not mean teaching each pupil individually. Organisational arrangements for individualising instruction can provide multimedia materials for pupils who learn best by seeing, doing, listening and talking. Adaptive aids can be integrated for exceptional pupils into classroom instruction.

Besides, a classroom for mainstreaming the mild mentally retarded would necessitate use of special teaching methods: use of developmentally appropriate examples and materials, ensuring success, limiting learning test to attention span, presentation of learning task in small, sequential steps, use of concrete concepts and modes, repetition, showing parallels with daily life and providing readiness for learning: reasoning, environmental experience, language, attention, visual discrimination, auditory discrimination. Each of these readiness can be developed in the mildly mentally retarded through systematic activities. Research evidences substantiate these basics.

Teaching for information processing is also achieved by using multisensory teaching techniques. Social skills and mental health and adjustments have been developed in these children with the limits of their educability. Cognitive learning is also achieved among EMR children through successful manipulation of informational and affective reinforcement techniques (Panda, 1971). Manipulation of achievement responsibility to the advantage of their achievement has been a positive strength for mildly retarded Further, a clear model has been suggested to understand the dynamics of mildly retarded by looking into their family.

The centrally sponsored scheme of IED envisages for early identification, assessment and education of mildly retarded and educable mentally retarded children in general schools. Most of these children are already in the schools unidentified. Unless EMR children are identified early and unless adequate measures are taken for their care, training and education that, will experience failure and later drop out from the school before completing the basic education. They will not only remain as burdens for the society but universalisation of elementary education will not be successful. EMIR children, like any other normal children have the same fundamental rights to exist.

Training, education and work and this calls for greater public understanding and awareness about the problems and special needs of such children. Care, training and education of such children are not the sole responsibilities of teachers. Parents and the community have also equal responsibilities in the care and training of such children.

The trainable mentally retarded children have I.Q. in the range of 25-55. These children are much more retarded than educable mentally retarded children. So their educational structure and curriculum are different. These children are mainly taught to take care of themselves and to do simple occupational jobs. Though physical anomalies like seizures, lack of control over elimination, etc., are very much prominent, regular schooling is difficult for these children. The primary objectives of TMR education are to teach the much more retarded children how to do their daily work without the help of anybody.

These daily works include washing, dressing themselves, eating properly, doing simple jobs and toilet training, etc. Recent reports reveal that in many cases, TMR education has proved a failure because they learn nothing more than what they would have learnt at home.

Here, less emphasis is given to the teaching of academic subjects and more time is devoted to the development of sensori-motor, self-care and daily living skills. As these children tire very quickly, a more definite timetable is necessary with short periods of activity. However, with the above objectives in mind, the curriculum should cover the following:

Self-Care: The curriculum school include a programme of simple habit training. This enables the children to develop skills of self-help in respect of their daily practical needs. Methods which are adopted for this purpose should be related to the real life experiences and everyday needs of the children.

Social Training: Priority should be given to group activities such as games, simple dramatic work and storytellings, etc. By this, the gregariousness and affiliation may be increased. The children become generally active and cooperative.

Sensory Training: Special emphasis must be laid on instructions by which the children will be able to make the fullest use of their senses.

Language Development: They must be provided with some aids through which they can have better speech development and proper understanding of verbal concepts.

Craft Work and Music: For developing the feeling of self-confidence in TMR children, the curriculum should include simple crafts training programmes like weaving, rug making, basketing, etc. By having this, economic self-sufficiency can be reached.

Research reports say that music is sometimes found as a means of releasing energy and provides a form of expression which the mentally retarded children enjoy. So this should find a place in the curriculum.

Besides all these above factors, emphasis is put on the group work. However individual study of each child is necessary for chalking out individual programmes related to different aspects of personality growth.

Individual-centred programmes are now being conducted at the Institute of Defectology in Moscow, Russia to educate the mentally retardates. Primarily the child is diagnosed as retarded by the age of six months. The time span from that age till the onset of puberty is very important for these children. During this span, individual programmes, from the multi-disciplinary points of view are prepared and implemented. It is observed that with the onset of puberty, the retardation is overcome. It is true that this programme is quite difficult and time consuming. It is also costly to manage individual based programmes. In a developing country like India, it is quite unthinkable, however, attempts should be made on an experimental basis to view the outcome.

Some psychologists have opined recently formalisation of education for retarded children. Of course, their argument is in support of EMR children. According to them, special education for mildly retarded children may only develop a complex in them in so far as they are inferior to and different from others.

They argue that mildly retarded children should be taught in regular classrooms instead of placing them in separate groups. The most prominent supporter of normalisation of education of EMR children, is Dunn who says that the past and present practices of special education are morally and educationally wrong.

Further researches of Robinson and Robinson (1976) also supported normalisation of education of mentally retarded. They are of the opinion that a special classroom is an isolating experience.

They are also of the view that EMR children are better able to succeed socially and academically if they are exposed to models other than their own. Meticulous observation confirmed that retarded children placed in regular classrooms may be less disturbed than those forced to remain in special classes. One of the reasons is that it is reality oriented. Mentally retarded children help other children to understand and accept them. As a result, the retarded child gets better scope for emotional security and adjustment. However, recently modern education for the EMR child involves a combination of special and regular classes.

Very often parents fail to understand their children, and prefer to keep the mentally retarded children at home. But they have to develop a right and positive attitude for bringing them up. If parents suspect that a particular child is mentally retarded, they should get him medically checked up first. If possible, they should take the child to the guidance of psychological centre to ascertain the degree of mental retardation. After confirmation, they must face the problem courageously and with determination.

They should not blame anybody or curse their fate for their child. The parents should know that the child needs basic security and he can have it through love and affection. Sometimes certain neighbours are so unsympathetic that became responsible for increasing the stress on the family.

But they should be a little cautious in dealing with such type of children. In some developed countries, baby sitters are prepared to deal with all possible dispositions of the mentally retarded children and they relieve the parents to go out together occasionally. But for a developing country like India, it is only a dream. The family members of mentally retarded child must see that their child is not bullied or teased by other children.

Duties of the Parents: Care and training of EMR children should start in the family by the parents:

1. Experienced mothers, the grandmother and other old women in the family are familiar with normal milestones of development. If a child is found to have delayed development

and if abnormalities are noticed in his physical and intellectual developments and if deficiencies are noticed in his adaptive behaviour he should be referred to paedriaticians and child psychologists for diagnosis and treatment.

2. Parents should not feel dejected and disappointed about the condition of their children. They should not loose patience but instead should take all possible steps to prevent further damage through proper care and training as per the advice of doctors, psychologists and teachers.
3. Home-based training is most effective and provides the foundation for later learning in the school. Parents and particularly the mother should create conditions and teach the child daily living skills, social skills, communication skills and pre-academic skills during the first few years under reinforced practice and through enjoyable activities. Listening skills, attending skills, naming objects, manipulating objects, awareness of self, responding to and greeting others, conversation, reading pictures, music, play, game and story telling should be emphasised in the home based training programme.

Disorders of Mind

There are two terms Mental retardation and 'Mental deficiency differ significantly to each other. The mental deficiency refers top lower level of intelligence or low intelligent quotient. Mental retardation refers to sub average intellectual functioning which originates during the developmental period.

The mental deficiency is due to the heredity factors where as mental retardation is due to both heredity as well as environmental factors. Mental retardation is remediable where as mental deficiency is not remediable. Mental retardation is to be diagnosed and remediation can be given. Mental deficiency, is due to nervous system but mental retardation is due to social and intellectual factors.

There are children who cannot mentally function as well as most children we find in society. These children are subnormal in intelligence and behaviour This retardation is pervasive and has been in all societies and cultures in varying proportions.

Students will get comprehensive and clear idea about mentally retarded children after reading the text presented here.

The Basic Issues: There are some important definitions of mental retardation.

"Mental deficiency is characterised by inadequate intellectual functioning in adaptive, associative and learning power, yet sufficient with I. Q. fifty (50) to become socially adequate and occupationally competent with the help of special educational facilities."

The most comprehensive definition given by the American Association on Mental Retardation. The definition given in 1983 which is as follow:

> "Mental Retardation refers to significantly sub-average general intellectual functioning, resulting in or associated with concurrent impairments in adaptive behaviour, and manifested during the developmental period."

The children with mental deficiency lack in mental development and possess less I.Q. their I.Q. is less than 75 but more than 50.

The Background: Mental retardation has been known for centuries and different terms have been used to explain it. Early in the twentieth century, the terms moron, imbecile and idiot explained the three levels of retardation. During the 1940s the term feeble-minded was used. In recent years terms like mental subnormality and developmental disability are being used.

Until the twentieth century, retardation was defined in terms of an individual's inability to meet the minimal demands of society. In 1905 Alfred Binet developed a method of identifying students who could be expected to fail in the regular school curriculum and who therefore required a special instructional programme, which was translated and used in the USA by Henry Herbert Goddard. Terman's 1916 edition of the Stanford Binet Intelligence Scale was quickly adopted as standardised, objective, norm-referenced way of identifying retarded children. I.Q. became standard for classification of mental retardation. However, David Wechsler, who devised a series of intelligence tests, warned against the rigid use of intelligence test scores as the sole criterion for diagnosing retardation.

The Mental Deficiency Act of 1921 in England considered "Mental defectiveness as a conditions of arrested or incomplete development of mind existing before the age of eighteen years, whether arising from inherent causes or induced by disease or injury".

One of the earliest definitions was given by Dool (1941). According to him mentally retarded children show different characteristics. These are:

1. Social incompetency.
2. Mental subnormality.
3. The deficiency is developmentally linked.
4. The retardation finally comes on maturity.
5. Retardation is Constitutional in origin.
6. It is essentially incurable.

Encyclopedia Britanica defines mental deficiency as "A state of subnormal evaluation of the human organism in consequence of which the individual affected is incapable of assuming the responsibilities expected of a socially adequate person, such as self-direction, self-support and social participation".

Sarason and Dorris (1969) defined, "Mental retardation refers to individuals who for temporary or long standing reasons function intellectually below the average of their peer groups, but social adequacy is not in question or if it is in question, there is little likelihood that the individual can learn to function independently and adequately in the community".

All the definitions were prevalent at different times and in different countries. But none of them could adequately explain mental retardation. The characteristics pointed out by different experts are also unrelated to one another. Therefore, the American Association of Mental Deficiency (AAMD) set up a committee under the Chairmanship of Rick Heber to develop a comprehensive definition of mental retardation.

Heber defined mental retardation as "significantly sub-average general functioning existing concurrently with deficits in adaptive behaviour and manifested during the developmental period".

This definition was subsequently restated as: "Mental retardation refers to significantly sub-average general intellectual functioning, resulting in or associated with, concurrent impairments in adaptive behaviour and manifested during the developmental period". This definition has three aspects:

1. Sub-average intellectual functioning
2. Developmental in origin, and
3. Impairment in adaptive behaviour.

Different Functions: Mentally Retarded Children who function at different levels of retardation require different educational programmes, curricula, methods, and materials. In recent years, differences observed among them have led to the use of four levels: mild, moderate, severe, and profound retardation. The mild group, which makes up approximately 75 to 80. I.Q students in the EMR range are capable of learning basic academic skills of reading, writing and arithmetic. Most children can learn vocational skills.

These children may enter school at the usual age, but formal reading and writing instruction may be delayed until about age eight or nine. During school years, they may be given instruction in simple arithmetical concepts, understanding of the home and community, and development of good work habits. Curricula are designed to provide basic skills for coping with the environment. Educable children usually develop language skills.

The moderate level of retardation (I.Q range about 35 to 60) includes essentially the same group as those called trainable mentally retarded (TMR) in schools. Until the 1950s, this group was usually not admitted to public schools. Gradually separate classes were started for them under the public school system. The curricula for TMR students differ from that of EMR curricula. TMR students are unlikely to develop independence as adults. They are unlikely to learn to handle finances beyond simple purchases and usually need some supervisory help. The academic skills taught include learning to recognise signs and common symbols, learning to recognise and use coins, and telling time to the half or quarter-hour. In addition to development of skills of self-care and simple skills, TMR students eventually develop language skills, but articulation problems are more common than that in the EMR children. Teachers use experiences as well as reinforcement techniques to teach the TMR.

Severely retarded (I.Q range about 20 to 35) and profoundly retarded (I.Q below 20) children are not considered for school placement. Educators usually referred to all retarded children below the TMR level as custodial. It was assumed that all such children would be in residential institutions.

Although today about 80 per cent of individuals who are in residential facilities are severely or profoundly retarded, many others have remained at home. With the deinstitutionalisation movement, many children in western countries are provided education through public schools.

Mental Disturbance

The development of child's personality and his general adjustment can not be ascribed by the influence of parents and family, of the community and the school practices but mainly depends on the mental health of the learners and the teacher. It is said that mother is first teacher or equal to the several teacher. It is said that mother is first teacher or equal to the several teacher. The home is the principal environmental factor contributing to his personality development and his adjustment, mid there after, during his school years, he is still subject to the influences of home and community. Especially his home should have provided for his basic organic needs and should have furnished an environment well suited to meet his needs for security and adequacy. The pleasant and satisfactory experiences should be provided for the personality development and adjustment of the student.

The knowledge and understanding of learning, intelligence, personality and motivation is sufficient for a teacher but the must understand the mental health of the students. Mental health influences the functioning of students and also their physical health. The mental health and physical health are very closely related to one another. A teacher has to deal with normal students in the class room as well as in the school. Mental and physical illness have the adverse effect on their performance and learning, outcomes. It is essential to understand the concept of mental health of students.

Basic Issues: Health is as freedom from ailments, it is the general notion about health. Mental health is like physical health, consists of the absence of serious defects or mental ailments. It is the approach of physician who gives you a physical test. He has a checklist of defects or ailments considered to be serious. If a person is free from these ailments considered to be serious. If a person is free from these ailments or symptoms is considered healthy. In considering either physical or mental health, such a checklist of ailments would emphasise defects which produce distress or interfere with the large functions of the individual.

Another approach to mental health is a number of feelings, attitudes or ways of behaving which lead to distress or interfere with larger goals and which are unusual or inevitable. These conditions are abnormal in the sense that there is departure from normal behaviour. This departure from normal is said to be ill mental health.

The concept of norm comes to act as an adaptation level. People to this norm are considered healthy but those are below the norm, it would draw our attention and are known unhealthy. In matters of health, mental or physical, this adaptation level or reference norm is not always a simple mathematical average. It is sometimes based on what would be expected if nothing unusual had occurred.

Health is also considered as positive attainment. Mental health should not be measured by the evils we avoid but by positive steps we take towards our true potential. In this view, descriptions of the healthy person are almost descriptions of the ideal person.

1. Minimal concept of mental health is considered as the absence of illness. It is the freedom from ailments, absence of mental disorder. He has the good resistance to stress.
2. Enlarged concept of mental health is considered as attainment of positive values and attitudes. He has enjoyable experiences,

happy, zestful and creative person. He has the potentialities for effective functioning day to day life.

The positive view mental health emphasise on effectiveness and competence. It is said that 'health mind in healthy body'.

During the present days mental ailments have increased tremendously and have involved serious problems at the national level in industrial development, social and economic changes. The problems of mental health has acquired importance in the national developmental programmes.

It is difficult to define the term Mental Health comprehensively. The definitions of mental health have great variations but the fundamental elements are more or less the same, inspite of workings used in their definitions.

Norma E. Cutts and Nicholas Moseley have defined the term Mental Health comprehensively:

> "Mental health is the ability to adjust satisfactorily to the various strains of the environment, we meet in life and mental hygiene as the means we take to assure this adjustment."

In the process of education mental health plays a significant role. The sound mental health is the first condition for the education. Mental health is most important condition for effective teaching and learning. It is, said that sound mind in sound body.

Thus, mental health and education are closely related to each other. The students learning or achievement depends on their sound mental health. It is essential to the learning process as intelligence. It is a crucial condition for education.

The following criteria have been identified of mentally healthy students or persons. It is also known as positive mental health signs:

1. Possesses socially adaptable behaviours.
2. He is emotionally satisfied.
3. He possesses adaptability and resilient mind.
4. His desires are in harmony with socially approved norms.
5. He is enthusiastic and reasonable.

6. He possesses good habits and constructive attitude.
7. He has insight into his own conduct.
8. He has own philosophy and values of life.

It is a fact that healthy person is in conscious control of his life. There is consistency in his behaviour and conduct. A healthy person is aware about his own strength and weakness. Psychological healthy person does not live in the past but he always plans and thinks for future and acts according into the present. His future orientation is very realistic according to his own capacities and resources.

Diseases of Brain: There are many positive aspects of mental health, the avoidance of specific ailments may not be the objective of mental health but it is one of important objective. There are several types of ailments of mental health.

1. Distortion of Reality or Denial
2. Unusual difficulties with anxiety.
3. Difficulties with Self-control and
4. Inadequate relation with other persons.

Distortion of Reality or Denial: An important feature of mental ailment is a distorted view of important facets of the world. The person may refuse to face his own hates, or fears or off beat desires. Some such moderate denials or distortion are of course quite typical. As a matter of fact, there may even be some advantage in temporarily turning our backs on some of the more unbearable pressures.

Unusual Difficulties with Anxiety: Anxiety is no mark of mental ill health. The lack of anxiety situation. Under these circumstances, reality anxiety as it is termed would be normal. It is only when such anxiety seems out of proportion to the menace that would consider that something is wrong. Such neurotic anxiety is unhealthful in and of itself. It brings serious distress.

Difficulties with Self-control: Lack of self-control has long been identified with poor adjustment. The self-control is regarded as the key test of emotional adjustment. Mental ill health may be associated with both the amount of control maintained and the type of the control that is used The self-control can not eliminate the basic urges or drives. On the contrary, the wholesome personality is endowed with strong urges or drives. The happy, admirable persons is well equipped with vigorous appetites and a full quota of needs. In a proper balance between drive and control there should be evidence of a happy and spontaneous energy. The balance maintains joyfully and zestfully to his task.

Inadequate Relations with other People: Social relations are related to mental health in at least two ways. First of all, to avoid ill health, we must have make some kind of adjustment to other people. Second, our must have made some kind of adjustment to other people. Second, our relations with other people often cast some light on other aspect of adjustment. They serve as an index by which other facts of mental health may be observed.

Positive Aspects: In describing some of the mental conditions are to be avoided and our attention should be on positive attributes which are as follow:

1. A Positive view of the self.
2. Striving towards a Confident mastery.
3. Specific. Positive goal.
4. Self-concept and
5. Mental health, Character and Morality.

A Positive View of the Self: The feeling about himself should be based on a view of himself that is reasonably, free about, himself should be based on a view of himself that is reasonably free from distortion. He should have some general notion and the notion he should not be too far from the objective truth or reality of life. He must also recognise the significant traits that given him some concern, his poor eyesight, his fear of rough and tumble games, his tendency to stammer. Self-acceptance has an intimate relation to freedom from distortion.

Striving towards a Confident Mastery: One of the attributes of positive mental health is that of commitment and striving. The healthy person does not merely avoid evils and handicaps, nor does he deal with them by simple retreat. As he gains success in these enterprises, he gains confidence in this ability to master other problems.

Specific Positive Goals: The several Psychologists who put forward the goals of positive mental health have, in total proposed a long list of desirable attributes.

Mental Health, Character and Morality: Mentally healthy child is the good child. The positive mental health called for a reasonable degree of socialisation and, sensitivity to the needs of others. Mentally healthy child generally possess good character and morality

Perfect Mental Health: The following are main indications of superior mental health:

Adaptiveness and Flexibility: It includes ability to deal with the world, to specific objectives and to carry them out, being guided by the results of the efforts.

Capacity to Gratify One's Needs: It means spontaneous actions in the relaxed enjoyment of life has sexual capacity. Ability to work for one's own interests.

Competence and Goodwill in Dealing with Other: He takes part in productive work and meets responsibility in a manner approved by other and fulfils the commitments to others ability to accept help. Trust and liking for people. He is capable of intimacy and warmness.

Intellectual Ability: He is accurate in his perception of reality and of self ability to solve problems in rational much common sense. He has broad comprehensive view of life.

Emotional Control: He is capable to handle anxiety and frustration, moral and conscientious. He is courageous and high morale.

Autonomy, Productivity and a Sense of Worth: He takes initiative, self-reliant in making contributions, Emotionally independent, detached, strong sense of identity and feeling of self-determination, He seeks self-actualisation, sense of achievement and self respect.

Integration and Equilibration: He maintains balance and consistency in dealing with opposing forces, mature unifying view of life and given impression of maturity.

Theoretical Basis: There are various theories of psychology which deal with the concept of mental health. Theories related to the needs provide the basis of mental health.

1. Maslow's Hierarchy of needs.
2. Murrays Need Theory, and
3. The Hygiene Theory of motivation.

Maslow's Hierarchy of Needs: Maslow (1948) developed hierarchy of needs with the primitive needs at the base and deferrable needs superimposed. There are five levels of needs psychological safety needs, love and belonging needs, esteem needs and self actualisation needs. Next to physiological-needs involved in avoiding danger or securing safety. One step beyond this is the need for esteem. Esteem need includes both the good opinion of other people and self approval. When pressure from these other needs is partially relaxed that the individual can get on with self-actualisation.

Throughout the hierarchy, any second order need will be at a disadvantage in competing with first order need. A fairly strong urge towards artistic creating, for instance, might be ruled out by weaker but more primitive need to avoid the contempt of others. When the basic needs are satisfied to some degree that the student can hopefully address himself to the more ambitious goals of competences and achievements.

Contribution to 'Education': The teacher of course, can not be the key person in helping the student meet the basic needs in such a way that he will be free to go on to higher level achievement. The teacher can, however, do much towards providing the student with some of the esteem and affectionate regard so important to his well-being. The teacher's warm emotional support can help make the classroom a less stressful place and enable him to take the risks necessary for self-actualisation.

Theory of Motivation: Fredrick HerzBerg (1966) formulated a new theory of motivation. He has explained the 'Need of theory' and classifies human needs into two factors:

Hygiene Factors: These hygiene factors are involved in the learning environment. These factors refer to the following components of learning situation: a) Working conditions, b) Administrative norms of schools, c) The form of supervision of school, and d) the safety and standard of school.

These factors provide the encouragement to the students to work hard. These factors are related to the environment or working conditions. These factors are prerequisite for higher order of learning.

Motivators: The factors are related to the activities and behaviour of the learners rather than the environment of learning. These are organised in teaching-learning situations such as reward, verbal praise, recognition, success, knowledge, of result and novelty. These factors are of four types: a) Achievement and performance, b) Recognition and Responsibility, c) Advancement and freedom, and d) Personal growth.

The factors have the permanent influence on the change of behaviour of the students whereas hygiene factors have temporary effect. The internal motivation is more effective than external one which is helpful in satisfying higher needs of esteem and self actualisation. A teacher's responsibility is in both factors hygiene and motivators. The hygiene factors are related to the school environment and organisational climate. The teachers and principal have to manage and organise hygiene factors in the school campus and in the classroom.

The students are encouraged and praised by the leachers for their good performance and desirable behaviour in the class and school by establishing rapport with them. These factors contribute to their mental health.

Dominating Agents

There are several factors which influence the mental health of child. The influence of parents and family life of the community and of school practices upon the personality or mental health of the child. The following are the main factors and areas of these influences:

Influences of the Parents and Family life.

The influence of Poverty on the child's personality.

A feeling of insecurity.

A feeling of inferiority.

The parents who reject the child.

Effect of Rejection on the child.

Expression of Rejection by the parents.

Origin of Rejection in the parents.

Unattractive children.

Relationship between husband and wife.

Immature parents.

Parents who over protect the child.

Expression of over protection by the mother.

Effects of over protection on the child.

The influence of the community on mental health.

Effects of school practices on mental health of children and their personality:

1. The effect of over competition in school.
2. Over restriction in the classroom.
3. Unsuitable curriculum.
4. Teachers method of handling the, class
5. The effect of the teachers personality on the class
6. Teachers report of behaviour problem in the class room
7. Treatment of behaviour problem in the classroom.

The influences of parents, and family life, community and school practices have been enumerated. There are four major factors of parents and family life and sex factors of school practices are listed here.

Role of Parents: The following are the main major for influence of the Parents and Family Life. The details have been given as follow:

Influence of Poverty on the Child's Personality: An excellent description of the effect of poverty on the personality of the child has been made by Plant. He points out that 'hardening' of the personality results from constant financial strain. He feels that "this is not a mechanisms of resignation, but the development of patterns of response.

That prevents each experience of want (it matters little how drastic) from resulting in the emotional reverberations which accompanied the first such experience". This is similar to reaction which Lewin calls 'encysting' in which the child attempts to make himself unassailable, in effect, by erecting a wall between himself and the environment.

A Feeling of Insecurity: Feeling of insecurity is a second resultant, according to Plant. Children who have suffered, repeated and serious blows to their sense of adequacy from a long-continued real fear of cold and hunger are likely to show a picture of anxiety and panic. This feeling becomes so firmly bound up with the personality structure that late acquisition of a sufficient income will not remove it.

A Feeling of Inferiority: According to Plant a third resultant is a feeling of inferiority. This may be found in children above the lowest economic levels; it occurs whenever there is a marked discrepancy between the economic status, reflected in type of home, clothes, belongings, etc. of the child and that of other children with whom, he is in contact, This feeling is likely to become heightened during adolescence when material and social problems are more in the focus of a child's interest.

A child is said to be rejected when he is disliked or not wanted by one or both parents, a situation which inevitably result in insufficient meeting off the child's needs for affection and belongingness. Children whose parents strongly dislike them at times; but love them most of the time are not considered to be rejected, consequently the following discussion is not applicable to them.

There are still many gaps in our knowledge of rejection. It cannot be distinguished as yet the supposedly different effects on the child of: 1) rejection by both parents as opposed to rejection by one, 2) the sex of the rejecting parent in relation to the sex of the child, and 3) the degree of affection shown by the non-rejecting parents. There have been however, a series of excellent studies which throw light on the problem, and we will draw freely from these in the course of our discussion.

Effect of Rejection on the Child: The pattern of behaviour of the rejected child is reported to depend primarily on, one or more of these factors: 1) a desire to win affection or at least attention, 2) a, wish to retaliate against people for the hostility shown him by the parents, or 3) feelings of worthlessness and anxiety. It is, of course, incorrect to attribute his behaviour entirely to one or another of these categories since, for example, one for of behaviour (that is activity calculated to annoy) maybe based on a desire for attention plus a wish to retaliate.

It is a very difficult to diagnose rejection from the behaviour of the child alone because children who are not rejected may show some of the same symptoms.

Expression of Rejection by the Parents: The sign of rejection exhibited by the parents vary from those which are obviously unequivocal to those which might possible indicate dislike for the child. Rejection is easily diagnosed when the parent's feeling is fully conscious and when there is no attempt to conceal it; not so easily diagnosed otherwise.

Some parents will frankly acknowledge that they heartily dislike their children and wish they had never been born. The majority of rejecting parents are not so outspoken, but express their feelings in the way they treat the child. Getting rid of the child is one of the most obvious signs of rejection. Desertion of the child or placement in an institution, boarding home or boarding school (for the higher income groups) is a common device among rejecting parents. Harsh treatment, being very strict with the child, using severe physical punishment, are all too frequent practices.

Some of the more subtle methods of expressing rejection are:

1. Expecting the child to live up to standards that, *i.e.* much too high for him,

2. Never saying anything favourable about the child,
3. Comparing him unfavourable with sibling or children in the neighbourhood,
4. Responding with surprise to favourable statements made by other about the child,
5. Taking conscientious care of the child needs but with an air of martyrdom.

Origin of Rejection in the Parents: The soil from which rejection grows is likely to be an unsatisfactory marital adjustment. The mother's feeling towards a disliked husband may be extended to the child. The husband may dislike the child of his unloved wife. Interference with the sources of satisfaction of the parents is an important cause. In homes of low economic level, the birth of a child means cutting down on necessities of life for the family in order to meet the baby's needs; on a somewhat higher level, parenthood often means giving up the possibility of further education, or drastic reduction in accustomed comforts. When the wife is employed in a job in which she takes a great deal of pleasure, childbirth means at least temporary and often permanent separation from the position.

Immature Fathers and Mothers who are still dependent on their own parents and who tend to take more interest in dancing, entertaining, and having a good time than in child-rearing are likely to continue to resent the presence of a son or daughter.

Unattractive Children are likely to be rejected. Unattractiveness need not be as obvious to an observer as lack of beauty, a malformed body or mental deficiency. A special quality or lack of it may maketh child seem unattractive to his particular parents – a boy to parents who keenly hoped for a girl; a frail child, even though charming, to parents who emphasise strength and agility; a slow child to parents who think quickness is the sumum bonum; even minor matters such as lack of interest in music when the parents put a high premium on this art-these traits and others may constitute special kinds of unattractiveness.

The relations between the husband and wife: for example when one parent becomes so occupied with the child that the previous degree of affection for the spouse seems to be lacking or to be greatly reduced the child may be rejected by the offended parent. The situation may be even, more critical when a step parent enters the home. It is normal for step parents to feel insecure in the new role at first, but one in whom this feeling is intense and persistent may easily begin to believe that the child is preventing a happy relationship between husband and wife.

Parents Who Overprotect the Child: A child is said to be over-protected when he is excessively cared for, shielded, and loved. As very little is known about overprotection by the fattier, probably because he assumes the responsibility for the child's care so rarely, this discussion will deal only with the overprotective mother. Much is still unknown about the causes and the effects of overprotection on the child, in spite of a number of excellent investigations in this field.

Expression of Overprotection by the Mother: Overprotection may result from either domination or indulgence, or vacillation between the two. In any type of overprotection, however the mother characteristically spends a great deal of time with the child, takes excessive care of him, and as a result succeeds in preventing the development of this independence. Specifically, she is likely to sleep with the child for years, amuse, play with, and found him for hours at a time.

Effects of Overprotection on the Child: Children of both dominating and overindulgent mothers often lack self-reliance. In both cases they have been for so long dependent on their mothers that they are unlikely to be able to assume responsibility for tasks or for minor life-problems. They continue to fine their security in the presence of their mothers, in whose absence they find it difficult to cope with the world.

Parents who Show Favouritism: When a strong preference is shown by the parents for one child the effect on both the favoured and the unfavoured child (for simplicity of discussion, only two-child families will be considered) is likely to be unfortunate. The favoured child may reflect, though in a mild form, the characteristics of the over indulged child. The unfavoured child is practically certain to show some form of jealousy.

Young children often make bodily attacks on the sibling, although direct aggression against the sibling is not always shown in their behaviour. Because of the feeling of injustice and lack of sufficient affection, they may exhibit negativism, restlessness, fighting, and attention-demanding activities especially in relation to their parents but also in relation to other adults and children. The behaviour of all unfavoured children does not show aggressive characteristics. Some will become despondent and withdraw. Others will throw great energy into competing with the sibling in socially approved activities, and still others will try to behave as differently as possible from their rival.

Parents who Have High Moral Standards: Children from homes with moral standards much more rigid than those of the rest of the community may be taught that sex is evil, that one thousand and one normal activities are sinful, *e.g.*, smoking, card-playing, going to the movies or the theatre, dancing, and reading modern novels.

This makes it inevitable that the child will meet numerous situations which would never have been a problem for him if it had not been for his rigid moral training. The most serious result is that children who accept this teaching acquire such severe consciences that they believe they are continually failing to live a proper life. Normal social relations are almost impossible for them in an average community and, all to frequently, they develop neurotic tendencies.

The child has as patterns parents who are dissolute, deliquent and of ten drunk one can not expect the child to the admirable personality traits. The effects of the home broken by divorce or separation are too familiar to relate. The poverty, rejection, over protection, favouritism and other specific condition cause for the ailment of mental health.

Community as a Force: Community influences on child personality adjustment are so multiform and the literature dealing with them is so indefinite that it is impossible to treat the topic adequately in a short space.

Some community conditions obviously important to children are:

1. The extent to which recreational facilities, social centres, and social agencies exist,
2. The degree of freedom allowed children by community-folk ways,
3. The disparity in economic levels,
4. The extent of race prejudice,
5. The extent of tolerance or intolerance of religious sects.

These are only a few of many community factors which indirectly affect the favourable or unfavourable development of children's personalities. A more general factor which should be mentioned is that the organisation of the community.

Practices in School: The school practices have significant influence on the children behaviour and their personality development. The important practices have been discussed in the following paragraphs:

The Effect of Over Competition and Examination in School: Authorities feel that the whole system of grades, examinations, and marks tends to place and undue emphasis on competition. The result in many cases is to discourage the slow learners and even many average pupils. The relatively fast learners are likely to get inflated notions of their own abilities. Excessive competition tends to breed an indifference to the welfare of others and to enhance self-interest.

Examinations, especially long ones, when used as even a partial basis for marks in a highly competitive atmosphere are likely to cause an undue strain and fatigue in many children..

The attendant strain may be increased in schools in which the results of examination are used as the primary criterion for rating the effectiveness of the teacher without taking into account the level of ability of the class. When examinations are used primarily for diagnostic purposes to detect areas of weakness in the children's knowledge and skill so that subsequent work may be better directed-then they are serving a worthy purpose.

Unsuitable Curriculum: If as too frequently occurs, the curriculum has little relation to the life. Problem of the children makes on contribution to their present needs, many unfortunate effects are produced. Antagonism to the school accompanied by misbehaviour may be expected, and a desire to "quit school" at the earliest legal age is likely to be born and nourished. Inquiries into the cause of delinquency have shown that some bright delinquents were first attracted to the questionable thrills of stealing as a result of their intense boredom with the curriculum of their school. Equally unfortunate is the plight of youngsters in many schools who are expected to master material beyond their ability.

Over Restriction in the Classroom: Many elementary and secondary schools unduly restrict the behaviour of their pupils. The ideal of many schools is pin-drop quietness and a place for every child and in the place. The traditional recess periods and the occasional working at the board are far from sufficient for most elementary school children's need for movement and activity. In the primary school the needs for movement and activity. In the primary school, the needs for both activity and rest are usually handled satisfactorily, but despite the difficulties adults themselves have in going for long periods without large-muscle activity the expectations that older children and adolescents can do so is seldom challenged in practice. Pupils not only suffer from over restriction in activity but also from lack of freedom to direct their own behaviour.

Teacher's Methods of Handling the Class: The teacher's methods of handling pupils can be considered primarily a function of his personality and his personality and his knowledge. His skill is dependent not only upon knowledge of children in general, but also upon knowledge of the individual children in his class and knowledge of how to meet the personality needs of children and control their behaviour in ways beneficial to them. There is likely to be a close relationship between the teacher's personality and the methods of controls he naturally tends to use.

The Effect of the Teacher's Personality on the Class: It may be surmised that the best liked teachers provide a warm, friendly and relaxed classroom atmosphere in which the children could not only do their best work and have the most enjoyable time, but also would have opportunity for wholesome personality development. The least liked teachers probably had the opposite effect. Some teacher really enjoy teaching and they have devotion to their job of teaching. They have high aptitude of teaching and high favourable attitude towards teaching have the positive effect on the class. The involvement in teaching according to Morrisan also contributes in the involvement of the class in their teaching activities.

Teacher's Report of Behaviour Problems in the Classroom: The Wickman study which demonstrated that teachers tended to consider violations of classroom order, dishonesties, and immoralities as more serious than recessive and withdrawing personality traits, while the opposite was true of mental hygienists, has had wide publicity. Although this study has been justly criticised as being unfair to the teachers because they were asked to rate the items on the basis of their seriousness in class. Other investigations not subject to this defect have shown substantially similar results.

Treatment of Behaviour Problems in the Classroom: These kinds of treatment technique used are even more revealing of the lack of appreciation of mental hygiene principles. A combination of categories I, II and III, all essentially punishment, totals 56 per cent of the techniques used. Constructive or non-punishment techniques comprise approximately 25 per cent. Deprivation – a method of meeting the immediate situation which may or may not have beneficent effects, depending upon the circumstances and type of deprivation-was employed 19 per cent of the time. Campbell comes to the following conclusions:

1. The teacher apply direct measures as punishment or reward for treating undesirable classroom behaviour of children. Skinner is of the view that undesirable behaviour should be ignored and desirable behaviour should be immediately rewarded or reinforced. This treatment avoids the adverse effect of punishment.
2. The teachers are rated highly successful in classroom control use rewards or reinforcement and provide direct help more frequently than the other teachers. The results the Skinner's thesis of ignoring undesirable behaviour, he is not in favour of the punishment for kind to the students in the classroom.

Adjustment Problems: There are some special problems or adjustment of children which cause the aliment of mental health. These have been listed as follow:

1. Physically handicapped child.
2. Schooly child.
3. Child with sensory defects.
4. Intellectually gifted child.
5. Dull child.
6. Isolated child.
7. Inferior child.

The above mentioned children have special problems which may cause their ailments or maladjustment. Wise handling may do much for such type of children. Their problems and treatments have been discussed there.

Physical Handicapped Child: Physically handicapped children because of their condition suffer more frustrations than the average child. The usual play and social activities are usually slower in their school work. Besides having fewer immediate opportunities for social recognition, most of them must look forward to a vocational future that is far from satisfying. As a result of their physical condition, also, unwise parents and teachers are likely to overprotect them.

It is not unusual, therefore, to find self-consciousness, sensitivity, timidity, self-pity, and a feeling of inferiority among their personality traits, and withdrawal as a favoured means of meeting difficult situations. Wise handing may do much for the physically handicapped child. To avoid in a natural manner, calling attention to his defect while at the same time arranging for special ways for him to receive merited recognition usually and markedly in this adjustment.

Sickly Child: The sickly child, is in many respects subject to the same restrictions as the physically handicapped child. He too cannot play as vigorously or do his school work as efficiently as the average child. He is likely to be considered lazy because he tires easily. Either as a reaction to the specific nature of his, discomfort or because of the pampering; he receives at home, may be easily irritated. When a server illness kept him out of school for a considerable length of time, he is likely to be unusually worried and tense about the work has missed.

The child who has been sickly but has since become healthy, has special problems too. Often it is harder to convince the parents than the child that he is really well. Occasionally, however, the child who has acquired the habit of non-participation in many play and social activities and bow feels inadequate in them is likely to continue his previous pattern of behaviour.

Child with Sensory Defects: Of the possible visual defects in childhood the most common are near-sightedness (myopia) and farsightedness (hyperopia). The effect on the personality is likely to be more serious for unsuspected hyperopics than for myopics because in addition to the inferiority feeling likely to result from repeated failures in schoolwork and in sports, farsighted children are plagued with headaches and often with nausea.. These conditions can make their school experience so unpleasant that truancy may result.

The child with unsuspected defective hearing is likewise handicapped in those phases of school work which depend upon the auditory sense and in games and social relations with his peers. He may appear to be inattentive and stupid. The most frequent reaction to defective hearing is excessive shyness and a tendency to withdraw.

Gifted Child: Louttit has very aptly enumerated the most frequent sources of difficulty in the adjustment of the superior child:

1. Lack of teacher's recognition of superiority leading to an antagonism towards the school as an institution.
2. Lack of parental recognition of superiority with resulting lack of stimulation or positive discouragement.
3. Superiority over available associates so marked that social adjustment is extremely difficult.

4. Development of poor study or work habits because of lack of stimulation of classroom work.
5. Development of inferiority feelings because the child's interests and activities are not socially recognised by his group.
6. Development of a boastful, conceited personality because of unwise emphasis by adults.
7. One-sided personality development because of lack of normal social activities resulting from parental intervention.

Dull Child: Dull children sometimes called 'low-normal' or dull normal, those with I.Q's roughly from 75 to 90, are confronted with unusually severe hazards in the ordinary public school. Few schools have a programme which meets their needs. Usually they are left to sink or swim (usually sink) in classes too, large to be handled satisfactorily even for the average child. The difficulty of the academic work, the speed expected of him as well as the frequent inability, because of lack of facilities, to demonstrate what talents he has, constitute the major sources of frustration in the school life of the dull child.

When to his, as sources of frustration in the school life of the dull child. When to this, as occasionally happens, is added the antagonism of the frequent humiliation he suffers at the hands of his classmates, it is little wonder that damaged personalities and annoying behaviour result.

Isolated Child: The excessive mobility of the family due to his father or mother job is transferable. When the family moves, the child friendships in school and neighbourhood are interrupted, and it is not easy to form new friendship in a neighbourhood or in school. The child feels isolated. The broken home also make him isolated child.

Isolated children often feel their plight keenly. They lack the status. Conferred by valued membership in a group and are likely to give up attempts at friendships and retire into a world of unreality. In addition, they feel that something is wrong with them, They in some way are inferior and different from the rest of the children.

Delinquent Child: 'Typical' delinquent is a boy who lies in a 'blighted area' of a city in home of low economic level with low moral standards as well. His parents are either not living together or are antagonistic to each other. They either utilise psychologically poor methods of discipline or reject the child altogether. His I.Q. is between 80 and 90 and he is retarded in school. Delinquency, however, may be found in children, in whom not one of these factors is present. Nevertheless, the environmental mass, approach to the prevention of deliquency is still the most feasible and rewarding.

Inferior Child: Children with a persistent feeling of inferiority are by no means rare in our school system. Ninety-two per cent of the men and 98 per cent of the women reported that they had an inferiority complex. Ninety per cent of the men and 91 per cent of the women reported a persistent feeling of inferiority during the current year.

The inferiority complex stems from large discrepancies between a child's level of achievement and his level of aspiration. Any factor which depress the first or raise the send enhance the suffering of the child. Some of the most important facts which tend primarily to lower the achievement level are:

1. Real or imagined physical defects,
2. Poor health, below average mentality,
3. Low organising above programmes. They should know the basic principles of social or economic status, and
4. Continued failure.

Factors which tend primarily to raise the level of aspiration are: an undue emphasis on the child's natural inability to do things as well as older children or his parents; excessive competition in school or sports and insistence by parents or teachers on too high standards.

The school, then has the responsibility of providing a hygienic, friendly environment with understanding teachers, of aiding the continuation of sound personality growth in well adjusted children; and of assisting the children whose personalities are already wrapped. Over competition, unsuitable curriculum over restriction, and poor methods of handling children are some of the factors which tend to retard personality development in any child.

Conditions of School

The role of parents and family is significant in the personality development of children. The teacher and school assume great responsibility in the process of development of children. They spend day time in school and the main focus of the school to develop the potentialities by satisfying their needs. The school provides the proper climate for their physical, social, emotional and intellectual development.

The following are the situations and activities are organised in a good school.

1. School environment or climate.
2. Democratic environment or freedom of expression.
3. Provision for co-curricular activities.
4. Social emotional climate of classroom.
5. Guidance and counselling services in school.
6. Supervised study or provision for assimilation.
7. Tutorial system in school and remedial teaching.
8. Educational Excursion or field trips.
9. Organisation of debates and group discussion.
10. Scouting and girls guiding, N.C.C. programme.
11. Teacher taught relation or rapport with students.

The above programmes and activities are helpful for generating conducive climate in the school. The students develop the positive attitude towards school and teachers. It should provide feelings of security irrespective cast, religion and socio-economic status. The environment should be free from fear and tensions.

Teachers must have the knowledge, understanding and skill for organising above programmes. They should know the basic principles of human behaviour problems and ailments of mental health. He must be emotionally stable and have positive attitude towards teaching and students. It is also essential that the teacher's mental health should be normal. The mental health of teacher and students are the significant ingredient for teaching learning process.

The understanding of ailment of mental health is enough for the teacher, but he should be capable of providing guidance and counselling for the problems of the students. The educational guidance is essential for the students. They should be given remedial teaching for their difficulties of learning. They should be provided recreational facilities in the school by organising the co-curricular activities and educational trips, etc.

Perfect Teaching

Mental health of teacher is much more important than the mental health of student. If a teacher is not sound in his mental health can not do justice to his students and can not provide guidance in their problems. His maladjustment may have the adverse effect on children. Therefore it is also essential to understand the cause of maladjustment or ailment of mental health as teachers or well as remedial measures.

Sources of Ailments of Mental Health of Teacher: The dissatisfaction in teaching arises from the following important sources:

1. The heavy pressure of work load on teacher.
2. Inadequate salaries to the teacher.
3. Occupational insecurity.
4. Restriction on outside activities.
5. The lack of acceptance by the society.
6. Autocratic administration and supervision and
7. The lack orientation courses or refresher courses.

The mental health of the teacher is necessary to improve by improving conditions of teaching and conditions of services. This can best be effected by means [illegible]trong professional organisation.

The teacher can improve his own mental health, if he is able to increase his understanding of himself, accept himself largely as he is and take an active part in directing his life rather than being content with responding to pressures.

Sources of Satisfaction in Teaching Procession: The following are the sources which arise satisfaction in teaching profession:

1. The socially useful character of the work.
2. The creative expression involve.
3. The stimulation of broad interest.
4. Personal growth and development in teaching.
5. The opportunity for association with youth.
6. The opportunity to influence social and national policy.
7. The merging of one's interests with those of the group.
8. The partial satisfaction of the needs for affection, respect, independence, freedom for expression and for maintaining the self-esteem.
9. The teaching is a naval profession and
10. Teaching involves a variety of activities physical, social, emotional and mental development.

Ways for Improving Mental Health of Teachers: There are various factors in school and outside the school which influence mental health of teachers. The listed factors help in maintaining mental health of teachers.

1. Improving teacher-principal relationship
   a. Democratic administration.
   b. Impartial behaviour of principal.
   c. Planning in advance.
   d. Seniority should be considered in assigning responsibilities.
   e. Proper distribution of work load.
   f. Principal should have helping attitude towards teachers.
   g. Teachers problems should be given due weightage.

2. Improving teachers relationship, should have cooperative spirit among teachers.
3. Organising refresher and orientation courses for the teachers.
4. Teachers should be allowed to attend seminars workshops and conference for their personal growth.
5. They should be encouraged for academic excellence.
6. Improving teacher community relations and community serve by teacher.
7. Improving teacher-taught relations, teacher should receive due regard and respect from the students.
8. Teachers should be rewarded or reinforced for better results or effective teaching or providing remedial teaching and guidance to the students by the principal and school management.

There is a tendency to criticise the teacher by principal, students and other colleagues in our school system. The principal should have the leadership qualities to encourage or praise the teachers for their good work and performance.

There is rapid development and advancement in every field of study and also in teaching methods and techniques. They should be encouraged to attend refresher courses, orientation programmes and workshops organised by different agencies for the excellence in jobs. In school library and reading facilities should be maintained having up-to-date literature. Teachers should also be encouraged for experimental projects and innovative ideas in teaching learning situation. Teachers should be well informed with new trends and technology in the field of education.

In the pre-service teachers training more and better courses should be offered in mental health and hygiene. The teachers trainees like such courses and many gain a great deal of insight through them. If in addition, enough psychological counsellors and psychotherapists and medical services could be provide to all teacher training institutions, great efforts could be made in increasing the mental health of the profession. The reading habit of books, provide guidance to the teacher related to his life:

1. Develop the habit of success in life.
2. Prepare teachers to face reality or hard facts of life.
3. He learns to react normally to emotional situation.
4. He begins to avoid worries of day-to-day working.

These are the realities of life, these may cause some sort of ailments, tension or anxiety. The above guidance is very realistic approach for avoiding causes of ailments and he may be able to maintain his sound mental health.

Mental Exercise for Reading

Significance of Reading

Since the new policy of education (1986) advocates placement of these disabled children in a integrated setting, so far as it is possible and it is a relatively new concept with which our classroom teachers will have to be familiar, it is important for all teachers in the school to understand what integration means; what are the models of placement of such children; what impact it has on the role and responsibilities of school personnel.

Some children have health problems that interfere with their education. Notable among these are rheumatic heart disease, and tuberculosis. There are cases of kidney ailments and infections such as asthma, eczema, hay fever, chronic health disorders such as: epilepsy, diabetes, migraine headache. But children with chronic illnesses are likely to be enrolled in any classroom.

As used in special education, integration refers to the education or pupils with special needs in ordinary schools. Integration provides a natural environment where these pupils are along side their peers and are free from the isolation that is characteristics of special school placement.

The concept of integration is a complex and dynamic one. It has evolved from a simple opposition to placement in a special school to encompassing a variety of arrangements in ordinary schools. This diversity is commonly described in Warnock Report (1978) wherein distinction has been made amongst different forms of integration – locational, social and functional.

The 'locational' integration relates to the physical location of special education provision. It includes special units or classes in ordinary schools. The special and the ordinary school share the same site. 'Social' integration relates to its social aspect, where children attending a special class or unit eat, play and interact with other children, and possible share organised lot of classroom activities with them.

The third and the fullest form of integration is 'functional' integration. This is achieved where the locational and social association of disabled children with their peers leads to joint participation in educational programmes. Where children with special needs join, part-time or full-time, the regular classes of the school, and make full contribution to the activity of the school. Another form of integration suggested by some authors is 'societal' integration.

The best environment for mainstreaming is a classroom that is appropriate to the needs of the handicapped students. A programme continuum provides full spectrum of services that may be tailored to the individual needs of each student at any given time during his educational career.

To meet the broad and many faceted changes occurring in schools in response to POA (1986) and (1992) envisaging integration, corresponding changes in teacher education are both necessary and inevitable. These may include the following programmes:

1. De-institutionalisation of many seriously handicapped children.
2. Rapid return of many handicapped students from special day class and school to regular classroom.

3. Decreasing direct service of special education teacher and emphasising indirect service such as consultative and support function.
4. Participation of regular classroom teacher in determining and writing individualised education plans (IEPs) for students with special needs.
5. Determination of education 'goals and programmes for exceptional students, based on specific individuals' learning needs rather than gross categories of exceptionality.
6. Formal involvement of parents of exceptional students in assessment, placement and planning activities.
7. Involvement of other school personnel.

Fundamental changes are being made in the governance of schools as well as in the role of most school personnel. Inevitably, there is gap between theory and practice and many pupils still go to special schools even if they do not need to. To bridge this gap, educational programmes must change to meet new school policies and to prepare school personnel for new roles.

Learner and Teacher

A teacher has to play the following roles for dealing H. I. Children:

1. Ease the child to the floor.
2. See that is not apt to injure himself by striking furniture or sharp comers while convulsions.
3. Turning the child's head to one side and carefully placing but never forcing a folded handkerchief of a soft object between back teeth is sometimes advised.
4. Do not use a pencil or other solid object for the teeth.
5. The teacher should help other children in the classroom to accept this seizure calmly and to understand that there nothing contagious or harmful about in convulsion.

Children with epilepsy do not have necessarily low intelligence due to seizures. They show some signs of maladjustment because social stigma and frustrating environment.

Majority of the children with this condition can attend regular school. Incidence is reduced by following ketogenic diet (high fact and carbohydrate) and anticotivulsive therapy.

The Complications

Epilepsy (Neurological Disease): This is one of the special health problems which is generally faced by children. The symptoms of this problem are:

1. the child shakes violently as if in the grip of hysteria,
2. there is constant recurrence of fits,
3. the child loses consciousness,
4. he falls and moves arm and legs violently,
5. the child may become pale,
6. he falls and moves arms and legs violently,
7. purposeless activities such as rubbing of arms and body parts,
8. the child starts taking off his clothes. The problem is due to brain injury or an extra growth in the brain. Some drugs are available to control the fits, and the extra growth can be removed by surgery. Epilepsy is treated as a special health problems.

Since the fits are painless to the victim, it is important that the teacher should remain calm and not attempt to restrain the child's movements. All sharp objects that may injure the child should be removed from around him, but the movements must not be interrupted. If the mouth is open some soft objects such as a handkerchief should be placed to prevent the tongue from being bitten.

The child should be allowed to rest after the fit and the parents and doctor should boycott among peers and to protect the child from such treatment, the teacher can use this opportunity to explain the problem to the entire class. The teacher should also explain to the other staff members and the community that the cause of epilepsy is not evil spirits but injury of the brain. The child is normal in his/her intellectual functioning. This will help in better social, emotional and academic integration of such children.

Diabetic Problem: Children with the problems show the following symptoms: Frequent urination, abnormal thirst, extreme hunger, frequent change in weight, generally rapid loss sleepiness, weakness, usual disturbances are felt more acutely and frequent skin infections such as boils and itching.

This problem can occur in both normal and disabled children studying in your school. As a teacher you are expected to identify these symptoms at an early stage. The problem is because the body not producing sufficient amount of the hormone called insulin and can be controlled by given insulin in the proper dose at the proper time. The teacher's role is to help the child to get medical examination and to take medicine and diet according to the doctors' prescription.

Asthma (Bronchial Problem): Generally, the problem of asthma is overlooked in our classrooms but since it creates some social and emotional problems for the child so it is better if the teacher is made aware of it. The child suffers from breathing trouble due to allergy. The commonly seen symptoms are: difficulty in breathing. The child takes large gulps of air becomes pale, breathes noisily and perspires too much. Asthma is caused by allergens such as dust and the pollen of some plants. It may also occur due to excessive physical activity or emotional reaction.

Drugs can be given orally or by injection, which help to control the problem, but it is not completely curable. Teachers who have such children in their class should help these children by keeping them away from dust and pollen. They should not be asked to do strenuous exercises. The teacher is also required to help the affected child to adjust to the problem and to involve in social activities that are not too rigorous.

Juvenile Rheumatoid: Pain in the joint which occurs in younger children is known as juvenile rheumatoid. Such children have a skin rash and swelling and redness of the eyes. There could be some retardation in growth since it is a disease that attacks the joints. It may cause stunted growth. Swelling and pain occur in the fingers, wrists, elbows, knees, hips and feet. In severe cases, it left untreated the joints become stiff, making movements difficult and painful. Juvenile rheumatoid is a chronic infection of the connective tissue of the body. Drugs and special exercises can prevent the disease from becoming too severe. In the case of such children the role of teacher is very important.

The teacher must be understanding and at the same time, not overprotective. Such children require more time to finish their assignments. Various adjustments such children require more time to finish their assignments. Various adjustments such as writing aids and special paper and pencils can be provided to the children who have stiffened upper limbs. Since such children are physically weak, the teacher should not insist on their participating in all the activities.

Anaemia health problem is a condition in which the child suffers from severe loss of blood. Children who suffers from anaemia have periodic attacks of acute pain, may be weak and prone to jaundice and leg ulcers. They have pain in the abdomen, knees, elbows and other joints in the body. They suffer from constant headaches and may occasionally faint, feel ringing in the ears and see spots before the eyes. The major cause of this loss of blood is the loss of the red pigment of blood cells known as haemoglobin.

The shape of the red blood cells change to sickle-shaped. A complete cure is not possible in server cases of the disease. Children afflicted with the disease need to rest frequently and be protected from further infection. The teacher should allow them more time to finish their assignments. Since it also leads to lack of oxygen, frequent hospital treatment is required. Teacher should get the children medically examined if he suspects any such problems in them. The children with mild type of anaemia need only periodic medical check ups and medicines according to doctors' prescription. They can be integrated without any problems.

The following are the main areas health problem impaired children:

Psychomotor: There are several type of epilepsy – psychomotor, petitmal, grandmal. In psychomotor epilepsy the individual is violent, vigorous and is doing some automatic action which appear to other as meaningful but are meaningless. During the seizure the child's behaviour is inconsistent. The makes sucking noises with his mouth, move his hand aimlessly, strikes a child, tears up paper, move about the room. But the individual does not remember what he has done. Such behaviours include temper tantrums also.

Petitmal: In petitmal, the child loses consciousness for a few seconds but does not fall. His eyes may roll up or there may be a rhythmic blinking of eyelids. He drops things, appears to be staring straight ahead, or stands still, unaware of what is going on around him.

The teacher often thinks that he is not paying attention. He quickly recovers and goes on what he was doing not inconvenience him or to any one to great extent. But if such seizures occur quite frequently the child is apt to lose the thread of a lesson and be handicapped by gaps in continuity. The teacher should watch for sign that indicate a child is having a seizure and repeat directions. He may have missed or checked to see that he has understood what was going on in the class.

Grandmall: A child who has grandmal seizures has less consciousness and fall rigidly on the floor. This is preceded by strange sensation known as aura (warning) and by a shrill cry. His muscles first tighten, then accompanied by salivation, twitching and tremors may follow. Then comes a deep sleep, come or stuper. The seizure may last for a minute or two and when he recovers he may be dull or disoriented. He may want to sleep for some more time and consequently his school programme may be impaired.

The following are main symptoms of health problem impaired children:

1. Shortness of breath
2. Frequent cough
3. Blue appearance of skin
4. Increased appetite
5. Gets easily tired

6. Restless inattentive
7. Slow and inactive
8. Irritable
9. Temper tantrums
10. Abnormal thirst, frequent irritation
11. Itching
12. Perspires often
13. Dust allergy
14. Loss of weight.
15. Very easily tired.
16. Excessively restless.
17. Extremely slow and inactive.
18. Unusually breathless after exercise.
19. Subject to frequent dry coughs or complains of chest pain after physical exertion.
20. Cheeks, lips of finger tips have a slightly bluish colour.
21. Has slight temperature most of the time.
22. Extremely inattentive.
23. Faints frequently.
24. Complains of pains in the arms, legs, or joints.
25. Easily irritated-gets angry easily, loses temper, may exhibit destructive, aggressive tendencies without proper reason.

A teacher in the integrated classroom teaching can identify the children of health problems by observing their behaviours, of special health problem. He can deal with such children according to their individual special needs.

The Problems

Michael (1994) summarised the causes of epilepsy as follows:

1. Ideopathic-causes not known – (30-50) per cent.
2. Genetic – (10-20) per cent by inheritance.
3. Metabolic errors – PKU, Maple syrup wine.

4. Congenital and perinatal infections.
5. Encephalitis and meningitis (brain fever) and severe dehydration.
6. Brain tumours – Intra Cranial space occurring lessons.
7. Brain injury before birth at last among 1/3 of epileptics.
8. Cerebral haemorrhage.
9. Drugs and lead poisoning, and
10. Cerebral palsy and epilepsy often occur together.

Brain damage can be prevented during pregnancy. Avoid marriages between close relatives. Anti-fits medicines are to be taken for 3 to 4 years to prevent epilepsy occur further.

The Solutions

There are no medicines that can cure epilepsy. There are no vaccinations that can prevent epilepsy. However, medicines can prevent occurrence of fits if these are taken regularly. Sometimes preventing fits for a long time seems to help stop epilepsy permanently.

Treatment for epilepsy generally consists of four parts:

1. Identification and eliminating of factors that cause or precipitate attacks.
2. Sustaining of general mental and physical health and social integration.
3. Pharmacological therapy that raise the convulsive threshold to prevent attacks.
4. Surgical therapy for carefully selected patients with seizure of focal origin or for those for whom medication has proven completely ineffective.

The commonly used anti-convulsant medications in pharmacological therapy are Diantin, Mysoline. Sarontin, Tegretoe, Clonopin, Depakene for different types of seizures. The most significant treatment in epilepsy is the growth of good physical and mental health. A nutritious balanced diet and adequate muscular activity will be paralleled by the relief of emotional stress, and the creation of an atmosphere of productive and normalcy.

Core Factors

The term physically handicapped has been used in literature in various ways: Physically disabled, crippled, orthopaedically impaired, or otherwise health impaired. Physical handicaps and divided into two types: Orthopaedically impaired and health impairments for the purpose of special education. The legal definition of the term orthopaedically handicapped is a severe, orthopaedic impairment that adversely affects a child's educational performance. The term includes impairments caused by a congenital anomaly, *e.g.*, dub foot, absence of somebody organs, impairments caused by disease, *e.g.*, cerebral palsy, amputations, and fractures or burns that cause contractures. A similar definition has also been adopted by Department of Social Welfare, Government of India.

A physically disabled child be defined as one whose physical or health problems result in an impairment of normal interaction with society to the extent that specialised services and programmes are required. This group is extremely heterogeneous group and includes varied disabilities and conditions out of which the commonly encountered are:

Cerebral Palsy (CP): is a non-progressive disorder that affects gross and fine motor coordination. It is often associated with convulsions, speech disorders, hearing defects, vision problems, deficits in measured intelligence or combination of these problems. Main types of cerebral palsy are Spasticity, Ataxia, Athetosis, Rigidity and Floppiness.

Myopic Dystrophy: A disease in which the muscles progressively weaken and degenerate until they can no longer function.

Policmyelitis (infantile paralysis): Viral infection that affects or destroys some cells in the spinal cord leading to paralysis of part or parts of body or entire body.

Spina Biflida: A congenital defect that result when the bones or a part of the spine fail to grow together resulting in gap in the spine. The area affected and symptoms very depending on the location of spine affected and the extent or disorder.

Amputation: It is the absence of some limb.

Physical and health problems may have grave, little or no effect upon the school performance of the student. The legal definition for other health impairments is having an acute condition that is manifested by severe communication and other developmental and educational problems, or having limited strength, vitality or alertness because of acute health problems, *e.g.*, heart condition, tuberculosis, rheumatic fever, nephritis, asthma, haemophilia, epilepsy, lead poisoning, leukaemia, or diabetes that adversely affect a child's educational performance.

Certain crippling and chronic health disorders in children are seen as a result of infection after they are born. Some of the common examples are poliomyelitis, estomyelitis, tuberculosis, cerebral palsy. Although, the first three do not invariably lead to brain injury, perception, vision and audition deficiencies yet these children demand special educational treatments.

However, there are certain neurological disorders which are not categorised as either crippling or a special health problem, *e.g.*, aphasia language disorder due to brain injury. Hence, from an educational point of view crippling and neurological impairments would include all children with non-sensory physical impairments whether they are accompanied by a neurological damage or not, and whether they resulted in chronic health condition of not.

Basically non-sensory physical impairments may be classified as crippling and chronic health ailments. The cripples have muscular and skeletal deformities which are obvious. They may wear braces, prosthetic devices such as artificial limbs or may be moving with crutches or wheel chairs.

The second category of children are confined to bed for relatively long periods of time and just do nothing. The crippled children are known as orthopaedically handicapped or motor impaired whereas the second category were known as special health problem cases.

Some students with physical and health disorders begin their school careers with an identified handicap. With others the problem is first noted after they have entered the school, or it may result from an accident or disease that occurs during the school years. Because of heterogeneity in this group, a single list of signs to identify them is not possible. However, all of them have a common problem of posture, mobility, difficulty in performance of physical activities.

Almost all children with locomotor handicaps, sensory impairments, speech impairments and with mild and even moderate intellectual disabilities can be conveniently placed in ordinary schools. However children with more moderate and severe intellectual deficits and multiple handicaps will still have to be placed in special schools or classes depending on the nature and degree of disability. Thus special education will be provided in (i) Integrated; and (ii) Special Schools.

Other Factors

Some children with epilepsy are intelligent. Others are mentally slow. Occasionally fits that are very frequent and severe can injure the brain and cause of increase retardation. Treatment to control fits is important.

Some children may have both minor and big fits or they may have first minor ones and later develop high one's. There is a sign of warning or aura. They may suddenly cry and then are finds suddenly jerks or are thrown immediately. These fits vary in duration.

After the fit is over the child may be very sleepy and confused. He/she may feel body-ache and feel weak.

Children with severe problems, like heart problem, diabetic, epilepsy, need to rest after 10-15 minutes of studying. It is difficult to accommodate them in general classroom since they require constant medical care and the full attention of the teacher.

Epilepsy is the most common neurological disease. In 1870, Jackson defined epilepsy as a group of disorders with paroxysmal and excessive neurocal discharge that cause a sudden discharge in neurological function. There is a sudden change in intellectual, sensory, motor, autonomic, or emotional activity, limited in length and presumably associated with neuronal over-activity.

Those who have poor physical condition, make them inactive and who require special health precautions in school. Such children can be categorised into the following groups.

Children With Mild Health Problems: It Comes under the educable IED group. Their health problems do not interfere with educational learning. But precautions need to be taken in terms of getting adequate medical check-ups and support.

There are children with severe health problems who cannot be integrated in regular schools. The severity of their health problem interferes with educational planning. They will need constant medical care and are therefore not be able to participate in the academic and non-academic activities of general classrooms.

Children with severe problem, like heart problem, diabetic, cepilepsy, need to rest after 10-15 minutes of studying. It is difficult to accommodate them in general classroom since they require constant medical care and the full attention of the teacher. Such children need to be educated either at home/hospital or in special classes in general schools. Some health problems are discussed below:

> The problem may occur in disabled children hence the knowledge of the symptoms and their implications can help the teacher in minimising these problems and helping the disabled to develop their talents like others.

Intellect for Reading

In contrast to animals man is considered to be endowed with certain cognitive abilities which make him a rational being. He can reason, discriminate, understand, adjust and face a new situation. Definitely he is superior to animals in all such aspects of behaviour. But human beings themselves are not all alike. There are wide individual differences. A teacher easily discovers these differences among his pupils. Some learn with a good speed while others remain lingering too long. There are some who need only one demonstration for handling the tools properly while for others even the repeated individual guidance brings no fruitful result.

What is that causes one individual to be more effective in his response to a particular situation than another. No doubt, interest, attitude, desired knowledge and skill, etc., count towards this achievement. But still there is some thing that contributes significantly towards these varying differences. In Psychology it is termed 'Intelligence'. In ancient India our great Rishis named it 'Viveka'.

Reader's Assessment

Above we have given some definitions, more of such definitions can further be cited. All these definitions when taken separately, give an incomplete picture because they partly emphasise that:

1. intelligence is the ability to learn,
2. it is the ability to deal with abstraction,
3. it is the ability to make adjustment or to adapt to new situations.

The definition given by Wechsler seems to combine all the three view points presented above but this definition too has come under criticism due to difference of opinion among Psychologists. Several attempts have been made to reach some general agreement but all have been in vain. However, the British Psychologists are said to have reached some measures of agreement regarding a suitable definition of intelligence.

To them intelligence consists of the ability:

1. to see relevant relationships between objects or ideas, and
2. to apply these relationships to novel situations.

It makes us conclude that intelligent behaviour is divided into two categories – theoretical and practical, abstract and concrete. The theoretical operations make an individual capable to face and solve the actual life-problems and make adjustment to the environmental situations.

If we try to analyse the factor which determines the success of an individual's activities, we can by all means say that cognitive or mental abilities have a dominant role to play in the success or failure. "Intelligence", as Rex and Margaret knight have put it "is the factor that is common to all mental abilities". (1952, p. 124) and therefore, the judgement about intelligence can ever be taken with the evaluation of the task one performs, how he reacts and responds to a situation. In this way, if we try to come to the practical ground, we can define intelligence as follows:

Intelligence consists of an individual's those mental or cognitive abilities which help him in solving his actual life-problems and leading a happy and well contented life.

1. *The Relation of Intelligence with Nature and Nurture:* There have been too many attempts on the, part of Psychologists to weigh the relative importance of nature and nurture. The conclusion of their studies reveals that intelligence is the

product of heredity and environment. Both are necessary for the intellectual growth of an individual, neither can be considered moiety necessary than the other.

2. *Distribution of Intelligence:* There are individual differences with regard to the distribution of intelligence in nature like wealth, health, etc. This distribution is governed by a definite principle that is "the majority of the people are at the average, a few very bright and a few very dull".
3. *Growth of Intelligence:* As the child grows in age, so does the intelligence as shown by intelligence tests now the question arises-at what age does this increase cease? The age of cessation of mental growth varies from individual to individual. However, in majority of cases, intelligence reaches its maximum, somewhat at the age of 16 or 20 in the individual, after that the vertical growth of intelligence ceases. But the horizontal growth accumulation of knowledge and acquisition of skills-continues throughout the life span of an individual.
4. *Intelligence and Sex Differences:* Various studies have been conducted to find out whether women are less intelligent than men and vice versa. The result of these researches hangs in one way or the other. In some of the cases, no significant difference has been found. Therefore, it is proper to think that difference insex does not contribute towards difference in intelligence,
5. *Intelligence and Racial or Cultural Difference:* Whether a particular race, caste, or cultural group is superior to others in intelligence-the hypothesis has been examined by so many research workers. In USA it has been a problem for centuries. The results of earlier studies which take the whites to be a superior race in comparison to the Negroes have been questioned. Now It has been established that intelligence is not the birth right of a particular race or group. The 'bright' and the 'dull' can be found in any race caste or cultural group and the differences which are found can be explained in terms of environment influences.

There are a number of misconceptions prevalent about the nature and concept of intelligence. For the clarification let us be clear that what is not meant by intelligence.

1. Intelligence is not knowledge though acquisition of knowledge depends, to a great extent, on intelligence and vice versa.
2. Intelligence is not memory. A very intelligent person may have a dull memory, and vice-a-versa.
3. Intelligence is not guarantee against abnormal behaviour, backwardness and delinquency in spite of the fact that it is one of the major factors contributing towards achievement, adjustment and character formation.

Values of Wisdom

With the help of definitions, we can be able to understand how intelligence operates or what type of behaviour of an individual makes him intelligent or unintelligent or in other words, what are the different components or elements of intelligence The theories of intelligence propagated by Psychologists from time to time have tried to answer this question. These theories can be grouped under two heads, namely, factor theories and cognitive theories. However, in the text we will limit our discussion to factor theories.

Factor Theories of Intelligence: Let us try to discuss some of these theories below:

1. *Unitary Theory or Monarchic Theory:* This theory holds that intelligence consists of one factor simply a fund of intellectual competency, which is universal for all the activities of the individual

   A man who has vigour can move so much to East as to the West in a similar way if one has a fund of intelligence he can utilise it to any area of his life and can be as successful in one area as in the other depending upon his fund of intelligence. But in actual life situations, the ideas propagated by this theory do not fit well. We find that the children who are bright in Mathematics may, despite serious interest and hard work, not be so good in Civics A student very good in conducting Science experiments does not find himself equally competent in learning language. This makes us conclude that there is nothing like one single unitary factor in intelligence. Therefore, the unitary theory stands rejected

2. *Anarchic theory or Multifactor Theory:* The main propagator of this theory was E. L. Thorndike. As the name suggests this theory considers intelligence a combination of numerous separate elements or factors, each one being a minute element of an ability. So, there is no such thing as general intelligence (a single factor) and there are only many highly independent specific abilities which go into different tasks.

   In this way, Monarchic and Anarchic theories hold the two extremes. Just as we cannot assume good intelligence, a guarantee of success in all the fields of human life, we cannot also say with certain specific type of abilities one will be entirely successful in a particular area and completely unsuccessful in the other area. Actually Gardner Murphy put it, "There is a certain positive relationship between brightness in one field and brightness in another and so on". (1968, p. 353). This brings us to the conclusion that there should be a common factor running through all tasks. The failure to explain such phenomena gave birth to another theory named Spearman's Two Factor Theory.

3. *Spearman's Two Factor Theory:* This theory was advocated by Spearman. According to him every different intellectual activity involves a general factor 'g' which is shared with all intellectual activities and a specific 's' which it shares with none.

   In this way, he suggested that there is something which might be called general intelligence, a sort of general mental energy, running through all the different tasks but in addition to this general factor there are specific abilities, which make an individual able to deal with particular kinds of problems. For example an individual's performance in Hindi is partly due to his general intelligence and partly some kind of specific ability in language which he might possess, *i.e.* g + s1 or in Mathematics his performance will be due to g + s2 in drawing it will be due to g + s3 and so on. The factor g (in lesser or greater degree) will enter in all specific activities. The total ability or intelligence of such an individual (symbolised as A), thus, will be expressed by the following equation A schedule.

$$g + s1 + s2 + s3 + \ldots\ldots = A.$$

This two factor theory of Spearman has been criticised on various grounds. The two main reasons are given below:

a. Spearman said that there are only two factors expressing intelligence but as we have seen above there are not only two but several factors (g, s1, s2, s3, ...etc.).
b. According to Spearman each job requires some specific ability. This view was not proper as it implied that there was nothing common in the jobs except a general factor and profession such as those of nursery; compounders and doctors could not be put in a group. In fact the factors s1, s2, s3, s4....etc. are not mutually exclusive. They overlap and give birth to certain common factors.

This idea of overlapping and grouping has given origin to a new theory called Group Factor theory.

4. *Thurstone's Group Factor Theory:* For the factors not common to all of the intellectual abilities but common to certain activities comprising a group, the term 'group factor' was suggested. Prominent among the propagators of this theory is L. L. Thurstone. While working on a test of primary mental abilities he came to the conclusion that certain mental operations have in common a primary factor which gives them psychological and functional unity and which differentiates them from other mental operations. These mental operations constitute a group factor. So, there are a number of groups of mental abilities each of which has its own primary factor. Thurstone and his associates have differentiated nine such factors. They are:

   a. *Verbal Factor (V):* concerns with comprehension of verbal relations, word and ideas.
   b. *Spatial Factor (S):* involved in any task in which the subject manipulates an object imaginatively in space.

c. *Numerical Factor (N):* ability to do numerical calculations, rapidly and accurately.

d. *Memory Factor (M):* involving the ability to memorise quickly.

e. *Word Fluency Factor (W):* involved whenever the subject is asked to think of the isolated words at a rapid rate.

f. *Inductive Reasoning Factor (RI):* ability to generalise through specific examples.

g. *Deductive Reasoning Factor (RD):* ability to make use of generalised result.

h. *Perceptual Factor (P):* ability to perceive objects accurately.

i. *Problem-solving Ability Factor (PS):* ability to solve problems independently.

The weakest link in the group factor theory was that it discarded the concept of common factor. It did not take Thurstone very long to realise his mistake and to reveal a general factor in addition to group factors.

5. *G. H. Thomson's Sampling Theory:* This theory was propagated by G. H. Thomson, a brilliant psychologist. It assumes that the mind is made of many independent bonds or elements. Any specific test or school activity sample some of these bonds. It is possible that two or more tests sample and utilise the same bonds., then a general common factor can be said to exist among them. It is also possible that some other tests sample different bonds, then the tests have nothing in common and each is specific.

   This theory seems to combine various theoretical viewpoints as :

   a. It appears to be similar to Thorndike's multifactor theory except that it concedes to the practical usefulness of a concept like 'g'.

   b. At the same time Thomson seems to maintain that the concept of group factor (G) is of equal usefulness,

6. *Vernon's Hierarchical Theory:* R.E. Vernon, a British psychologist has propagated the theory of intelligence by

suggesting a hierarchical structure for the organisation of human intelligence.

Thus, according to Vernon, intellectual abilities or factors of intelligence lie in hierarchical order. On top we have G, a general type of major factor representing an overall intelligence of the individual. Under G, there are two prominent group factors namely Ved (Concerning with the verbal, numerical and educational abilities) and KM (connected with practical, mechanical, spatial and physical abilities). These two major factors may be divided with minor group factors and these minor factors may be further subdivided into various specific factors related with minute specific mental abilities.

7. *Gullford's Theory Involving a Model of Intellect:* J.P.Guilford and his associates have developed a model of intellect on the basis of the factor analysis of several tests employed for testing intelligence of the human beings. They have come to the conclusion that any mental process or intellectual activity of the human being can be described in terms of three basic dimensions or parameters known as operation (the act of thinking or way of processing the information); contents (the terms in which we think or the type of information involved): and products (the ideas we come up with, *i.e.* the fruits of a thinking).

This model proposes that intelligence consists of 150 independent abilities that result front the interaction of five types of contents, five types of operations, and six types of products (after Guilford, 1982).

Each of these parameters-operations, contents and products-may be further subdivided into some specific factors or elements. As a result, operations may be subdivided into 5 specific factors, contents into 5 and products into 6. The interaction of these three parameters, according to Guilford, thus results into the 5 x 5 x 6 = 150 different elements or factors in one's intelligence. In a figural form, these 150 factors or independent abilities of the human beings along with the basic parameters and their divisions can be represented through a model named as Guilford's Model of Intellect or Intelligence.

What is implied by these contents, operations and products can be understood through the following brief description, Contents (The type of Information involved):

- Figural (Visual) – The properties of stimuli we can experience through the visual senses, e.g. colour, size, shape texture and other visual characteristics of figure.
- Figural (Auditory) – the properties of stimuli we can experience through the auditory senses, e.g. voice and sound.
- Symbolic – numbers, letters, symbols, designs.
- Semantic – the meaning of words, ideas.
- Behavioural – the actions and expressions of people. Operations (The way of Processing the Information).
- Cognition – recognising and discovering.
- Memory – retaining and recalling the contents of thought.
- Divergent Production – producing a variety of ideas or solutions to a problem.
- Convergent Production – producing a single best solution to a problem.
- Evaluation – taking decision about the nature of the intellectual contents or gathered information whether it is positive or negative, good or bad, etc.
- Products – (The results obtained through Operations).
- Units – Individual, pieces of information limited in size, *e.g.* a single number, letter or word.
- Classes – groups of units of information related to each other on the basis of some common characteristics involving a higher order concept (e.g. men + women = people).
- Relations – a connection between concepts.
- Systems – an ordering or classification of relations.
- Transformation – altering or restructuring intellectual contents.
- Implication – making inferences from separate pieces of information.

In this way, according or Guilford's model of intellect, there are 150 factors operating in one's intelligence. Each one of these factors has a trigram symbol, *i.e.* at least one factor from each category of three parameters has to be present in any specific intellectual activity or mental task.

Let us illustrate this basic fact with an example. Suppose in case a child is asked to find out the day of the week on a particular date with the help of a calendar. In the execution of this mental task he will need mental operations like convergent thinking, memory and cognition. For carrying out these operations, he has to make use of the contents.

In this particular case, he will make use of semantics, *i.e.* reading and understanding of the printed words and figures indicating days and dates of a particular month in the calendar. By carrying out mental operation with the help of contents he will finally arrive at the products. The day of the week to which the date in questions, refers represents the factor known as "relations". He may further transform and apply this knowledge to identify the days for contiguous dates or vice versa.

Each of the seven theories of intelligence described above attempt to provide a structure of intelligence in term of its constituents or factors. These theories exhibit wide variations in terms of the numbers of factor that they consider important. The range of all such factors also varies from 1 (Unitary theory) to 150 (Guilford's Intellect Model). However, for understanding what goes on inside one's intelligence we must try to build an eclectic view by incorporating the essence of all the workable theories of intelligence. Consequently, any intellectual activity or mental task may be said to involve the following three kinds of basic factors (arranged in the order as suggested by Vernon or in the form of a model suggested by Guilford).

1. General factor (g) (common to all task).
2. Specific factors s1, s2, etc. (Specific to the task).
3. Group factor G (Common to the task belonging to a specific group).

The Measurement: We are only familiar with that intelligence of an individual which is manifested by him on an intelligence test or tests. Psychologists have devised so many such tests for the measurement of intelligence.

The Classification

1. As far as the administrative point of view is concerned the intelligence tests can be classified into two broad categories namely:
   a. *Individual Tests:* In which only one individual is tested at a time.
   b. *Group Tests:* In which a group of individuals are tested at a time.
2. Another way of classifying the intelligence tests is based on the form of the test. Accordingly there are two types of tests.
   a. Verbal tests or Language tests.
   b. Non-verbal tests or Non-Language tests.
      i. *Verbal or Language Tests:* These tests make use of language. Here the instructions are given in words (either in written or oral form or both). Individuals are required to use language as well as paper and pencil for giving the responses. The test content is loaded with verbal material.
      ii. *Non-Verbal and Non-Language Tests.* These tests involve such activities in which the use of language is not necessary. The use of language is eliminated from test content and response except in giving directions.

The typical examples of such non-verbal tests are Performance Tests. The principal characteristics of these tests are given below:

1. Test contents of these tests are in the form of material objects.
2. What an individual has to do is indicated by the tester either through oral instructions or by pantomime or signs.
3. Individual's responses depends upon what he does or performs rather than by anything he says or writes.

4. Generally these tests are individual tests. As Dr. Pillai observes:

   "These cannot be used as group tests, chiefly because it is necessary to supervise the individual testee at work and give him necessary direction."

   (1972, p. 265).

If we try to have a final picture of all types of tests in intelligence we will have to keep in view both the ways of classifying them as mentioned above. All these types of intelligence tests can be represented-diagrammatically as follows:

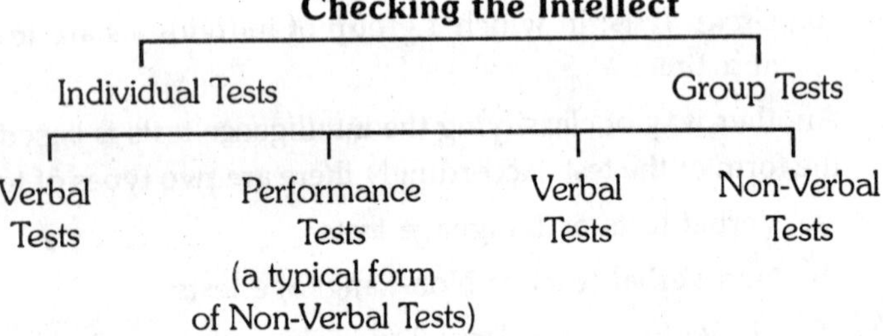

Now we will discuss these types one by one.

Individual Verbal Tests: The tests involving the use of language and administered to an individual at a time belong to this category. As and example of such tests we can quote Stanford-Binet Scale. It is the revised form of the Binet-Simon test. Actually, French Psychologist Alfred Binet, father of intelligence test construction movement along with Theodore Simon prepared a test as early as in 1905, containing 30 items (arranged in order of increasing difficulty) graded for different level. The test included such items as:

> At age 3-Point out to nose, eyes and mouth. At age 7 Tell what is missing in the unfinished picture.

In 1931, the first American revision of this test was published by Terman at Stanford University and in 1937 another revision was carried on with the help of Maud A. Merril. This as well as 1960s revision is called Stanford Binet Scale and widely used as an individual intelligence test. The tests in this scale are grouped into age levels, extending from age 2 to 22 years. The tasks to be performed by the tests in these various tests range from simple manipulation to abstract reasoning.

Binet Tests have been adopted in India too. The first such attempt was made by Dr. C.H. Rice in 1922 when he published his "Hindustani! Binet Performance Point Scale". This was an adaptation of the Binet test along with some performance tests in addition. The State Manovigyan Shala of Uttar Pradesh has made a Hindi Verson of Stanford Binet test. This test is divided into several age-groups and named as Budhi Pariksha Anooshilan.

The other common Verbal Individual Intelligence test (used in India) is Samanya Budhi Pariksha (Pt. 1 and 2). This test is an Indian adaptation of the well-known test of William Stephenson. It has been prepared by State Bureau of Educational and Vocational Guidance, Gwalior (MP).

Individual Tests: As said earlier the complete non-verbal or non-language tests of intelligence for testing an individual at a time come into this classification. In these the contents and reponses are in the form of performance and language is not used at all. In these tests the items which require responses in terms of motor activities are included. Generally the activities, on which the performance of an individual is tested, are of the following types:

1. *Block Building or Cube Construction:* Where the subject is asked to make a structure or design by means of blocks or cubes supplied to him. The examples of the tests involving such type of activities are Merril Palmer Block Building, Koh's Block Design Test, Alexander's Pass along Test, etc.
2. *To Fit the Blocks in the Holes:* Test material of such types provides numerous blocks and a board in which there are holes corresponding to these blocks. The subject has to fit the blocks in these corresponding holes (in the board). Examples are Seguin Form Board Test and Goddard Form Board Test.
3. *Tracing a Maze:* Test material consists of a series of mazes of increasing difficulty, each printed on a separate sheet. The subject is required to trace with pencil, the path from entrance to exit. Porteus Maze Teat is an example involving such type of activities.

4. *Picture Arrangement or Picture Completion:* In picture arrangement test, the task is to arrange in series the given pictures whereas in picture completion test the subject is required to complete the pictures with the help of given pieces cut of each picture. The Healy pictorial completion test is a good example of such test which provides a good estimate of the intelligence of the subject without making use of language.

As seen above, these tests try to emphasise upon one or the other types of performance. Instead of using one or two tests a group of performance tests, organised either into a scale or battery, are used for a comprehensive picture of an individual's mental ability. Some of the popularly known scales are:

1. The Pinter Patterson Scale.
2. The Arthur Point Scale.
3. Alexander's Battery of Performance Tests.

In India too the attempts for constructing such batteries have been made. Dr. Chander Mohan Bhatia's work, in this regard, deserves special mention. He has developed a battery of performance tests known as 'Bhatia's' Battery of Performance Tests.

It contains the following five sub-tests:

1. Koh's Block Design Test.
2. Alexander's Pass-along Tests.
3. Pattern Drawing Test.
4. Immediate memory test (with an alternative form suitable for illiterates).
5. Picture Construction Test.

Last three tests in this battery have been constructed by Mr. Bhatia himself while the former two have been borrowed.

This scale is available in two forms. The one form WISC is used for children and the other WAIS for adults. It is an individual test which has a unique quality of being named as verbal and performance scale simultaneously.

The scale consists of eleven sub-tests. Sub-tests make up a verbal scale and five performance scale. These tests are listed below in the order in which they are administered.

1. Test of General information
2. Test of General comprehension.
3. Test of Arithmetic reasoning.
4. Test of distinction between similarities.
5. Test of Digit span.
6. Test of vocabulary.
7. Digit symbol test.
8. Picture completion test.
9. Block Design test.
10. Object assembly test.

The scores on these sub-tests are added to given an idea of an' individual's intelligence.

Meaning and Factors

Since time immemorial attempts have been made to have understanding about the meaning and concept of intelligence. Let us be acquainted with the nature and meaning of intelligence by throwing light on the following aspects:

1. Meaning and Definition of Intelligence.
2. Some established facts about Intelligence.
3. Misconception about intelligence.

The Problems

1. They may not be able to predict scholastic success in schools as do the verbal tests simply because school work itself is predominantly verbal.
2. They specially performance tests, are very costly and pose difficulty in carrying from one place to another.
3. They are more susceptible to practice-effects and chance successes are more frequent than in the case of verbal tests. Therefore, they are less reliable then verbal tests.

4. These tests are limited in a range of mental functioning tested, such as they do not require much use of the ability to make abstractions and to deal with concepts. That is why they are not able to differentiate among above-average individuals.

In this way, we come across the merits and limitations of these tests. In fact, the testing of mental ability is a comprehensive task and cannot be solely left either to the verbal or performance tests. For taking a reliable view of a person's intellectual ability the following things should be kept in mind:

1. Performance test should be taken as a supplement to verbal tests and vice versa.
2. No single test or tests is suitable for this purpose. There should be an attack from so many angles.

Increase in Checking

The tests which necessitate the use of language and are applied to a group of individuals at a time come under this category. Some of the earlier tests belonging to this category are:

1. Army Alpha Test (developed in World War).
2. Army General Classification Test (developed in the World War).

Today we have so many group verbal tests. In India too, the attempts have been made to construct such tests. Some of the popular tests of this nature are:

1. C.I.E. verbal Group Test of Intelligence (Hindi) constructed by Prof. Uday Shankar.
2. The Group Test of General Mental Ability (Samuhik Mansik Yogyata Pariksha) constructed by Dr. J.S. Jalota (Hindi).
3. Group test of intelligence, prepared by Bureau of Psychology, Allahabad (Hindi).
4. Prayag Mehta's Group Intelligence Test (Samuhik Budhi Pariksha, Hindi). This test has been published by Manasayan, Delhi.
5. General Mental Abilities Test Prepared by Dr. P.S. Hundal of Punjab University (Panjabi).

6. Group verbal intelligence test prepared by Dr. P. Gopala Pillai of the Kerala University (Malayalam).
7. Samuhik Budhi Pariksha (Hindi), prepared by Sh. PL. Shrimali Vidya Bhavan G.S. Teacher College, Udaipur.
8. Samuhik Budhi Ki Jaanch (Hindi, prepared by Shri S.M. Mohsin, Educational and Vocational Guidance Bureau, Bihar, Patna.)

Group Non-verbal Intelligence Tests: These tests do not necessitate the use of language and are applicable to the group of individuals at a time. The difference between performance tests (used for an individual) and non-verbal tests (used for a group) is of degree as far as their non-verbal nature is concerned. The performance tests require the manipulation of concrete objects or materials supplied in the test, by the subject. Responses are purely motor in character and seldom require the use of paper and pencil (except in a case like Maze Test, etc.). Where the test material in the non-verbal tests, used for group testing, is provided in booklet and requires the use of pencil by the testee.

Still in these tests, material does not contain words or numerical figures. It contains pictures, diagrams and geometrical figures, etc. printed in a booklet. The subject is required to do such activities as to fill in some empty spaces, to draw some simple figures, to point out similarities and dissimilarities, etc. In this way, although the subject uses paper pencil he does not need to know words or numerical figures. What he is to do is explained clearly by the examiner usually through clear demonstrations so as to make the least possible use of language.

The examples of such type of tests are:

1. *Army Beta Test:* It was developed in I World War, in USA for testing the intelligence of those soldiers who were either illiterates or were not used to English language.
2. *Chicago Non-verbal Test:* This non-verbal test has been proved most useful for the young children aged 12 and 13 years.
3. *Raven's Progressive Matrices Test:* This test was developed in UK. It is a very much popular non-verbal group test of

intelligence. The test has been designed to evaluate the subjects ability:

a. to see relationship between geometric figures or designs.
b. to perceive the structure of the design in order to select the appropriate part for completion of each pattern.

4. *C.I.E. Non-verbal Group Test of Intelligence:* Originally prepared by J.W. Jenkins, the test is printed by C.I.E. for adaptation into Hindi medium schools. The test contains such terms as instructed.

Individual v/s Group Tests: Individual and group tests have their advantages as well as disadvantages. We can compare them on the following lines:

Individual Tests	*Group Tests*

1. With these tests only one individual is tested at a time. They cannot be administered to a group and this makes them costly in terms of time, labour and money.
2. Individual tests have the unique advantage of being used for children as well as adults.
3. An examiner has a close contact with the subject, he can take into account all personal and emotional factors and like – wise have all those additional pieces of information which may prove useful for the interpretation of an individual's test scores.
4. Individual tests are not as objective and standardised as group tests. Their administration, scoring and interpretation require well trained and competent examiners.

1. These tests have two fold advantage. In addition to their applicability in testing a group of individuals at a time, they can also be administered to the individuals separately. Testing of so many individuals at a time gives them the advantages of saving time, money and labour.
2. Group tests cannot be given to young children below 9 or 10 years of age.
3. The examiner does not have a desirable contact with the subject. He cannot detect and rectify influence of such factors as ill health, mood, poor social background or practice and coaching that might have been given to a subject for boosting his score. What the

examiner gets at all is the numerical score and nothing of additional information as obtained in individuals tests.

4. Group tests are more objective and standardised in comparison to individual tests. The manuals and instructions provided with these tests make their administration, scoring and interpretation so easy that a need of such trained personnel is seldom felt.

Verbal Tests v/s Non-verbal and Performance: What led to the construction of non-verbal and performance when verbal tests were there for testing the intelligence, is a relevant question to be asked. Verbal tests as already said, gave emphasis on linguistic ability. They were loaded with verbal material words and numerical. Hence, the persons having linguistic superiority were always on the side of advantage in comparison to the persons having language weakness. To do away such evils, non-verbal and performance tests were put to use. In brief, the advantages of these tests over verbal tests are as under:

1. Performance tests are useful for those who have language handicaps due to some of the following reasons:
   a. They may belong to the foreign language speaking groups.
   b. They may include illiterates not knowing how to read and write.
   c. They may have difficulties in reading, writing and listening due to defects in their sense organs (persons like deaf, dumb, etc.).
   d. They may be younger children who are not yet able to read and write well.
   e. They may be mentally retarded or mentally deficient children and therefore, are very slow in grasping and responding of the verbal items.
   f. They may belong to unprivileged class or strata of the society and hence have got limited education opportunities.
2. Verbal test belonging to one region contains the material which has a direct relationship with the language or culture

of that region or country. Non-verbal and performance tests are more of less language and culture free and hence can be used for cross cultural and linguistic study of intelligence.

3. They can be proved useful in the efforts to determine aptitude and promise in shop work, mechanical job, etc.

Explaining the Ideas

As discussed earlier, in a day to day conversation an individual is said to be intelligent in proportion as he is successful in meeting general life situations. What is there is intelligence, that contributes towards this success, is a question which has been attempted by Psychologists in different ways resulting in so many varied definitions. Below we give some of these important definitions.

1. *Woodworth and Marquis:* "Intelligence means intellect put to use. It is the use of intellectual abilities for handling a situation or accomplishing any task." (1948, p. 33)
2. *Stern:* "Intelligence is a general capacity of an individual consciously to adjust his thinking to new requirements. It is general mental adaptability to new problems and conditions of life." (1914, p. 3)
3. *Terman:* "An individual is intelligent in proportion as he is able to carry on abstract thinking." (1921)
4. *Wagnon:* "Intelligence is the capacity to learn and adjust to relatively new and changing conditions." (1937, p. 40)
5. *David Wechsler:* "Intelligence is the aggregate or global capacity of an individual to act purposefully to think rationally, and to deal effectively with his environment." (1944, p. 3)

Ideas for Reading

What goes in the process of learning? How do we learn? How can a child learn to solve mathematical problems? How does a girl learn to cook the food or sew the clothes? There are so many questions, the answer of which needs a thorough explanation of the phenomenon of learning. Psychologists have tried to perform experiments for throwing light on the phenomenon of learning and as a result have developed various learning theories. Each theory with its systematic body of knowledge explains the nature and process of learning. These theories represent broad principles and techniques of learning. The set of rules and the laws of learning, having wide applicability, are drawn from these theories. In another sense, these theories also put forth various methods of learning and suggest the teacher and learner to take proper steps for the effective learning.

Modern learning theories may be classified into two broad types, namely:

1. Stimulus response-associationist type of theories.
2. Gestalt field or field cognition type of theories.

The former interpret learning in terms of the change in behaviour of the learner brought about by association of the response to a series of stimuli. The chief exponents of this type of theories are-Edward L. Thorndike (1874-1949); John B. Watson (1878-1958) and Evan Petrovich Pavlov (1849-1935) and Burrhus Frederic Skinner (1904). While the ideas and system propagated by Thorndike is called 'Connectionism', the system presented by Watson and Pavlov is known as Classical Conditioning and the system given by Skinner is called Operant Conditioning.

The second type of theories look upon learning as the change in the field consisting of the learner and his environment and the learner's Perception of field. These theories emphasise the role of purpose, insight and understanding in the process of learning. The chief exponents of these type of theories are Max-Wertheimer (1880-1943); Wolfgang Kohler (1887-1967), Kurt Koffka (1886-1941) and Kurt Lewin (1890-1947).

All these theories belonging to one or other type represent the viewpoints, held by their propagators about the nature and process of learning. None of these theories are said to be complete in all aspects for explaining the phenomenon of learning. Each one of them gives a partial description. For example, one theory is good in explaining the learning process in one situation while the others hold equally good in the other different situations. Therefore, it is essential to have a working knowledge of some important theories. Below, we try to think over some of the most important theories. These are:

1. Thorndike's Trial and Error or S.R.Theory of Learning.
2. Watson's & Pavlov's Classical Conditioning.
3. Skinner's Operant Conditioning.
4. Kohler's Gestalt or Insightful Learning.

Environment of Classroom

After performing various experiments upon the subjects like dogs, rats and cats, psychologists like Watson and Pavlov gave birth to a new theory of learning known as Conditioned Response Theory or simply as Learning by Conditioning. For understanding what is Conditioning and what does this theory imply, it is desirable to have an idea of the type of experiments performed by these psychologists.

Experiment by Pavlov: In one of the experiments, Pavlov kept a dog hungry for the night and then tied him on to the experimental table which was fitted with certain mechanically controlled devices. The dog was made comfortable and distractions were excluded as far as it was possible to do so. The observer kept himself hidden from the view of the dog but able to view the experiment by means of a set of mirrors. Arrangement was made to give food to the dog through automatic devices. Every time when the food was presented before the dog, he also arranged for the ringing of a bell. When the food was presented before the dog and the bell was rung, there was automatic secretion of saliva from the mouth of the dog. The activity of presenting the food accompanied with a ringing of the bell was repeated several times and the amount of saliva secreted was measured.

After several trials, the dog was given no food but the bell was rung. In this case also the amount of saliva secreted was recorded and measured. It was found that even in the absence of food (the natural stimulus), the ringing of the bell (an artificial stimulus) caused the dog to secrete the saliva (nature response).

It considers the learning as a habit formation and is based on the principle of Association and Substitution. It is simply a stimulus-response type of learning where in place of a natural stimulus like food, water, sexual contact, etc. the artificial stimulus like sound of the bell, sight of a definite colour, etc. can evoke a natural response.

When both the artificial or neutral stimulus (ringing of the bell) and natural stimulus (food) are brought together, several times, the dog becomes habituated or conditioned to respond to this situation. There becomes perfect association between the types of stimuli presented together. As a result, after some time natural stimulus can be substituted or replaced by an artificial stimulus and this artificial stimulus is able to evoke the natural response.

Diagrammatic Presentation of the Experiment

Natural Stimulus (Presentation of food)	Natural response (Salfivation)
S1	R1
S2	R2
Artificial stimulus (Ringing Bell)	General alertness

In this experiment, the dog learned to salivate at the sound of the bell. This kind of learning was named as Learning by Conditioning.

Another Experiment: In one of the experiments done by Wateon, the subject was a human baby of 11 months. The baby was given a rabbit to play. The baby liked it very much and was pleased to touch its fur. He watched carefully the pleasant responses of the baby. After some time in the course of the experiment, a loud noise was produced to frighten the baby. As soon as the baby touched the rabbit, the baby was frightened. Each time when he tried to touch the rabbit, the loud noise was produced and he gave fear response. After some time he began to fear the rabbit, even if no loud noise accompanied it. In this way, he learned to fear the rabbit through conditioning.

From these experiments, Watson and Pavlov, etc., concluded that all types of learning can be explained through the process of conditioning. What is this process can be understood through the following conclusion;

It is a learning process whereby artificial stimulus is able to behave like a natural stimulus when both natural and artificial stimuli are presented together. In this land of learning, association plays a great role since the individual responds to an artificial stimulus because he associates it with the natural stimulus.

The conditioning theory of learning put forward by Watson and Pavlov actually involves the conditioning of the Respondent behaviour though a process of stimulus association and substitution. Here the responses of the learner become so much conditioned – behaving in the same way or responding similarly to the similar situation, that he does not care for the natural stimuli for evoking the related natural response. As a result the new substituted stimulus behaves like original stimulus and is able to evoke the desired response.

Educational Implications: The phenomenon of conditioning does not limit itself to such laboratory experiments only. The day to day learning at home, school, etc., consists of plenty of examples where the child learns through conditioning. Fear, love and hatred towards the subjects are created through conditioning. A mathematics teacher, with his defective methods of teaching or improper behaviour, may be disliked by students or by a particular student. He without caring to know the basic reason, always rebukes and punishes the child while returning him the checked home-assignments. Gradually, the child begins to fear home assignments of any sort. He also develops a distaste and hatred towards the subject of Mathematics.

On the contrary, the sympathetic treatment given by the teacher and his interesting and effective methodology can bring a desirable impact on the students through the process of conditioning. They develop a positive attitude towards the subject and love their teacher as well as the subject taught by him.

The use of audiovisual aids in the teaching-learning process involves the conditioning theory in making the students learn so many things. The child gets an idea of a particular object or phenomenon through this aid. For example, the teacher shows him the picture of a cat, along with the written words 'cat'. The teacher speaks out 'cat' and asks the student to say 'cat' every time when the picture is presented. After some time the picture of the cat is not presented, only the written word 'cat' is shown. But the child responds to it by saying 'cat'. He associates the written word 'cat' with the picture of the cat and sound of the word.

In developing desirable habits, interests, attitudes, sense of appreciation in the children, etc., the conditioning process may help the others and parents a lot. Not only it helps the development of proper behaviour in them, but also is helpful in removing so many bad habits-unhealthy attitudes, superstition, fear and phobias-through deconditioning. A child who fears a particular object can be made to seek pleasure with it. Another child who thinks it a dangerous sign if a cat crosses his way can be made to give up his misbelief. In this way, the conditioning theory throws light on so many aspects of learning and helps the teacher and parents in their task.

Dominating Conditions

Although classified and included in the category of conditioning, operant conditioning differs a lot from the classical conditioning advocated by Pavlov and Watson. The most outstanding difference lies in the order related with the initiation and response, *i.e.,* stimulus response mechanism. In classical conditioning the organism is passive. It must wait for something to happen for responding.

The presence of a stimulus for evoking a response is essential. The behaviour cannot be emitted in the absence of a cause. The child expresses fear only when he hears a loud noise, the dog waits for food to arrive before salivating. In each of such instances, the subject has no control over the happening. He is made to behave in response to the stimulus situations. Thus, the behaviour is said to be initiated by the environment, the organism simply responds.

Skinner revolted against "no stimulus, no response" mechanism in the evolution of behaviour. He argued that in practical situations in our life we cannot always wait for things to happen in the environment. Man is not a victim of the environment. He may often manipulate the things in the environment with his own initiative.

Therefore, it is not always essential that there must be some known stimuli or cause of evoking a response. Quite often, most of our responses could not be attributed to the known stimuli. The organism itself initiates the behaviour. A dog, a child, or an individual "does" something, "behaves" in some manner, it "operates" on the environment and in turn the environment responds to the activity. How the environment responds to the activity, rewarding or not, largely determines whether the behaviour will be repeated, maintained or avoided.

From where Skinner got the cue for such ideas is a question that can arise at this stage. Definitely, it was from the studies and observations of an earlier psychologist named Edward Lee Thorndike. Through his experiments, for propagating his famous trial and error theory of learning, Thorndike concluded that the rewards of a response (like getting food after a chance success through the randomised movements) leads to repetition of an act and the strengthening of S-R associations.

These conclusions made Skinner begin a series of experiments to find the consequences of the rewards in repeating and maintaining behaviour. Based on the finding of his experiments, he concluded that "behaviour is shaped and maintained by its consequences. It is operated by the organism and maintained by itself". The occurrence of such behaviour was named as operant behaviour and the process of learning, that plays the part in learning such behaviour, was named by him as operant conditioning. For understanding what Skinner propagated through his theory of operant conditioning, let us try to build a base by defining and explaining some of the concepts used by him for bringing out his theory.

Respondent and Operant Behaviour: As we have seen, the earlier theories of learning assumed the existence of a known stimulus as a necessary prerequisite for evoking a response. Skinner, first time, got the idea that most of the responses could not be attributed to the known stimuli. He defined two types of responses-the one 'elicited' by known stimuli which he called as "respondent behaviour" and the other "emitted" by the unknown stimuli which he called as "Operant behaviour". Examples of respondent behaviour may include all reflexes such as jerking one's hands when jabbed with a pin and the pupillary constriction on account of bright light or salivation in the presence of food.

In the respondent behaviour the stimulus preceding the response is responsible for causing the behaviour. On the other hand, in the operant behaviour the stimulus causing such behaviour is unknown and it is not important to know the cause of the behaviour. Here it is not the stimulus but the consequences of the behaviour which are more important and hence the operant behaviour is controlled by the strength if its consequences instead of stimuli. Examples of such behaviour may include the behaviour like moving one's hand, arms or legs arbitrarily, and abandoning one toy in favour of the other, eating a meal, writing a letter, standing up and walking about and similar other everyday activities.

Operant: Skinner considers an operant as a set of acts that constitutes an organism's doing something, *e.g.*, raising its head, walking about, pushing a lever, etc.

Reinforcer and Reinforcement: The concept of reinforcement is identical to the presentation of a reward. A reinforcer is the stimulus whose presentation or removal increase the probability of a response re-occurring. Skinner thinks of two kinds of reinforcers – positive and negative.

A positive reinforcer is any stimulus the introduction or presentation of which increase the likelihood of a particular behaviour. Food, water, sexual contact, etc., are classified as positive reinforcers. A negative reinforcer is any stimulus the removal or withdrawal of which increases the likelihood of a particular behaviour. Electric shock, a loud noise, etc., are said to be negative reinforcers.

The Schedules of Reinforcement: Skinner put forward the idea of planning of Schedules of reinforcement of conditioning the operant behaviour of the organism. The important schedules are as under:

1. *Continuous Reinforcement Schedule:* It is hundred per cent reinforcement schedule where provision is made to reinforce or reward every correct response of the organism during acquisition of learning. For example, a student may be rewarded for every correct answer he gives to the questions or problems put by his teacher.
2. *Fixed Interval Reinforcement Schedule:* In this schedule the organism is rewarded for a response made only after a set interval of time, *e.g.*, every 3 minutes or every 5 minutes. How many times he has given correct response during this fixed interval of time does not matter; it is only on the expiry of the fixed interval, that he is presented with some reinforcement.
3. *Fixed Radio Reinforcement Schedule:* In this schedule the reinforcement is given after a fixed number of response. A rat, for example, might be given a pallet of food after a certain number of level presses. A student may be properly rewarded after answering a fixed number of questions, say 3 or 5. Fixed ratio schedule is used in some factories, and by employers of casual workers or labourer where salary is paid on a piecework basis, number of garments sewn and number of baskets of fruit packed.

4. *Variable Reinforcement Schedule:* When reinforcement is given at varying intervals of time or after a varying number of responses, it is called a variable reinforcement schedule. In this case reinforcement is intermittent or irregular. The individual does not know when he is going to be rewarded and consequently he remains motivated throughout the learning process in the wait of reinforcement. The most common example of such schedule in human behaviour is the reinforcement operation schedules of gambling devices. Here rewards are unpredictable and keep the players well-motivated though occasional returns.

Reinforcement and its schedules play a key role in the conditioning of operant behaviour and acquisition of a learning. Where a continuous reinforcement schedule increases the response rate, the discontinuation of reinforcement may result in the extinction of that response or behaviour. Continuous reinforcement schedule thus yields the least resistance to extinction and the lowest response rate during learning. Therefore, learning of a response takes place quickly if every correct response is rewarded, but it is easily forgotten when the reinforcement is stopped. If reinforcement is given after a varying number of correct response or at varying intervals of time the response is remarkably resistant to extinction.

However, the fixed interval reinforcement schedules are found to provide the lowest yield in terms of performance as the individual may soon learn to respond correct only when the time or turn of reinforcement arrives. Similarly, he may lose interest in getting reinforcement after a fixed interval or fixed number of correct response. Weighing all these properly, Skinner suggests to begin with 100 per cent schedule, practice the fixed interval or fixed ratio schedule and finally arrive at the variable reinforcement schedule for better results in learning or training.

The Definition: Operant conditioning refers to a kind of learning process whereby a response is made more probable or more frequent by reinforcement. It helps in the learning of operant behaviour, the behaviour that is not necessarily associated with a known stimuli.

The Distinction: Classical or respondent conditioning is based on respondent behaviour. Specifically, it deals with responses that invariably follow a specific stimulus and are thus elicited, *e.g.*, blinking at a bright light, an electric shock, salivation at the sight of food, and so forth. In this, greater importance is attached to the stimulus for eliciting the desired response. That is why, it is also called a type conditioning.

On the other hand, operant conditioning helps in conditioning or learning of operant behaviour – behaviour that is emitted (rather than elicited). The organism seems to initiate operant behaviour on his own without a single, explicit, preceding stimulus. In this type of learning much emphasis is placed on the response rather than the stimulus causing the response. That is way, it is also named as type R conditioning. In type S conditioning, the problem with the trainer or teacher is to select appropriate stimuli for evoking desired response.

On the other hand in R type conditioning, out of many responses which an organism is capable of giving the problem with the trainer or teacher is to evoke only the appropriate responses and then fix them properly with the help of suitable reinforcement.

The Difference between these two Types of Conditioning may thus be Summarised as under:

Classical Respondent Conditioning	*Operant Conditioning*
1. It helps in the learning of respondent behaviour.	1. It helps in the learning of operant behaviour.
2. It is called type S conditioning to emphasise the importance of the stimulus in eliciting desired response.	2. It is called type R conditioning because of the emphasis on the response.
3. In this type of conditioning beginning is being made with the help of specific stimuli that into bring certain responses.	3. Here beginning is made with the responses as they occur "naturally" or "unnaturally" shaping them existence.
4. Here strength of conditioning is usually determined by the magnitude of the conditioned response, *i.e.*, the amount of saliva (as in the case of classical experiment of Pavlov with dog).	4. Here strength of conditioning is shown by the response, *i.e.*, the rate with which an operant response occurs as a result of some reinforcement.

Experiments Regarding Operant Conditioning: B.F. Skinner conducted a series of experiments with animals. For conducting the experiments with rats, he designed a special apparatus known as Skinner's Box. It was a much modified form of the puzzle box used by Thorndike for his experiments with cats.

The darkened soundproof box mainly consists of a grid floor, a system of light or sound produced at the time of delivering a pallet of food in the food cup, a lever and a food cup. It is 'arranged so that when a rat (hungry or thirsty) presses the lever the feeder mechanism is activated, a light or a special sound is produced and a small pallet of food or small drops of water is released into the food cup. For recording the observations of the experiments, the lever is connected with a recording system which produces a graphical tracing of the lever pressings against the length of time the rat is in the box.

To begin with, Skinner, in one of his experiments, placed a hungry rat in the above described box. In this experiment pressing of the bar in a desirable way by the rat could result in the production of a click sound and presence of a food pallet. The click-sound acted as a cue or signal indicating to the rat that if it responds by going to the food cup, it will be rewarded. The rat was rewarded for each of his proper attempts for pressing the lever. The lever press response having been rewarded, was repeated and when it occurred, it was again rewarded which further increased the probability of the repetition of the lever press response and so on. In this way, ultimately the rat learned the art of pressing the lever as desired by the experimenter.

For doing experiments with pigeons, Skinner made use of another specific apparatus called "pigeon's box". A pigeon is this experiment had to peck at a lighted plastic key mounted on the wall at head high and was consequently rewarded by receiving grain.

With the help of such experiments, Skinner put forward his memory of operant conditioning for learning not only the simple responses like pressing of the lever but also for learning the most difficult and complex series of responses like pressing of the lever but also for learning the most difficult and complex series of responses.

The Mechanism: Operant conditions as emphasised earlier is correlated with operant behaviour. An operant is a set of acts that constitutes an organisms in doing something. Hence, the process of operant conditioning may start with the responses as they occur "naturally" or "at random". In case they do not occur naturally, then attempts may be made for shaping them into existence. How it can be done will be explained ahead under the heading "Shaping".

Once a response (as desired by the trainer, experimenter or teacher) occurs, it is reinforced through a suitable reinforcer (Primary or Secondary, positive or negative). In due course, this response gets conditioned by constantly reinforcing, it. In Skinner's experiment a pallet of food worked as a positive primary reinforcer for the hungry rat.

He got the reinforcement after emitting a certain response (pressing of the lever as desired by the experimenter). The secondary reinforcement may also produce the some results as brought about by the primary reinforcement. It is a sort of neutral stimulus which acquires the reinforcing properties (rewarding value) after getting paired or associated with a primary reinforcer (*e.g.,* food or water). The clicking of a sound and lighting of a bulb in Skinner's experiment may work as sefendary reinforcement if they are paired with the appearance of a pallet of food.

The important thing in the mechanism of operant conditioning is the emitting of a desired response and its proper management through suitable reinforcement. Here the organism is to respond in such a way as to produce the reinforcing stimulus. The subsequent reinforcement gradually conditions the organism to emit the desired response and thus learn the desired act.

There are situations especially in case of the acquisition of complex behaviour and learning of difficult skills, etc., where there may arise very remote chances of nature occurrence. In such cases, waiting for an organism to behave in specific way at random (the natural occurrence) may take a lifetime. For example, the chances for a pigeon to dance in a specific way are extremely remote. The same holds true for a child learning Russian or even table manners. In these situations, where the desired responses do not occur at random (or naturally) efforts are made for eliciting the appropriate responses. It is done by building a chain of responses through a step by step process called "shaping".

In one of his experiments for shaping the behaviour of a pigeon to teach it to walk in a figure eight — Skinner watched its activity and gave it a small amount of grain (reward) for its every proper movement. At first the pigeon got his reward for simply turning its head in the right direction, then for taking a step in the right direction, then for making the correct turn, and so on, until it had learned to do a complete figure eight.

Shaping, in this way, may be used as a successful technique for making individuals learn difficult and complex behaviour and also for introducing desirable modifications in the behaviour. Behaviour modification technique and aversive therapy used in treating the problem behaviour and abnormality have come into existence through the use of shaping of behaviour mechanism.

Implications of the Theory of Operant Conditioning: Theory of operant conditioning has revolutionised the field of training or learning by bringing forward the following practical ideas and implications:

1. A response or behaviour is not necessarily dependent (contingent) upon a specific known stimuli. It is more correct to think that a behaviour or response is dependent upon its consequences. Therefore, for training an organism to learn a particular behaviour or response, he may be initiated to respond in such a way as to produce the reinforcing stimulus. His behaviour should get the reward and in turn he should again act in such a way that he is rewarded, and so on. Therefore the learning or training process and environment must be so designed as to create minimum frustration and maximum satisfaction to a learner to provide him proper reinforcement for the desired training or learning.
2. The principle of operant conditioning may be successfully applied in the task of behaviour modification. We have to find something which is rewarding for the individual whose behaviour we wish to modify, wait until the desired behaviour occurs and immediately reward him when he does. When

this is done, the rate with which the desired response occurs goes up. When the behaviour next occurs, it is again rewarded, and the rate of responding goes up even more. Going in the same way, we will be able to make the individual learn the desired behaviour.

3. The task of the development of human personality can be successfully manipulated through operant conditioning. According to Skinner. "We are what we have been rewarded for being. What we call personality is nothing more than consistent behaviour patterns that summarise our reinforcement history. We learn to speak English, for example, because we have been rewarded for approximating the sounds of the English language in our early home environment. If we happened to be brought up in a Japanese or a Russian home, we would learn to speak Japanese or Russian because when we approximated sound in that language, we would have been attended to or rewarded in some other way" (Hergenhahn, 1976, p. 87).
4. The theory of operant conditioning does not attribute motivation to internal processes within the organism. It takes for granted the consequences of a behaviour or response as a source of motivation to further occurrence of that behaviour. Food is reinforcing to a rat or pigeon. Knowledge of correct response is reinforcing to a learner. Secondary reinforcers also prove very important sources of motivation for a learner. Verbal praise, positive facial expressions of the trainer or teacher, feeling of success, scores, grades, prizes, medals and the opportunity to do the work of one's liking, all constitute good motivator. In this way operant conditioning provided an external approach to motivation.
5. Operant conditioning lays stress on the importance of schedules in the process of reinforcement of the behaviour. In trying to train or learn a behaviour, therefore, great care is to be taken for the proper planning of the schedules of reinforcement.
6. This theory advocated the avoidance of punishment for unlearning the undesirable behaviour and for shaping the

desirable behaviour. Punishment proves ineffective in the long run. It appears that punishment simply suppresses behaviour and when the threat of punishment is removed, behaviour returns to its original level. Therefore, operant conditioning experiments suggested appropriate behaviour and ignoring the inappropriate behaviour for its gradual extinction.

7. In its most effective application, theory of operant conditioning has contributed a lot towards the development of teaching machines and programmed learning. The theory of operant conditioning had led us to think that learning proceeds most effectively if
   a. The learning material is so designed that it creates less opportunities for facing failure and more opportunities for gaining success.
   b. the learner is given rapid feed-back concerning the accuracy of his learning, and
   c. the learner is able to learn at his own pace.

These principles originating from operant conditioning have revolutionised the training and learning programmes. As a result, mechanical learning in the form of teaching machines and computer assisted instructions have replaced usual class room instructions.

Kohler's Gestalt or Insightful Learning: The learning theory named as "Learning by Insight" is the contribution of Gestalt Psychologists. Gestalt Psychology began with the work of German psychologists who were studying the nature of perception. Wertheimer is, generally, considered to be the Gestalt Psychology founding father. Wertheimer, Kohler, Koffka and Lewin all four of these men, originally German, eventually settled in America, are the leaders of what is historically known as Gestalt Psychology.

"Gestalt" is a German noun for which there is no English word equivalent, so the term was earned over into English psychological literature. The nearest English translation of Gestalt is 'configuration' or more simply an organised whole in contrast to a collection of parts. Gestalt psychologists consider the process of learning as a Gestalt – an organised whole. A thing cannot be understood by study of its constituent parts but only by study of it as a totality, is a basic idea behind this theory.

In the practical sense, Gestalt Psychology is primarily concerned with the nature of perception. According to it, an individual perceives the thing as a whole while the Behaviourists and Stimulus-Response theorists define perception in such a way as to make it analogous with taking photographs. They think that sensation comes prior to meaning and consider these two acts as separate. But the Gestalt Psychologists do not separate sensation of an object from its meaning.

They are of the opinion that unless a person sees some meaning in an object he will pay little or no attention to it. Furthermore, to a Gestalt Psychologist, the meaning of sensation or perception is always related to the total situation. According to them perception always involves a problem of organisation. A thing is perceived as a relationship within a field which includes the thing, the viewer and a complex background incorporating the viewer's purposes and previous experience.

Gestalt Psychologists tried to interpret learning as a purposive, exploratory and creative enterprise instead of trial and error or simple stimulus-response mechanism. Learner, while learning, always perceives the situation as a whole and after seeing and evaluating the different relationships takes the proper decision in an intelligent way. He always responds to the proper relationship rather than the specific stimuli.

Gestalt Psychology used the term 'insight' to describe the perception of the whole situation by the learner and his intelligence in responding to the proper relationships. Kohler, first of all, used this term (insight) to describe the learning of his apes. Kohler conducted many experiments on chimpanzees and brought out a book *'Mentality of Apes'* in 1925 which was the result of his experiments, conducted during the period 1913-17 on the Canary Island. These experiments show learning by insight. Some of them are given below:

1. In one experiment, Kohler put the chimpanzee, Sultan, inside a cage and a banana, was hung from the roof of the cage. A box was placed inside the cage. The chimpanzee tried to reach at the banana by jumping but could not succeed. Suddenly, he got an idea and used the box as a jumping platform by placing it just below the hanging banana.

2. In an other experiment, Kohler made this problem more difficult. Now it required two or three boxes to reach the banana. Moreover, the placing of one box over the other required different specific arrangements.
3. In a more complicated experiment banana was placed outside the cage of the chimpanzee. Two sticks, one larger than the other, were placed inside the cage. One was hollow at one end so that the other stick could be thrust into it to form a longer stick. The banana was so kept that it could not be picked up by one of the sticks.

The chimpanzee first tried these sticks one after the other but failed. Suddenly, he got a bright idea. The animal joined the two sticks together and reached the banana. In these experiments, Kohler used many different chimpanzees. Sultan, who was the most intelligent of Kohler's chimpanzees, could solve all the problems. Other chimpanzees could solve the problems only when they saw Sultan solving them.

With such experiments, Kohler concluded that in the solution of problems, his apes did not resort to blind, Trial and Error mechanism. They reacted intelligently. Kohler used the term 'Insight' to describe the learning of his apes. Insight involves the following criteria:

1. The situation as a whole is perceived by the learner.
2. The learner tries to see and judge the relationship between various factors involved in the situation.
3. As a result, the learner is helped in the sudden grasping of the solution of the problem.

On the similar line experiments were conducted by the Gestalt Psychologists. All the experiments have shown that at some stage there is a new organisation of the perceptual field resulting in getting a solution ail of a sudden.

Therefore, the learning according to them is restructuring the field of perception through insight. As a whole, Insight depends upon the following factors:

1. *Experience:* Past experiences help in the insightful solution of the problems. A child cannot solve the problems of Modern

Mathematics unless he is well acquainted with its symbolic languages.

2. *Intelligence:* Insightful solution depends upon the basic intelligence of the learner. The more intelligent the individual is the greater will be his insight.
3. *Learning Situation:* How insightfully the organism will act depends upon the situation in which he has to act. Some situations cue more favourable than the others for insightful solution. As a common observation, insight occurs when the learning situation is so arranged that all the necessary aspects are open for observation.
4. *Initial Efforts:* Insightful learning has to pass through the process of trial and error. But this stage does not last long. These initial efforts, in the form of simple trial and error mechanisms, open the way for insightful learning.
5. *Repetition and Generalisation:* After having an insightful solution of a particular type of problem, the organism tries to repeat it in another situation, demanding similar type of solution. The way found in one situation helps him to read insightfully in the other identical situations.

Educational Implicationing of the Theory of Insightful Learning: This theory brings the following important facts into the limelight:

1. The whole is greater than the parts and, therefore, the situation should be viewed as a whole.
2. The use of blind fumbling and mechanical trial and error should be minimised. The learner should try to see relevant relationships and act intelligently.
3. The purpose or motive plays the central role in the learning process.

Based on the appeal of this theory, teachers are required to pay attention to the following aspects:

1. Subject-matter (learning material) should be presented in Gestalt form. While teaching the topic, parts of a flowering plant or flower the initial start should not be made by presenting the different parts. The plant or flower as a whole

should be presented before them and later on the parts should be emphasised. The problem of Mathematics requiring solution should be presented as a whole and after grasping it as a whole, it should be tried for the solution.

2. In the organisation of the syllabus and planning of the curriculum, the Gestalt principles should be given due consideration. A particular subject should not be treated as the mere collection of isolated facts or topics. It should be closely integrated into a whole. Similarly, the curriculum, comprising of different subjects and activities should reflect unity and cohesiveness.
3. This theory has brought motivation in the forefront by assigning purpose and motive, the central role in learning process. The child should be motivated by arousing his interest and curiosity and he should be acquainted well with the specific aims and purpose of his learning.
4. The greater contribution of the Insight theory of learning is that it has made learning an intelligent task requiring mental abilities instead of blind fumbling and automatic responses to specific stimuli. It has called a halt to age, old mechanical memorisation, drill and practice work which lack in basic understanding and use of thinking, in reasoning and creative mental powers.

Evaluation of All the Above Theories of Learning: All the theories mentioned above have contributed significantly to Education thought and practice. Each, in its own way, tries to explain the nature and process of learning. But the explanations given by the propagators of these theories are completely one sided and reflect their own point of view. Each one of these theories throws light on only one or me other aspect of the whole phenomenon of learning and each is right in its own field of application.

Theory of Trial and Error explains, satisfactorily, the learning of so many skills through repetition and practice. In learning to walk, swim, cycling, driving and typing, etc., it is useless to try any method other than that of Trial and Error. The learning of small children, and the initial attempts in solving any problem, not only by the children but by the older and intelligent persons require trial and error. Also it is not wise to waste the precious time and energy by attempting the problems blindly without understanding them.

Human beings are endowed with adequate mental powers and are required to use them properly, therefore, learning in their case should involve the use of mental powers. All types of higher learning which requires basic intelligence can only be explained in terms of insight approach.

On the other hand, the acquisition of habits and development of interests and attitudes can be better explained through the Conditioning Theory of Learning. A child acquires the language through this method, Although he learns to hate or love somebody or something through conditioning.

In this way these various theories of learning throw light on some or the other aspects of the total phenomenon of learning and each is right in its own field of application. Each one of these theories claim that every mode of learning is covered by it. Thorndike and others reduce all types of learning into mechanical trial and error or blind fumbling. Pavlov, Watson and Skinner, etc., tried to explain every mode of learning through conditioning and later on Gestalt Psychologists made it a subject of pure 'insight', requiring specific mental abilities.

The situation resembles the plot of the story where some blind men tried to describe an elephant by touching its different parts – leg, trunk, ear and tail, separately. Each one of the gentlemen described the elephant in their own way and was sure that he was correct and others were wrong. Similarly, the propagators of these theories try to describe the phenomenon of learning through its various aspects. Actually, the real picture can only be obtained through the happy combination of these theories. Therefore, a wise teacher and the learner should give due consideration to all of these theories and methods of learning. The field of learning can only be covered by the joint front of these theories.

Exploratory Reading and Learning

Thorndike propagated his theory with the help of the experiments performed on chickens, rats and cats for this purpose he put them under different learning situations, Pierre Fboure (1794-1857) proposed that conclusions drawn from animal experimentation would be equally applicable to man. This proposition started the chain of experimentation, in the field of learning with animals. Thorndike selected chickens, rats and cats for experimentation. He placed them under different learning situations and studied them artfully. With the help of these experiments he tried to evolve certain laws and propagated his theory m connectionism or trial and error learning. It is interesting to know the type of experiments he performed with these animals. For illustration, below we narrate one of his experiments.

He put a hungry cat in a puzzle box. There was only one door for exit which could be opened by correctly manipulating a latch. A fish was placed outside, the box. The smell of the fish worked as a strong motive for the hungry cat to come out of the box. Consequently, the cat made every possible effort to come The situation is described by Thorndike (1911) himself as "It tries to squeeze through every opening; it claws and bites at the bars or wires, it thrusts its paws through any opening and claws at everything it reaches". In this way, it made a number of random movements. In one of the random movements, by change, the latch was manipulated. The cat came out and got its reward responses. Now it was able to open the door without any error or in other words, learned the way of opening the door.

The experiment sums up the following stages in the process of learning:

1. *Drive:* (In the present experiment it was hunger and was intensified with the sight of the food).
2. *Goal:* To get the food by getting out of the box.
3. *Block:* The cat was confined in the box with a closed door.
4. *Random movements:* The cat, persistently, tried to get out of the box.
5. *Chance Success:* As a result of this striving and random movement the cat, by chance, succeeded in opening the door.
6. *Selection (of proper movement)*: Gradually, the cat recognised the correct opening way by manipulating the latch out of its random movements.

7. *Fixation:* At last, the cat learned the proper way of opening the door by eliminating all the incorrect responses and fixing only the right response. Now it was able to open the door without any error or in other words, learned the way of opening the door.

Thorndike named the learning of his experimental cat as "Trial and Error Learning". He maintained that the learning is nothing but the stamping in of the correct responses and stamping out of the incorrect responses though trial and error. In trying for the correct solution the cat made so many vain attempts. It committed errors and errors before getting success. On subsequent trials, it tried to avoid the erroneous ways and repeated the correct way of manipulating the latch.

Thorndike called it "Learning by selecting and connecting" as it provides an opportunity for the selection of the proper responses and connect or associate them with adequate stimuli. In this reference, Thorndike has written: "Learning is connecting. The mind is man's connection system" (1931, p. 122).

As a result learning is caused by the formation of connection in the nervous system between stimuli and responses. There is definite association between sense, impression and impulses to action. This association can be known as bond or connection. Since it is these bonds or connection, which becomes strengthened or weakened in the making and breaking of habits Thorndike's system is, sometimes, called a "bond psychology" or simply "connectionism".

Thorndike propounded the following laws of learning on the basis of his theory:

1. *The Law of Readiness:* The statement runs as under:

> "When any condition unit is ready to conduct, for it to do so is satisfying. When any condition unit is not in readiness to conduct, for it to conduct is annoying. When any condition unit is in readiness to conduct, for it not to do so is annoying

This law is indicative to learner's state to participate in the learning process. Readiness according to Thorndike is preparation for action. It is very essential for learning. If the child is ready to learn he learns more quickly, effectively and with greater satisfaction than if he is not ready to learn. It warns us not to make the child learn till he is ready to learn and also not to miss any opportunity of providing learning experience if the child is, already, prepared to learn.

The right movements concerning the learning situation and the learner's state of mind should be very well-recognised and maximum use of this knowledge should be made by the teacher. He should also attempt to motivate the students by arousing their attention, interest and curiosity.

2. *The Law of Effect:* In the words of Thorndike, the statement of the law runs as under:

> "When a modifiable connection between situation and response is made and is accompanied or followed by a satisfying state of affairs, that connection's strength is increased. When made and accompanied or followed by an annoying state of affairs, its strength is decreased."

In simple words, it means that the learning takes place properly when it results in satisfaction and the learner derives pleasure out of it. In the situation when the child meets a failure or gets dissatisfaction, the progress on the path of learning is blocked. All the pleasant experiences have a lasting influence and are remembered for a long time, while the unpleasant ones are soon forgotten. Therefore, the satisfaction and dissatisfaction, pleasure or displeasure obtained as a result of some learning ensures the degree of effectiveness of that learning.

In the words, this law emphasises the role of rewards and punishment in the process of learning. Getting reward as a result of some learning motivates and encourages the child to proceed on the same path with more intensity and enthusiasm while the punishment of 'any sort discourages him and creates distaste and repulsion towards that learning.

3. *The Law of Exercise:* This law has two sub-parts-law of use and law of disuse. The statements regarding these sub-parts run as under:

Law of Use: "When a modifiable connection is made between a situation and response that connection's strength is, other things being equal, increased".

Law of Disuse: "When a modifiable connection is not made between a situation and response, during a length of time, that connection's strength is decreased".

In this way, law of use refers to the strengthening of connection with practice while the law of disuse to the weakening of connection or forgetting, when the practice is discontinued. In brief, it can be said that law of exercise as a whole, emphasises the need of repetition, practice and drill work in the process of learning.

Changed form of the (2) and (3) Laws. In the later years of his life, Thorndike changed his stand on the laws of exercise and effect.

He experimented upon a blindfolded man who was asked to draw a line of 3 inches in length. Mere repetition did not bring any change or improvement. So, he concluded that practice without rewarding the response was meaningless, which follows that in the process of learning connection get strengthened by being rewarded and not by just occurring.

Regarding the Law of Effect he began to think that rewards and punishment were not equal and opposite in effect. Rewards strengthen the connection considerably whereas punishment does not weaken the connection to the same degree. The intensity and speed of reward in casting influence upon learning is greater than that of punishment. It also brings healthy and desirable improvement in the personality of the child. In this way, he began to give more importance to rewards and praise in place of punishment and blame.

All these three laws-law of readiness, law of effect and law of exercise-have a wide field of application in the teaching-learning process. These laws imply the truth of the well-known proverbs and maxims like "You can lead a horse to water but you cannot make him drink. "Nothing succeeds like success". "Practice makes a man perfect".

Some More Laws of Learning:

1. *Law of Multiple Response or Varied Reactions:* The law implies that when an individual is confronted with a new situation he responds in a variety of ways before arriving at the correct response.
2. *Law of Attitude:* Learning is guided by a total attitude or 'set' of the organism. The learner performs the task properly if he has developed a healthy attitude towards the task.
3. *Law of Analogy:* An individual responds to a new situation on the basis of the responses made by him in similar situations in the past. He makes responses by comparison or analogy.
4. *Law of Associative Shifting:* The statement of law runs thus "We can get any response from the learner of which he is capable, associated with any situation to which he is sensitive". In other words, any response, which is possible, can be linked with any stimulus. Thorndike clarified his stand through one of his experiments in which he demonstrated how a cat can be trained to stand up at command. He concluded that first of all, a bit of fish is dangled before the cat while you say "Stand up". After enough trials, there will be a stage when you would not need the help of the fish. The oral signal or command will alone evoke the response. The idea put through this law gave birth to a new theory of learning known as Theory of Conditioning.

Educational Implications: Thorndike's theory of trial and error has enough educational significance. It tries to explain the process of learning, carefully on the basis of actual experiments performed. Not only the animals but human learning also, to a greater extent, follows the path of trial and error. A child while confronted with a mathematical problem tries so many possibilities of its solution, before he arrives at a correct one. Even the discoveries and inventions in the various fields of knowledge are the results of trial and error process.

For example, let us take the discovery made by Archimedes in the form of his well-known principle. He was confronted with a problem given by his Emperor. There was a Drive that he will be beheaded if he could not get the solution of problem. There was a Block, as he could not think of any solution. The problem was difficult. He went on experimenting and made a number of attempts (trials) for the solution of his problem. One day while taking his bath, he got chance success in one of his attempts and this led to the formulation of the law of floating bodies.

But the excessive use of the method, trial and error, without caring for the development of understanding should, not be encouraged in any circumstances. We cannot reduce the human learning as mechanical and blindfolded as advocated by this theory. It must be supported by reason, understanding and insight. Trials and practice coupled with insight will make the process of learning more effective than either of the methods adopted alone.

As far as the Thorndike's laws of learning are concerned, it goes without saying that Thorndike has done a valuable service for the field of learning and teaching by providing these laws. These laws imply the following things in general:

1. In the process of teaching and learning, the main task of the teacher is to see what things he likes to be remembered or forgotten by his students. After this, he must try to strengthen the bonds or connections between the stimuli and responses of those things, which are to be remembered, through repetition, drill and reward. For forgetting the connections should be weakened through disuse and annoying results.
2. The child must be made ready to learn. His interest, attitude and mental preparation is essential for the smooth sailing in the teaching-learning process.
3. It is also emphasised that the past experiences and learning give an adequate base for the new learning. Therefore, the teacher should try to make use of the previous knowledge and experiences of the students. The child must, also, be encouraged to see similarities and dissimilarities between the different kinds of response to stimuli and with the help of comparison and contrast should try to apply the learning of something in one situation to the other similar situations.
4. The child should be encouraged to do his work independently. He must try the various solutions of the problem before

arriving at a correct one. But every care should be taken to see that he may not waste his time and energy. He should not be allowed to repeat his mistakes and proceed blindly without using his reasoning and thinking powers and utilises the past learning experiences.

In short, Thorndike's theory and laws of learning have contributed a lot to educational theory and practice. It has made the learning purposeful and goal-directed and has brought motivation in the forefront, it has also given impetus to the work of practice, drill and repetition and realised the psychological importance of rewards and praise in the process of teaching and learning.

Reader's Role

Significance of the Individual

Etymologically the word personality has been derived from the Latin word 'persona'. At first this word was used for the mask worn by the actors to change their appearance but later on it began to be used for the actors themselves. Since then, the term personality has been used to depict outward appearance or external behaviour, etc.

It is in this sense we have developed a wrong notion about the term personality. We often listen to such comment as this man has a fine or magnetic personality or that man has a poor personality. We try to paste such labels as fine, good or poor on the individuals on the basis of their physical make-up, manner of their walking, talking, dressing and host of other similar characteristics.

Sometimes, we use personality as equivalent to one's character. It is also a wrong notion. Character is, by all means, a moral or ethical term which refers to the standards of right and wrong. While personality is purely a psychological term and hence it is not proper to use it in reference to the study of ethical values.

Thus, we cannot take personality as an equivalent word for outward appearance or behaviour. It is a very superficial approach.

We cannot ignore the inner aspect of one's personality. Personality includes the totality of one's behaviour and hence, both inner and outer (covert as well as overt) behaviour should be taken into consideration.

Concept of Personality

The psychologists adopting Type approach advocate that human personalities can be classified into a few clearly defined types and each person can be put in one or the other type depending upon his behavioural characteristics, somatic structure, blood types, fluids in the body, or personality traits. Based on such approach, the physicians of ancient India broadly categorised all human beings into three types.

This classification was based on the three basic elements of the body, *i.e. pitt* (bile), *bate* (wind), and *kuff* (muscus). Almost the same approach was followed by the Greek physicians like Hippocrates, one of the disciples of the great philosopher Aristotle. In the subsequent years many more scholars and psychologists tried to divide persons into certain types depending upon their specific criterion. Let us describe a few of such approaches.

Hippocrates' Classification: According to Hippocrates the human body consists of four types of humours or fluids – Blood, yellow bile, phlegm (mucus) and black bile. The predominance of one of these four types of fluids in one's body gives him unique temperamental characteristics leading to a particular type of personality summarised as below:

Dominance of fluid	*Personality in the body*	*Temperamental Characteristics types*
Blood	Sanguine	Light hearted, optimistic,, happy, hopeful and accommodating.
Yellow bile	Choleric	Irritable, angry but passionate and strong with active imagination.
Phlegm (mucus)	Phlegmatic	Cold, clam, slow or luggish, indifferent.

Black bile	Melancholioc	Bad tempered, dejected, sad, depressed, pessimistic, deplorable and self-involved.

Kretschmer's Classification: Kretschmer classified all human beings into certain biological types according to their physical structure and has allotted definite personality characteristics associated with each physical make-up as follows:

Personality types	*Personality characteristics*
I. Pyknic (having fat bodies)	Sociable, jolly, easy going and good natured.
II. Athletic (balanced body)	Energetic, optimistic and adjustable.
III. Leptosomatic (lean and thin)	Unsociable, reserved, shy, sensitive and pessimistic.

Sheldon's Classification: He too like Kretschmer, classified human beings into certain types according to their physical structures and attached certain temperamental characteristics to them as under.

The approach adopted by the above psychologists to have classification on the basis of correlation between structure of the body and personality characteristics, is lopsided. It is somewhat misleading. There does not exists such perfect body-mind or body-heart correlation as the propagators of these approaches have assumed.

Jung's Classification: He divided all human beings basically into two distinct types-Introvert and Extrovert-according to their social participation and the interest which they take in social activities. Later on, he further sharpened his two-fold division by giving sub-types. In this process he took into consideration the four psychological functions-thinking, feeling, sensation and intuition, in relation to his previous extrovert and introvert types.

The classification has been criticised on the grounds that in general, such different types or classes as suggested by Jung do not exist. Most of us, on the basis of typical characteristics prescribed for extrovert and introvert, may belong to both of the categories, as may be called ambivert. This brings complication and hence this type of approach does not give a clear picture of the classification or description of personality.

Process and Meaning

Psychologically speaking personality is all that a person is. It is the totality of one's behaviour towards one another. It includes everything about the person, his physical, emotional, social mental and spiritual make-up. It is all that a person has about him.

In this way, definitely, the term personality signifies something deeper than mere appearance or outward behaviour. How should it be given a proper meaning or definition is a difficult problem. Actually its subjective nature does not allow to reach a clear-cut, well agreed definition. That is why, it has been defined by so many psychologists in so many ways according to their own points of view. Some of these well known attempts at defining personality are presented below:

1. *Watson:* "Personality is the sum of activities that can be discovered by actual observations over a long enough period of time to give reliable information." (1930)

   In this manner, Watson gives emphasis upon the behaviour of an individual and says that personality is nothing but the useful effect one makes upon the person coming into his close contact.
2. *Morton Prince,* accepting the role of both heredity and environment, defines it as;

   "Personality is the sum total of all the biological innate dispositions, impulses, tendencies, appetites and instincts of the individual and the dispositions and tendencies acquired by experience." (1929, p. 532)
3. *Allport:* After evaluating 49 definitions of personality written by so many eminent persons, Allport summarises his own concept in the following words:

   > "Personality is a dynamic organisation within the individual of those Psycho-physical systems that determine his unique adjustment to his environment." (1948, p.28)

Although Allport has tried to give a comprehensive definition of the term personality including the words organisation, dynamic, psycho-physical system, unique adjustment and environment, etc. yet he, like other pervious ones, only describes it. By emphasising merely on theoretical aspect and describing it in terms of behavioural or dynamic concepts the true nature of personality cannot be understood. The contemporary psychologists like R.B. Cattell and Eysenck are of such opinion. They feel very strongly that if personality cannot be demonstrated, measured and quantified it should be called philosophy or art and not personality theory in psychology.

Below we give their ideas in connection with the meaning of the term personality.

4. *R.B. Cattell:* "Personality is that which permits a prediction of what a person will do in a given situation." (1970, p. 386)
5. *Eysenck:* "Personality is the more or less stable and enduring organisation of a person's character, temperament, intellect, and physique, which determine his unique adjustment to the environment," (1971, p.2)

He has tried to make certain terms clear in the following way: Character denotes a person's more or less stable or enduring system or organisation of conative behaviour ("Will").

Temperament denotes a person's more less stable or enduring organisation of effective behaviour ("Emotions").

Intellect denotes a person's more or less stable or enduring organisation of congnitive behaviour (intelligence).

Physique denotes a person's more or less stable or enduring organisation or bodily configuration and neuro-endocrine endowment (glands + nervous system + bodily configuration).

Major Characters

As pointed out in deriving meaning and nature of personality. Our personality is a unique organisation of so many things belongs to our self. How all what we possess is integrated for shaping our personality thus needs to be investigated. The structure and composition of personality should be known properly so that we can understand us and others in a proper way. Psychologists have tried to think over this issue and as a result have propounded a number of theories explaining structure and integration of personality. The theories so derived, in general, can be classified as below into four broad categories according to their modes of approach.

1. *The Theories which Adopt Type-approach:* The viewpoints of Hippocrates, Kretschmer, Sheldon and Jung belong to this category. They hold that human personalities can be classified into a few clearly defined types and each person can be put in one or the other types according to his personality traits.
2. *The Theories which Adopt Trait-approach:* Worth mentioning in this category is Cattell's theory of personality. This approach believes in the mathematical analysis and quantification of the personality constituents and helps in the prediction on human behaviour in a particular situation.
3. *The Theories which Adopt Type as well as Trait-approach:* Eysenck's theory of personality belongs to this category. He goes a step ahead to the approach adopted by Cattell. He does not only mention the personality traits for assessing one's personality but also tries to give definite personality types.
4. *The Theories which Adopt Developmental Approach:* Eysenck's theory of personality belongs to this category. He goes a step ahead to the approach adopted by Cattell. He does not only mention the personality traits for assessing one's personality but also tries to give definite personality types.

Let us discuss some of these approaches and theories in detail.

Agents' Perception

R.B. Cattell, a British born American researcher tried to advance further the trait approach advocated by Allport. For this purpose he made use of the same 17953 dictionary words pointed out by Allport (capable of describing human behaviour and personality) for arriving at some fundamental dimensions or factors for the measurement of one's personality through the following simple non-technical description.

1. He began his task in 1956 with approximately 4000 of Allport's 17953 terms and narrowed the list down to 171 by eliminating the repeated ones and synonyms. In this way, he arrived at the final list of 171 words (dictionary words) related with personality and called these trait elements.
2. The next step was to find out how they are related. He found that each trait element correlated high with some and low with others. In this way, he managed to form some specific groups and called them Surface Traits. These surface traits identified were 35 in number.
3. Again he went on examining these surface traits in terms of their intercorrelations. There was overlapping. The removal of such overlapping gave him the desired basic dimensions which he called Source Traits, *i.e.*, the real structure influence underlying personality.
4. He ultimately concluded that 16 Factors or Basic Dimensions of personality given below are sufficient to describe one's personality. Each of these factors may be seen to carry a set of opposite personality traits, *i.e.*, Relaxed V/S Tense or Practical V/s Imaginative, etc. as shown in the following table:

The Set of Personality Traits Existing in Cattell's Sixteen Personality Factors

Name of the Factor	*Trait*	*Opposite Trait*
A	Reserved	Outgoing
B	Less intelligent	More intelligent
C	Affected by feelings	Emotionally Stable
E	Submissive	Dominant
F	Serious	Happy-go-Lucky
G	Expedient	Conscientious
H	Timid	Venturesome

Contd...

Name of the Factor	*Trait*	*Opposite Trait*
I	Tough-minded	Sensitive
L	Trusting	Suspicious
M	Practical	Imaginative
N	Forthright	Shrewd
O	Self-assured	Apprehensive
Ql	Conservative	Experimenting
Q2	Group-dependent	Self-sufficient
Q3	Uncontrolled	Controlled
Q4	Relaxed	Tense

Cattell made use of his 16 factors or basic dimensions of the personality in the construction of a personality inventory known as Cattell's Sixteen Personality Factors or Sixteen P.P. Inventory. This inventory is widely used for the measurement of the personality. In this way, efforts made by R.B. Cattell for knowing and measuring one's personality using trait approach may be said to be worth appreciating.

Educational Implication: Trait theories put forward by Allport and Cattell have a number of educational implication like below:

1. In the identification of the personality of the learners these theories put up an altogether new approach quite different from its earlier type approach. Both Allport and Cattell in their theories did not try to specify any relationship between the personality characteristics of the learners with their somatic structure, blood types, etc., but tried to lay emphasis on the behavioural traits, *i.e.*, a thing of qualification and measurement through the observation of one's behaviour in natural and controlled condition. It made the task of the assessment of the personality more objective and reliable. Thus, these theories were able to provide and recommend observation of one's behaviour as a method of assessing personality.

2. These theories put up the concept of trait for explaining the structure and integration of one's personality. According to them traits are the basic units or building blocks of one's personality or ways of behaving. If we know the traits of one's personality exhibited more often through his behaviour, we can be able to describe his personality and also distinguish his personality from other's personality. Therefore, these theories contributed a lot in emphasising the need of knowing about the personality characteristics of the learners in order to work for the wholesome development of their personality.
3. The distinction made by Allport in specifying one's behavioural characteristics or traits into certain categories like cardinal, central and secondary traits provided sufficient knowledge for laying emphasis on the development of certain important traits of one's personality while marginalising for the time being. It also explained that in case you want to develop the child into a specific personality, you have to take care of the development of specific cardinal and central traits for this task.
4. Cattell as we have noticed went too ahead in his trait approach by producing the factor analysis of all the observable behaviour traits in human behaviour and concluding that the learner's personality can be identified and assessed through 16 basic dimensions or factors of personality. The sixteen PF personality inventory constructed on the basis of these dimensions has very much helped the cause of education in providing quite a reliable and objective method of assessing the learners personality.
5. Both the theories put up by Allport and Cattell have been able to pin point the role of traits in building a good, poor or bad personality. Cattell even tried to suggest a clear cut distinction between positive and negative (desirable or undesirable) traits while mentioning the 16 basic dimensions or factors of learner's personality. The knowledge of the significance of the traits a builder of one's personality and distinction between desirable and non-desirable traits provided by these theories has thus served the cause of

education in putting right attempts for the development of desirable traits in the behaviour of the children.

Idea of Eysenck

H.J. Eysenck, the famous contemporary psychologist has adopted trait cum type approach for explaining the structure of personality.

Eysenck has tried to blend all which he could avail from the previous theories of personality.

While Cattell has tried to give dimensions to personality by giving traits, Eysenck gave it more specification by grouping traits into definite types. Hence his approach is trait cum type approach.

How the individual behaviour is organised and gets the shape of a definite type.

We have four levels of behaviour organisation:

1. At the lowest level we have specific responses.

   They grow out of particular responses to any single act. For example, 'blushing' is a specific response.

2. At the second level we have habitual responses. If the individual reacts in the similar fashion when the same situation re-occurs we get habitual responses. For example, the responses like.

   a. Not easily picking up friendship.

   b. Hesitant to talk to strangers, etc., are habitual responses.

3. At the third level we have organisation of habitual acts into traits. The behaviour ads which have similarities are said to belong to one group called trait. In the above example the habitual responses no. (a) and (b), etc. give birth to a group or trait called 'Shyness'.

4. At the fourth level we have organisation of these traits into a general type. A type is defined as group of correlated traits. The traits which are similar in nature give birth to a definite type which the traits like persistence, rigidity, shyness, etc., have been grouped into a type which is 'Introversion'.

Now at this final stage, ultimately we obtain a definite type. A person, now can be classified as introvert if he has traits as described at in level, habits and habit systems.

Eysenck has given the following distinct traits:

1. Introversion.
2. Extroversion.
3. Neurotism.
4. Psychotism.

He has also tried to link different traits and characteristics with each of these types.

The Classification

This classification of personality type is given by Meyer Friedman and Ray Rosenman. It classifies the people into two personality types, type A and type B on the basis of their personality traits and then points out which types of people are more prone to heart ailments particularly Coronary heart disease. In Coronary heart disease there is malfunctioning of the heart on account of the deficiency in supply and circulation of the blood through blood carrying arteries and veins. For a long time it was thought that cholesterol deposits in the arteries and veins put obstacles in the free flow of blood through them which in turn proves a potent factor for the deficiency in supply and circulation of the blood to the heart.

Friedman and Rosenman with the active assistance of some medical men tried to establish through their researches that stress is an important causative factor for the Coronary heart disease. They further established that a particular type of people possessing a set of particular personality traits named as type A are more prone to the stress producing behaviour in sharp contrast to the people belonging to type B. They further outlined the typical personality traits associated with these personality types A and B in the following way.

Type Personality: Emotionally unstable, tense, worried, irritating, competitive, high achieving motive, moody, indifferent, active and restless, aggressive, crazy, perfectionist, idealist, rigid, much worried about punctuality and rules, hasty, jealous, dissatisfied from the self and others, suspicious, sensitive, insecure, believer in action and not in fate and fortune, etc.

Type Personality: Emotionally stable, tension free, happy and jolly, average achieving motive, insensitive, patient, self-satisfied, calm and quite, flexible, tolerant, realist, optimist, having faith and trust in one's self and others, adjusted to one's self and others, believer in the philosophy of fate and fortune, sincere but not too serious about the execution and result of the work, etc.

The approach that makes use of the personality traits for identifying and describing the personality of an individual is known as Trait approach. The main propagators of this approach are the famous psychologists Gordon Allport and R.B. Cattell. Let us know about their attempts in this direction.

Concept of Properties

G.B. Allport (1897-1967) was the first personality theorist who adopted trait approach in providing a theory of personality. According to Allport personality trait are the basic units of the structure of our personality. Allport tried to search for these basic units of human behaviour. The problem before him was to decide the number of personality traits representing the human behaviour in its totality. He along with one of his colleagues pointed 17953 words in the English language with the help of available dictionaries for the description of the personality or behaviour of human beings. After analysis and rejection of the words on the basis of synonymy and inappropriateness, he arrived at 4541 words for classifying these into three main types named as cardinal traits, central traits and secondary traits.

Cardinal triats are the most active and dominant traits of one's personality. Although present in a very small number just as one or two, these are enough to colour the personality according to their characteristics. As an example we can cite sense of humour as a cardinal trait in one's personality. This trait may colour his personality in a specific way as much as that he may be identified or known through his behaviour almost dominated by the sense of humour at all the times and occasions.

Central Traits are those traits which are frequently employed for identifying and describing one's personality, e.g., honesty, kindness, timidity, shyness, rigidity, cruelty, etc. Usually seven or eight such central traits are enough for knowing and describing the personality of an individual.

Secondary Traits are those traits of an individual's personality which play quite a secondary or to say quite insignificant role in the identification and-description of one's personality. These are in fact not the essential part of one's personality. That is why these are reflected quite rarely in one's behaviour like a person named as miser, selfish and greedy or contributing generously for a common cause.

In this way, according to Allport, one's cardinal traits alongwith a few selected central traits may play a dominant and significant role in the proper identification of one's personality from others. Thus, they may provide speciality and separate identification to the different individualities of the persons. The rest of the central traits alongwith a few secondary traits, then can make a group of common traits which are generally found in most of the people. Hence, in the task of identification, naming and describing the individuals on the basis of their personality characteristics or traits we should mainly take into account the cardinal and central traits present in their behaviour.

Factors and Qualities

With all what has been said above we can conclude the following things about the nature and characteristics of personality.

1. Firstly, the personality is something unique and specific. Every one of us is a unique pattern in ourselves. No two individuals, not even the identical twins, behave in precisely the same way over any period of time. Everyone of us has specific characteristics for making adjustments.
2. The second main characteristic of personality is self-consciousness. The man is described as a person or to have

a personality when the idea of self enters into his consciousness. In this connection H.R. Bhatia writes. "We do not attribute personality to a dog and even a child cannot be described as a personality because it has only a vague sense of personal identity." (1968, p. 371)

3. Personality includes everything about a person. It is all that a person has about him. It includes all the behaviour patterns, *i.e.* conative, cognitive and affective and covers not only the conscious activities but goes deeper to semi-conscious and unconscious also.
4. It is not just a collection of so many traits or characteristics which is known as personality. By counting the bricks only how can we describe the wall of a house? It needs something more and actually personality is more than this. It is an organisation of some psycho-physical system or some behaviour characteristics and functions as a unified whole. Just as to tell what an elephant is, we cannot say that it is like a pillar only by examining its legs. In the same way by looking through, one's physique or sociability, we cannot pass judgement over one's personality. It is only when we go carefully in all the aspects biological as well as social – we can make an idea about his personality.
5. Personality is not static, it is dynamic and ever in process of change and modification. As we have said earlier that personality is all that a person has about him. It gives him all that is needed for his unique adjustment in his environment. The process of making adjustment to environment is continuous. One has to struggle with the environmental as well as the inner forces throughout the span of his life. As a result, one has to bring modification and change in one's personality patterns and it makes the nature of personality dynamic instead of static one.
6. Every personality is the product of heredity and environment. Both contribute significantly towards, the development of the child's personality.
7. Learning and acquisition of experiences contribute towards growth and development of personality. Every personality is the end product of this [illegible]cess of learning and acquisition.

8. Every person's personality has one more distinguishing feature that is, aiming to an end towards some specific goals. Adier asserts this view frankly in his book *'Individual Psychology'*. He is of the opinion that a man's personality can be judged through a study and interpretation of the goals he has set for himself to achieve and the approaches he makes to the problems of his life. In this way, he gives very concise meaning to the personality of an individual by calling it by the name 'lifestyle of an individual'.

Indeed this short and concise explanation of the term has a wide meaning. It draws a beautiful portrait of an individual's totality. It may be understood to mean as the sum total of one's way of behaving towards oneself and others as well. It also predicts one's nature of behaviour as how one will behave in a particular situation and one's pattern of adjustment to the ever changing forces of environment.

Determinants of Personality Development: The personality of an individual is all that what a person is in his totality. It includes everything about a person, his internal body system and outward appearance, his covert as well as overt behaviour, his conative, cognitive and unconscious layers of behaviour. What we are today as a person are the result of a constant process of growth and development, the forces of heredity and environment 'play their interactive role in pushing us up at our present personality make up.

Our life starts with the conception in the mother's womb and right then, the game of shaping our personality is played covertly as well as overtly by so many forces, the key of which lies in the heredity contributions, biological factors, our psychological make up and the various social and cultural factors present in our environment. All of them and factors which try to shape our personality make up from the conception till death are termed as determinants of our personality.

These factors determine the course of our personality make-up and influence its development in so many ways. A personality characterised as good or bad, poor or magnificent, weak or strong, extrovert or introvert, social or unsocial, normal or abnormal is the result and outcome of these determinants.

Classification of Determinants of Personality: The things and factors which are said to play a determining and decisive role in the development of personality can be categorised in two different ways outlined below:

1. The one way of categorising the determinants of personality is to divide them into two broad categories – internal or personal and external or environmental.

   Internal or personal factors include the factors that lie within the individual and not externally in the environment. These may include the factors like physical structure of the individual, (his physique, sex, nervous system and glands, etc.); his intelligence, motivation, emotions reactions, attitudes, interests, temperament and sentiments, etc.

   External or environmental factors are associated with the forces of environment lying outside the individual. The influence of physical environment, like climate and other physical facilities available to the individual as well as the impact of culture and sociai forces like home, family, school and society are included in this category.

2. Another way of classifying the determinants of personality is based upon the viewpoints and angles from which personality is conceptualised. It includes the biological perspective, the psychological perspective and social and cultural perspective. Accordingly the determinants of personality may be classified as:

   a. Biological determinants,

   b. Psychological determinants and

   c. 'Social and cultural determinants.

Let us try to discuss the determinants of personality now by taking into account the later mode of classification.

Biological Determinants: The Biological determinants of personality include the factors like: i) Hereditary influences, ii) Nervous system, iii) Ductless glands, iv) Physique or somatic structure, and v) Body chemistry.

1. *Hereditary Influences:* Heredity influences transmitted at the time of child's conception through genes and chromosomes provides the base and structure for the future development of the personality. One can grow and develop in proportion he is helped by the hereditary forces in the course of his personality development. In case he gets less from the hereditary stock he has to work hard for attaining desired level of personality development. The somatic structure one inherits, the nervous system he gets, the nature of intelligence and abilities-he receives, all prove quite important in his future personality development.
2. *Nervous System:* Our behaviour, to a great extent, is controlled by our nervous system. How we will behave in a particular situation depends upon the judgement of our brain. The sense impressions., which we receive through our sense organs, are meaningless unless they are given meaning by our nervous system. How intelligently we would react or make use of our mental power is again decided by our nervous system, particularly by the brain apparatus. The proper growth and development of nerve tissues and nervous system as a whole, helps in the task of proper intellectual development. Any defect in spinal cord or brain apparatus affects seriously the intellectual growth. Similarly, physical as well as emotional development is also influenced by our nervous system. Our autonomic nervous system play a leading role in this direction. It controls the activity of involuntary processes like circulation of blood, digestion, respiration and action of the glands.

   These processes do not only control the physical or emotional activity of an individual but also exercise a great deal of influence over the physical and emotional development of an individual. Nerve tissues also cause the change in the secretion of hormones by some glands and consequently influence the emotional behaviour of an individual. Moreover, the nervous system acts as a coordinating agency for many operations going inside the body and harmonises the activities and functions of the body parts — internal as well as external.

In this way, nervous system should be considered as one of the important components of the human machine that plays a significant role in the growth and development of the personality of an individual.

3. *Ductless Glands or Endocrine Glands:* The ductless glands through the secretion of their specific hormones exercise a great influence in the shaping of behaviour and personality of an individual. Let us try to discuss the location of these glands and their influence on the development of our personality.

   a. *Thyroid Gland:* It lies at the base of the neck in front of the wind pipe. It secretes the hormone called thyroxin, the main constituent of which is iodine. The thyroid plays a leading role in controlling the process of oxidation of food. It regulates the body's oxygen consumption and the rate of metabolism. Underdevelopment of this gland results in the undergrowth of the individual. The deficiency of thyroxin causes under activity of the thyroid gland which does not only retard the growth of the body but also causes mental retardation and disorders. Over activity of this gland is equally harmful. It produces unusual excitement, restlessness and irritability.

   b. *Parathyroid Glands:* These glands are located in the back surface of the thyroids and are generally four in number. The parathyroid hormone tries to counter-balance the exciting activity of the thyroid hormone. These glands remove the toxic products from the body and restore the nervous system to relative calm. Their under activity produces muscular tenseness and over activity produces lack of interest, fatigue and lethargic conditions.

   c. *The Pituitary Gland:* The pituitary gland is situated at the base of brain. It is called the "master gland" because its hormones affect most of the other glands. This gland has two lobes – an anterior and a posterior.

      The anterior lobe exercises great influences on the growth of bones. Its underactivity causes incomplete development and we have a dwarf, whereas an overactive, anterior lobe results in gigantic growth and we have a giant. The hormones produced by the lobe also supplement the activities of other glands like thyroid, adrenal and sex glands.

The posterior lobe also secretes valuable hormones. These hormones help in regulating blood pressure.

d. *Adrenal Gland:* These glands two in number, surround the two kidneys separately. They are believed to secrete two separate hormones – cortin and adrenaline. The function of cortin is not definitely known. But adrenaline is known to exercise great influence over nervous, muscular and sexual functions. Adrenal glands are generally, known as glands of survival as their underactivity makes an individual progressively weaker day by day.

   During emotional current the adrenal gland is observed to perform a useful function. In such a situation more adrenaline is secreted that prepares an individual's organs for the particular emotional state. Their over activity makes an individual highly active and energetic. It may also cause sexual maturity at an early age. A little girl or a boy may acquire secondary sex characteristics of nature of man or woman. In some case over-development of the adrenal glands results in increased characteristics which in the case of women may produce extremely masculine characteristics like the growth of beard and moustache.

e. *The Sex Glands or Gonads:* The sex glands or Gonads are different in different sexes. Men possess male gonads and women the female gonads. The male sex glands or gonads are located in the testes. The hormones produced by the testes are known as androgens. The female sex glands are located in the ovaries. The hormones produced by the ovaries are known as estrogens.

The underactivity or overactivity of these glands caused by the deficiency or excess of the hormones secreted by them as well as by the co-acting influence of other glands like Thyroid, Pituitary and Adrenal, affects not only the sexual growth and development of the individual but also his entire behaviour and development process. A slight imbalance of these glands cause restlessness, anxiety and weakness.

Our physical strength, morale, thinking and reasoning power and decision making ability – all depend upon the health of these glands. In short, these glands are found to play a dominant role in one's life. Without their proper functioning a man or woman finds difficulty in leading a happy normal life.

'All the Endocrine or Ductless glands discussed above exercise a great influence on various aspects of growth and development. These glands affect the behaviour of an individual by controlling his emotional behaviour and physiological activities. In this way, they have a direct bearing upon the total personality of an individual. Actually, there are the hormones, secreted by these glands, which are responsible for developing the typical personality characteristics in an individual.

These hormones are circulated throughout the body and influence all those tissues on which functioning of body system, emotional actions and every thought depends. As Gardner Murphy remarks. "These hormones, ultimately, may be regarded as bathing the nervous system, including the brain and all the organs of the body in their own appropriate chemical juices" (1968. p. 52).

Thus, the hormones secreted by different endocrine glands control the behaviour as well as the overall personality development of an individual.

4. *Physique or Somatic Structure:* Physique or somatic structure besides being one of the important components of one's personality affect the personality development in a significant way. The somatic structure and physical characteristics of the individual concerning his height, weight, physical appearance, physical strength or general health, physical deformities and abnormalities, etc., influence the development of personality of an individual. This influence is exercised in two ways:

a. The individual's gain or loss in these physical characteristics may influence his style of life-his modes of behaviour, action, tendencies, goals of life and the ways of striving towards these goals, etc. Every person walks a sizeable distance along a course according to his strength and stamina and so is the case with the process of the development of personality.

b. The physique itself does not directly contribute towards the development of personality but the self image formed by the individual through the reactions of his associates and other members of the society to his physical appearance play a significant role. It makes him conscious of his superiority or inferiority and develops such complexes as to affect his behaviour pattern.

5. *Body Chemistry:* The Chemistry of one's body also exercises a great influence in determining one's behaviour and developing one's personality. Our body gets essential energy for its functioning on account of the chemical changes going inside our body. The sugar is converted into glucose, the food is digested, oxidation takes place through the intake of oxygen and similarly a number of chemical actions take play day and night continuously in our body. Our behaviour and functioning is too much governed by our body chemistry. In case there is some irregularity or malfunctioning in our body chemistry it seriously affects our behaviour and personality make up. For example a slight increase in the amount of nervous fluid in the body may cause nervousness in the individual. Similarly, the low level or high level of sugar in the body may seriously affect the physical and mental state of the individual.

Psychological Determinants: Ductless Psychological factors play a big role in the functioning of the human behaviour and development of one's personality. A few important ones are discussed below:

1. *Intelligence and Mental Functioning:* One's intelligence and mental functioning plays a significant role in the development of this personality. How one behaves is almost determined

by his power of intellect and adjustment, learning, acquisition of knowledge, and skills, the way of taking decisions and dealing with the people and situation. The behaviour pattern of the individual is effectively controlled by his intellect and his personality is shaped according to the functioning of his mental powers.

2. *Interests and Attitudes:* The pattern of one's interests and attitudes try to colour one's behaviour, ways of looking towards the things and people, his learning and striving for the goals in his life. He tries to move towards the things and people in which he has interests and favourable attitudes and it determines the development of his personality.
3. *Level of Aspiration and Achievement Motivation:* One can get success in a designed direction depending upon the level of his aspiration and achievement motivation. He, who does not aspire or desire for a thing cannot be expected to attain satisfactory progress. The people who have high achievement motivation are found to struggle for their accomplishment, demonstrating distinct lifestyle in comparison to those who have no aspiration or achievement motivation.
4. *Will Power:* One's will power determines his way of behaviour and personality make up. The persons with strong will power are found to be credited with emotional stability, decision making ability and persistence, etc. While the persons having weak will power are found to possess the negative traits in their personality.
5. *Emotional and Temperamental Make-up:* The emotional and temperamental make up of an individual cast a strong influence over his behaviour pattern and personality development. The presence of negative and positive emotions, the quality of emotional maturity, his temperament and "the organisation of habits and sentiments, etc., colour his way of behaving and dealing with the things, ideas and people. He reacts according to his emotional, potential and temperamental make up and his personality is fashioned accordingly.

Social and Culture Determinants: Most of our behaviour is learned and learning is controlled almost by the environmental factors lying in one's society and cultural setup. Consequently, the development of one's personality is largely carried out by the social and cultural determinants outlined below:

1. *Home and Family:* No matter whatever the traits of the personality may be, their development and fundamental pattern is always initiated and directed by home life. From the very birth of the child, the parents and the home, and family atmosphere provide the atmosphere for the normal growth and development of his personality. If the child finds a healthy atmosphere at home, he has all chances for the development of personality in the right direction. On the other hand, poor and uncongenial atmosphere develops him into maladjusted personality. Below are given some important constituents of home and family environment which influence the development of personality.
   a. *Parents:* Their education, personality characteristics, their emotional and social behaviour, their mutual affection, love and quarrels their interests and attitudes and general character, etc.
   b. *Parental Attitude:* How they behave with the child and their over protecting or rejecting attitude towards the child.
   c. *Size of the Family and Birth Order:* How many sisters or brothers the child has, the number of male and female children in the family, his own birth order, etc.
   d. *Economic and Social Status of the Family:* Not only of the parents but the behaviour and personality traits of other members of the family cast a desirable impact on the personality development of the children.
2. *School Environment:* School atmosphere also contributes a lot in the development of the personality of child. The personality characteristics of the teachers, headmaster, classmates the teaching methods; curriculum; opportunities for co-curricular activities; the values and ideals maintained by the institution and the general atmosphere of the classroom and school –

all influence the personality development of the child. It is why there is great demand and rush for the admissions in the good and reputed schools as they try to provide all what is desired for the balanced personality development of the children.

3. *The other Factors in the Social Environment:* Besides one's home family and school influences, there are so many other social agencies and institutions that play vital role in growth and development of the personality of the child. These can be named as under:

   Neighbourhood: Its nearness to the child and his family makes it a potent factor for casting its influence on the behaviour pattern and personality of the developing child. What the child observes in his neighbourhood do not only provide him the simple company but also affect his behaviour and set the direction of his personality development.

   Religious Institution: Religious institutions like temple, church, gurudwara and their religious activities, fairs and ceremonies, etc., make a silent and sound appeal for the shaping of the child's personality according to their ideals.

   The other social groups and institutions: There are other social groups agencies and institutions like social clubs, means of entertainment and communications (Radio, television films) advertisement material, newspapers, magazines and other material and literature, etc., available in the social environment of the child which are capable of casting strong impact on the personality of the developing children. A child sees crimes and fighting on the TV screen at his home and it may prove quite enough for his bullying and aggressive behaviour in the school or with his brothers and sisters at home. Similarly, he or she may be greatly influenced by the role of a character read in the novel and may like to imitate personality traits of the character in his own behaviour. In this way, what is observed and experienced in the society by the children through his contact with various social groups, means and agencies plays a significant role in this personality development.

4. *The Cultural Environment:* The cultural environment of the child possesses a vital; potential for shaping and determining his personality. The environment is characterised by the mode of the living of the people of the society, caste, and social group to which the child belongs. How do these people mix, eat, dress, feel, behave with each other, deal with the strangers, respect the members of other sex and observe rituals and ceremonies, what is their style of living and philosophy of life, etc., cast a strong influence on the behaviour of the developing children and their personality is almost fashioned and tailored according to the pattern of their culture environment. A cultural environment in which parents and elders are neglected by the young generation and no responsibility is shared for their looking after especially in the old age will definitely shape the behaviour and personality of the concerned individuals in the same way. On the other hand, in Indian society where old cultural values of respecting the old age are present, the behaviour patterns and personality of the young and old generations will be tailored in the different style, respecting and feeling obligation to each other in the environment of mutual love, cooperation and trust.

In this way, the development of the behaviour pattern and personality of the children is influenced and determined by so many factors, things and conditions broadly categorised as biological, psychological, social and cultural determinants. However, these can never be said to act independently for exercising their influence on the development of the personality of an individual.

The determinants, in one way or the other have affiliation with one's heredity and environment. Since it is quite impossible to separate the influences of one's heredity and environment in the task of personality development of the individual it is easy to think that all these three determinants of personality act and interact with each other for influencing and shaping one's personality.

Step by Step Growth

1. The definition gives a balanced consideration to heredity and environment in building one's personality.

2. Eysenck stresses the concept of structure and organisation and criticises just naming of some of the behavioural characteristics like bricks in describing a home.
3. This definition gives personality a physiological base.
4. It gives a complete picture of the human behaviour patterns by including cognitive, conative, affective and somatic (constitutional aspects).
5. This definition aims at making personality somewhat measurable and assessable and thus gives it a scientific base.

The above mentioned characteristics do not suggest that Eysenck's definition has explained everything about the term personality or it does not have any weakpoint. Like other definitions, this also suffers from some limitations and drawbacks,, which are given below:

1. Eysenck advocates that personality must have a physiological base, but it is not a case always. Everytime we cannot have a physiological base due to the very complex nature of personality.
2. His definition leads us to form an opinion that personality is fixed and cannot be changed.

This is an extreme approach. It is true that personality should be evaluated on the basis of generality of the behaviour (the behaviour must be consistent in a number of situations) but on the other hand, changes cannot be denied. The person who is extrovert may turn into introvert depending upon so many intervening factors.

In this way, for understanding of the concept of personality, the evolution of an ideal definition still needs further research. In fact, the concepts like personality are difficult to be explained as they have the identity like sound, electricity, etc. the impact of which can be felt but the real nature of them is always a matter of secrecy. Something about them can be known by their utility or describing some of their characteristics and distinguishing features. Let us seek the meaning of the term personality also on similar lines.

Psychology of Reading and Learning

Significant Factors

Whatever we learn, we learn through experiences gained in our environment. Learning in no way can be said to be a gift or contribution from our hereditary stock. It is always regarded as a coefficient of friction between our self and the environment. It is therefore the environment which is supposed to influence and shape our learning. The contribution of the mechanism of motivation is also nowhere less than the actual efforts and attempts made by a learner in learning a thing. This motivation also is influenced by so many environmental factors like the process and product of learning.

Learning as you have studied can be defined as a process of bringing relatively enduring changes in the behaviour of the learner through experience and learning. An examination of this definition may reveal that the learning process is centred around the three elements namely:

1. the learner whose behaviour is to be modified,
2. the type of experience and training required for modification in the learner's behaviour, and

3. the men and material resources needed for providing desired experiences and training.

Therefore, the success or failure in the task of learning in terms of introducing desired modification in the behaviour of the learner will automatically depend upon the quality as well as control and management of the things and factors associated with the above cited main elements.

However a close analysis of these elements may clearly reveal that these elements can be easily grouped into two broad categories namely personal factors and environmental factors. The factors associated with the learner are nothing but the personal factors lying within the learner and whatever lying outside the learner is nothing but only the influence of his environment – on the processes and products of learning. Let us try to discuss now all the relevant factors that tend to influence the learning of learner.

Personal Factors: The learner is the key figure in any learning task. He has to learn or bring desired modification in his behaviour. How he will learn or what he will achieve, through a particular learning act depends heavily upon his own characteristics and way of learning. Such things or factors associated with him can be described as below:

1. *Learner's Physical and Mental Health:* Learning is greatly affected by the learner's physical and mental health maintained by him particularly at the time of learning. A simple headache or stomach can play a havoc with the process and products of learning. The children who did not keep up with satisfactory physical health, have to suffer adversely in terms of the gain in learning. Similarly, the mental state and health of the learner at the time of learning become potent factor in deciding the outcome of the learning. A tense, emotionally and mentally disturbed learner cannot be supposed to show satisfactory results in learning.
2. *The Basic Potential of the Learner:* The results achieved by the learner through a process of learning depend heavily upon his basic potential to undergo in such learning. Such potential may consist of the following things.

- Learner's innate abilities and capacities for learning a thing.
- Learner's basic potential in terms of general intelligence and specific knowledge, understanding and skills related to particular learning area.
- Learner's basic interests, aptitudes and attitudes related to the learning of a particular thing or area.

3. *The Level of Aspiration and Achievement Motivation:* Learning is greatly influenced by the level of aspiration and nature of achievement motivation possessed by the learner. How can we expect from a learner to achieve a thing for which he has no aspiration? One has to maintain the level of his aspiration and achievement motivation to a reasonable level neither too high causing frustration for non-achievement nor too low as not to try for the things for which he is quite capable. In this way, one's level of aspiration and achievement motivation works significantly towards gains in learning.
4. *Goals of Life:* The philosophy and immediate as well as ultimate goals of one's life affect the process and products of learning. His mode and ways of looking towards the things, his inclination towards the learning in a particular area and patience and persistence maintained for continuing his learning despite the heavy odds all depend upon his goals and philosophy of life.
5. *Readiness and will Power:* Learner's readiness and power to learn is a great deciding factor about his results in learning. No power on earth can make a learner learn if he is not ready to learn, Contrarily, if he has a will to learn a thing then automatically, he will himself find the way for its effective learning.

Environmental Factors: In the process of teaching-learning whatever exists besides the personal factor involving the self of the learner may be included in the boundaries of environmental factors influencing learning. Thinking in the way we may name the following two sub-categories in the broad generalisation of environmental factors.

1. Factors Associated with the type of learning experiences.
2. Factors Associated with the men and material resources.

Let us discuss now environmental factor influencing learning under these two heads.

Experiences Factor: The type of changes or modification to be aimed in the learner's behaviour depends much on the type of learning experiences and training received by him for this purpose. This task involves a variety of factors like below:

1. *The Nature of the Learning Experience:* The learning is influenced by the nature of the subject material and learning experiences presented to the learner like below:
   a. Whether the nature of the learning experiences is formal or informal, incidental or organised, direct or indirect, etc.?
   b. Whether the learning experiences are suitably selected on the basis of the principle of child-centredness, principle of activity, criterion of activity, age, grade and experiences of the learner, etc.?
   c. Whether the learning experiences are suitably organised for the attainment of desired educational objectives or not?
2. *The Methodology of Learning Experiences:* In learning, much depends upon the methods, techniques and approaches employed for the teaching and learning of the selected contents and learning experiences. Let us weigh the truth of this statement from various angles.
   a. *Linking of the New Learning with the Past:* The quality of the result in learning depends much on the abilities of the teacher and the learner to link the present new learning with the past experiences of the learner. Past experiences help the learner to assimilate and understand the new learning by providing success as well as cementing force for this purpose.
   b. *Correlating the Learning in one Area to the Other:* Correlation facilitates the task of learning as it allows maximum transfer of training or learning from one area to another.

Accordingly one can expect good results in learning if learning experiences are given in view of seeking correlation: i) among the different subjects or areas, ii) within the branches or experiences of the same area, and iii) with the real life happening and situation.

c. *Utilisation of Maximum Number of Senses:* Senses are said to be the gateway of knowledge and consequently the results in earning are very much influenced by the nature and type of the utilisation of one's senses for the acquisition of learning experiences. A learner who learns through the utilisation of his maximum senses like sense of sight, hearing, touch, smell, tastes and also tries to learn by doing the things himself does always reach at an advantageous point.

d. *Provision of Work Revision and Practice:* Review and practice always brings good results in the achievements of learning. A learner who makes use of sufficient drill work, practice work, revision and review of his learning can be expected to harvest a good yield in terms of its good retention, reproduction and utilisation at the proper time.

e. *Provision of Proper Feed Back and Reinforcement:* The learning yields are much dependent upon the nature and quality of the feed back and reinforcement provided to the learner in his learning task. One must be acquainted with the progress of his learning in terms of his strength and weaknesses and remedial action, if needed may be taken at the proper time. The knowledge of the results and progress may work well for providing immediate reinforcement to the learner. In addition to it, the learning process can be suitably designed if we take due care for the planning of proper reinforcement schedules. The results are unmatchable, so much so as a simple reinforcement technique in the shapes of approval of the learning response, nodding of the head, smiling, saying good-bye, etc., bring a magic in terms of learner's interest and achievement.

f. *The Selection of the Suitable Learning Methods and Teaching:* There are sufficient methods and number of good techniques available for the teaching and learning of the different subjects and areas of experiences. The results in learning are always influenced by the nature and quality of the methods and techniques employed for the teaching and learning of a particular content, subject matter or learning experiences like those given below:

   i. Whether or not methods and techniques are helpful in learning at memory, understanding or reflective level?

   ii. Whether or not these are teacher dominated, learner centred or allow useful teacher-pupil interaction?

   iii. Is it possible to proceed on the path of self learning through them?

Resources Factor: The learner is helped by the available resources (men and material) for bringing desirable changes in his behaviour. How effectively such changes will be introduced in his behaviour depend much on the quality and management of these resources. Such things and factors affecting learning may be listed as below:

1. The quality of the teacher in terms of his mastery over the subject matter, teaching-skills, rich experiences and teacher like qualities and behaviour.
2. The socio-emotional climate available in the institution in the shape of teacher-pupil relationships, pupil-pupil relationships and school-staff relationships, etc.
3. The availability of appropriate learning material and facilities in terms of teaching-learning aids, text books, library and laboratory facilities, project work, etc.
4. The proper conducive environment and learning situations like those given below:
   a. Proper seating arrangement.
   b. Quite calm and peaceful environment.
   c. Management and control of the factors leading to distraction.

d. Cooperative and competitive group situations.

e. Congenial learning environment at home.

f. Provision of proper change, rest and recreation.

g. Provision of opportunity for creativity and self expression.

In this way the processes and products of learning are said to be influenced by the personal factors associated, with the learner himself and the external factors lying within the teaching learning environment.

Practical Aspects

Learning is a process and not a product. This process has a continuity and is carried over through various steps. While summing up these steps, Smith gives the following verdict:

> "In short, the learning process involves a motive or drive, an attractive goal and a block to the attainment of the goal. All these are essential" (1962, p. 262).

Let us try to examine the statement of Mr. Smith. The first step in the process of learning is motive or drive. Motives are the dynamic forces that energise behaviour and compel the child to act. Every individual has to take care of the satisfaction of his basic motives and needs. As long as our present behaviour, knowledge,, skill and performance are adequate to satisfy all our needs, we do not feel any necessity to change our behaviour or acquire new knowledge and skills. It is this requirement which initiates a learner to learn something.

Motives and needs of the learner demand their satisfaction. When the need of a learner is strong enough, he is compelled to strive for its satisfaction. For this purpose, he has to set definite goals and aims for achievement. Definiteness of the aim and setting of the goal helps in making the learning purposeful and interesting. The goal attracts us to learn.

Then comes the third step in the process of learning which is equally essential as the previous ones. It is in terms of some obstacle or block or barrier that keeps us from attaining that goal. If we face no difficulty of any kind in attaining our goal, we need not bring any change in our present behaviour, stock of knowledge and skills. This means that we have no necessity to learn. In this way the block or problem is an essential step in the learning process. We try to change or modify our behaviour only when there is a need to do so to reach the goals that our unsatisfied motives create.

Let us clear the above views by taking an example. Suppose, you wish to be included in your college Hockey Team, playing game that appeals to many of your psychological needs. You want the esteem of your colleagues, and your teachers. You are also motivated by the interesting experiences that you may enjoy. But you are blocked by your lack of skill in dodging, tackling and handling the ball. These obstacles and blocks in the path of goal achievement will set you make up your deficiency and acquire essential skill through sufficient practice and coaching.

By these steps, Smith has tried to consider the problem, why we learn, and has emphasised the role of motivation, needs and goals in the process of learning.

But the process of learning remains incomplete with these three elements — motives, goals and blocks — which Mr. Smith has suggested. It is, rather, a preparatory stage for learning, then being, the stage for actual learning. With these three steps, strong desire and essential readiness is produced in the child for learning something. It is very essential, for any scheme of learning.

The child's readiness, his positive attitude towards learning is to be ascertained before beginning the learning programmes. There are many factors which contribute towards the learning readiness. The worth mentioning among them are his physical and mental maturity, previously acquired knowledge and skills and his ability in goal setting. With the help of all these factors, teachers or the parents should try to fix an appropriate level of aspiration for the child so that he may proceed properly on the path of learning.

The next steps in the process of learning, after the preparatory stage, are concerned with the task of actual learning by the learner. One of such important steps is the teaming situation. The learning situation provides opportunity for learning. The quality, speed and effectiveness of learning depends much upon the kind of learning situation and environment available to the learner. Healthy and favourable learning environment brings satisfactory results in learning while the poor and unfavourable learning environment proves an obstacle in the path of learning. In a particular learning environment, when the learner strives to learn something, the process of learning involves constant interaction. According to Udai Pareek "Interaction is the process of responding to a situation and getting *or* thwarting the needs. Learning results from such interaction (Kuppuswamy, B, 1964, p. 112).

In fact, when the child strives to learn something in order to achieve his desired goal, he is very curious to know the results of his striving. On this path when he acquires some new knowledge and skills or brings changes in his behaviour, he is desirous to know, whether or not, with these changes he is able to cherish the desired end. If he finds that all that which is learned so far is useful and feels satisfied with his progress, he is sure to gain speed in the path of his learning. Moreover, the learning process has a continuity in its flow. What has been learnt to far in the path of learning, works as a running capital and base for further learning.

Learning at a particular moment in a learning environment brings essential changes in the behaviour of an individual. These changes later on become part and parcel of the learning behaviour. These learned acts are retained for a longer time, depending upon the nature of the learner and effectiveness of the learning process and used in similar situations when the need and opportunity arises. Therefore, the process of learning does not end, only with the acquisition of certain knowledge, skill and changes in behaviour in one particular situation.

It is a never ending process. The change once acquired or the learning once accomplished, gets its fixation in other likewise situations. It stands for its modification and thus seems always in a process of continuous change and development.

Characteristics of Acquired behaviour, i.e., Learning: The changes brought out in our behaviour through learning by all means are accounted as an acquired phenomenon. Learning in this way can't be attributed to some or the other hereditary influences.

It is earned and acquired by us like other attributes of our personality and that is why learning of all types is given a common name, i.e. acquired behaviour. It has its special nature and characteristics, a glimpse of which you may find through the following description.

1. *Learning is the Change in Behaviour:* Learning in its any form or shape is always associated with some or the other changes in learner's behaviour. That in why learning is always directed or aimed for bringing changes in learner's behaviour. However, these changes in learner's behaviour should always be desirable ones as the undesirable changes, if these are allowed to happen, prove detrimental to the welfare of the learner as well as to the society.
2. *Change in Behaviour Caused by Learning is Relatively Enduring or Permanent:* Change in behaviour caused by learning is neither too permanent (as caused through maturation) nor too temporary (as caused by the factors like fatigue, illness, etc.). They lie between these two states and are usually referred to as relatively permanent changes implying that although frequent or unwanted changes in the learned behaviour can't take place, yet the needed changes can be introduced in the manner such as getting rid of the bad habits or unlearning a wrong method of doing things, etc.
3. *Learning is a Continuous Life Long Process*: Learning is, although not inherited, yet its beginning can be very well made right from the conception of the child. The environment available in the womb of the mother may work as facilitator for such learning. We have Abhimanyu before us as an example who was able to learn the art of 'Chakravueh Bhedari from his father 'Arjuna' in the womb of his mother 'Shubhadra'. After birth the process of learning picks up a greater speed with the constant interaction and stimulation received from the physical social and cultural environmental forces and it does not stop till one's death. Regarding its continuity we have

enough evidences that one activity leads to another and the individual engages himself to learn more and more. Every day new problems are faced, new situations are created and the individual has to face these situations and bring essential changes in his behaviour. Thus it is a never changing process and it is why we refer that it goes from womb to tomb.

4. *Learning is a Universal Process:* We all the living creatures on this earth have the abilities and capacities for learning irrespective of the nature of our species, caste, colour, sex, geographical location or some other such individual differences. Therefore the myths like that members of the upper castes especially Brahmins have more capacity of learning than the members belonging to the lower castes and untouchables, women have inferior learning capacity than men, or the blacks possess sub normal capacities for learning in comparison to whites, etc., have no substantial ground. On the contrary, the truth remains that every living being on the earth has been favoured by the nature to possess the capacity to learn according to the species specific characteristics and environment as well as opportunities available for learning.

5. *Learning is Purposive and Goal Directed:* All learning is goal-directed. It is the definiteness of the aim and clear understanding of the purpose which makes an individual learn immediately the techniques of performing a particular task. It is the purpose or goal which determines what he sees in the learning situations and how he acts therein. Therefore, the purpose or goal is the pivot, around which the entire system of learning revolves. In case where there in no purpose, definitely, there would, hardly, be any learning.

6. *Learning Involves Reconstruction of Experiences:* We learn something at a particular stage and it is stored in our learning experiences in the shape of previous experience or learning for the learning of a future task However, what has been learnt by us at a particular occasion, always remains in the state of modification in the light of the new or richer experiences gained by us in this respect. As a result the old

learning is replaced by the new learning and our previous experiences are restructured and reorganised for giving birth to a new structure composed of the reconstructed experiences. It is therefore education, *i.e.* the process of learning is often referred to as the process of continuous reconstruction of experiences.

7. *Learning is the Product of Activity and Environment:* The basic condition of the emergence of any learning essentially lies in one's responding activity to the stimuli belonging to one's environment. In case the child is not willing to respond to the stimuli present in his learning environment, he can't be persuaded to proceed on the path of his learning journey. More the learner will respond actively to the stimuli present in his learning environment the more progress he will be able to make in terms of his learning outcomes. Therefore the key of a successful learning in any teaching learning-process always lies in the active responding of the learner to the stimuli present or the activities going on in the teaching-learning environment.
8. *Learning is Transferable from one Situation to Another:* Learning has a special characteristic of being transferred from one learning situation to another having positive as well as negative effect. In its positive transfer the learning in one situation helps the learning in another situation but in the case of negative transfer we may observe the adverse effect when learning in one situation hinders or obstructs the path of learning in another situation.
9. *Learning does not Necessarily Imply Improvement:* Learning is often considered as a process of improvement with practice or training. This means that all types of learning helps the child in the path of his progress towards desired ends or results. But this is not always true. The child learns so many things in the class room that do not at all help him to achieve his goal. Habits of idleness, disrespect towards authority, truancy, developing poor hand writing and defective pronunciation and exposition, etc., are among these.

Therefore, it should be known clearly that learning does not necessarily imply improvement (with respect to the achievement of an end).

10. *Learning does not Necessarily Imply the Development in Right Direction:* In a similar way, while defining learning as a process of development, the word development should never be confined to mean 'progress in right direction to achieve certain ends or results' as Woodworth clarifies in his definition, as a result of learning, the pattern of development is free to move to either direction – positive or negative. It is no guarantee that the individual will always pick up good knowledge, desirable habits, interest and attitudes. He has equal chances to be drifted to the debit side of the human personality.
11. *Learning helps in Bringing Desirable Changes in Behaviour:* Learning is the process of bringing changes in behaviour. It can help in introducing desired changes in the behaviour of the learner in all its three domains, *i.e.*, cognitive, conative and affective.
12. *Learning helps in the Attainment of Teaching-learning Objectives :* The teaching-learning objectives and teaching-learning situation can be effectively reached through the help of learning and consequently the children can be made to acquire essential knowledge, skills, applications, attitude and interests, etc.
13. *Learning helps in the Proper Growth and Development:* Learning helps in reaching to one's maximum in terms of the growth and development under various aspects of growth and development dimensions, namely physical, mental (cognitive) emotional, social, moral, aesthetic and language.
14. *Learning helps in the Balanced Development of Personality:* Our educational efforts are directed to bring an all-round development in the personality of the child. The process of learning results in bringing such an all-round development of the personality.
15. *Learning helps in Proper Adjustment:* Adjustment is the key of success in life. Learning helps the individual to seek adjustment with his self and environment.

16. *Learning helps in the Realisation of the Goals of Life:* Every man has his own philosophy and style of life and he strives to achieve the goals of his life. Learning process helps the individual to realise the goals of his life.
17. *Learning is a Very Comprehensive Process, Possessing Quite a Wide Scope:* The world of learning is considered to limit itself to the narrow walls of the activities concerning with intellectual and motor efficiency. It is often thought of as the acquisition of some knowledge and skills, memorisation of certain fads and principles, development of reasoning and thinking power, etc. These are some of the learning activities which formally go on inside the classroom or in any arranged learning situation. But learning is not only limited to these activities. It is a very comprehensive process which covers nearly all the aspects of the human personality. Its scope touches aspects like the formation of habits, development of interests, attitudes, a sense of appreciation and critical observation, acquisition of beliefs, perfection of values and ideals and setting of the goals and purposes.

Therefore, learning, as a whole, is not confined to the formal classroom learning activities. Life presents enormous opportunities to learn and learning activities are so numerous that it is difficult to limit them in any specific categories. How one eats, drinks, dresses, what are his specific hobbies, interests, attitudes, beliefs and aspirations, how he strives and what ideals and values he aims at, what is his concept of himself, etc., all are examples of learned and acquired behaviour. And the scope of learning, definitely, embraces all of these aspects into its domain.

Basic Ideas

In the process of education learning occupies quite a centre place. Whatever exists in our educational set up is meant for the learning of the learners, *i.e.* students. Therefore it is quite essential for you as a would be teacher to be acquainted with the concept of the term learning. Let us analyse the concept of the term learning by:

1. knowing about its meaning and definitions, and
2. knowing about the process of learning.

Definition and Concept

Learning situations are most natural and common in life and every one of us is learning one thing or the other although he may not necessarily be aware of it. An individual starts learning immediately after his birth. While approaching a burning matchstick, the child is burnt and he withdraws. Another time, when he faces a burning matchstick, he takes no time to withdraw himself away. He learns to avoid not only the burning matchstick but also all burning things. When this happens we say that the child has learned that if he touches a flame, he will be burnt.

In this way, the behaviour of an individual is changed through direct or indirect experiences. This change in behaviour brought about by experience is commonly known as learning. This is a very simple explanation of the term learning. But a complete understanding of the term needs more clarification and exact definition. Some well known definitions of the term 'learning' are given below:

1. *Gardner Murphy:* "The term learning covers every modification in behaviour to meet environmental requirements." (1968, p. 205)
2. *Henry R Smith:* "Learning is the acquisition of new behaviour or the strengthening or weakening of old behaviour as the result of experience." (1962, p. 260)
3. *Woodworth:* "Any activity can be called learning so far as it develops the individual – (in any respect, good or bad) and makes him alter behaviour and experiences different from what that would otherwise have been." (1945, p. 288).
4. *Kingsley and Garry:* "Learning is the process by which behaviour (in the broader sense) is organised or changes through practice or training." (1957, p. 12)
5. *Pressey, Robinson and Horrocks:* "Learning is an episode in which a motivated individual attempts to adapt his behaviour so as to succeed in a situation which he perceives as requiring action to attain a goal." (1967, p. 232)
6. *Crow and Crow:* "Learning is the acquisition of habits, knowledge and attitudes. It involves new ways of doing

things and it operates on an individual's attempts to overcome obstacles or to adjust to new situation. It represents progressive changes in behaviour. It enables him to satisfy interests to attain a goal." (1973, p. 225)

7. *Hilgard:* "Learning is the process by which an activity originates or is changed through reacting to an encountered situation, provided that the characteristics of the change in activity cannot be explained on the basis of native response, tendencies, maturation, or temporary states of the organism (*e.g.*, fatigue or drugs, etc.)." (1958, p. 3)

An overview of these above definitions may clearly reveal that learning may be termed as a process or its outcome in which necessary changes in the behaviour of the learner are brought through experience-direct or indirect.

Here it has been also emphasised that although changes in behaviour are also brought out by the factors other than experience yet all such changes in behaviour are not associated with the process and product of learning. In this connection special mention can be made about the Hilgard's definition. Let us reconsider this definition now.

On the basis of Hilgard's definition of learning the factors or forces responsible for bringing changes in our behaviour can be divided into following three main categories.

1. The factors or forces that bring permanent or enduring changes in our behaviour, *e.g.*, maturation.
2. The factors or forces that bring temporary changes in our behaviour like mental or physical fatigue, illness, drugs or intoxicating objects, medicines, sleeplessness, emotions like anger, fear, etc.
3. The factors or forces that bring relatively enduring or permanent changes (the changes lying between the temporary and permanent status-neither too temporary nor too permanent) in our "behaviour, *e.g.*, training, practice and experiences, etc.

Let us now analyse the type of changes brought out by these three category of factors or forces in our behaviour. First let us consider the effect of maturation.

1. *Learning and Maturation:* These two phenomena are so interrelated that sometimes it becomes difficult to say, definitely, as to which, of the behavioural changes are the results of learning and which are the consequences of maturation, For the clear differentiation let us try to make distinction between these two terms.

Maturation, in fact, is a natural process. It is the growth which takes place within the individual. The maturational changes are the results of unfolding and ripening of inherited traits and are relatively independent of activity, practice or experience. Biggie and Hunt clarify these ideas in the following words:

> "Maturation is a developmental process within which a person, from time to time manifests different-traits, 'the 'blue prints' for which have been carried in his cells from the time of has conception" (Biggie & Hunt, 1968).

In this way maturation involves changes that are associated with normal growth.

Learning, on the other hand, is a change in a living individual which is not heralded by his genetic inheritance. It is a process which takes place as a result of stimuli from without. The changes in the behaviour, in the process of learning, are always produced through some activity, training or experiences.

Maturation is learning's chief competitor as a modifier of behaviour. The distinction can be made on the following grounds :

> If a behaviour sequence matures (develops) through regular stages, irrespective of intervening practices or training, the behaviour is said to be developed through maturation and not through learning. If training procedures do not speed up or modify the behaviour, such procedures are not casually important and the changes do not classify as learning.

On this ground the relatively pure cases like the swimming of tadpoles and the flying of birds can be attributed, primarily, to maturation. But in most of the activities of human beings, it is difficult to decide whether these activities result from maturation or learning. The simplest example is the language development of the child. The child does not learn to talk until he reaches a certain stage or age in maturation, but it is also equally true that he does not learn the language just because he attains that stage. The language is taught to him. The language, which he learns, is that which he hears.

Therefore, the two processes – maturation and learning are closely related to each other. Maturation helps in the process of learning. Learning can only take place if the stage for that type of learning has been achieved through a process of maturation. If the teacher understands the complexity of the changes that are going on as the result of both processes and the interaction between the two, he is not apt to go far astray in his teaching. The reverse will be harmful.

For example, forcing a child to attempt to learn certain speech patterns, before a certain maturation has occurred, *can* disrupt the normal development of speech in the child and do damage. On the other hand, failure, at an appropriate time, to provide specific training in speech may be a cardinal educational error.

2. *Factors Associated with Temporary Changes in Behaviour*: Let us now think over the second category of factors responsible for bringing temporary changes in behaviour. Fatigue, illness, medicine, and intoxicating objects, fear, anger, etc. cause serious and quite effective changes in one's behaviour. The person who happened to be quite right when leaving home to his office in the morning may be seen to be quite fussy and irritable after returning home in the evening. This change in his behaviour is the consequence of his getting mentally and physically fatigued. However the change is quite temporary as the behaviour may turn again into a normal behaviour after taking some rest or refreshment. The same is true with the behavioural changes introduced on account

of taking drugs, alcohol and other intoxicating objects. The behaviour becomes normal as soon as one gets rid of the intoxication influences. Similarly under emotional current one may be drifted away from his normal behaviour but as soon as one comes to his senses after being cooled down, one realises his outburst and irrational behaviour and begins to behave as usual. In this way, the changes introduced in our behaviour on account of the factors falling in the second category are quite transitory and temporary. The changes in behaviour automatically vanish as soon as the impact of the factors or forces responsible for introducing such changes come to an end (you may very well equate these changes in behaviour to the type of changes called physical changes known to you as a student of physical sciences), like change of ice into water, lightening of an electric bulb, etc. On the other hand, the changes brought about by maturation are quite permanent like chemical changes, *e.g.*, burning of the piece of a paper, conversion of milk into curd, etc.

3. *Relatively Permanent Changes through Experience and Training:* The third category of changes in behaviour are neither too temporary (as brought out by the factors like fatigue, illness, alcohol, etc.) nor too permanent (as brought out by maturation). They somewhat lie between these two and are therefore may be termed as relatively permanent or enduring changes in one's behaviour. The factors or forces responsible for bringing such changes are named as experiences-direct or indirect, involving training, practice, and formal as well as informal education attempts. Only such type of relatively permanent changes in our behaviour brought out through experience may be associated with the process and product of learning.

Their characteristics of being neither too permanent nor too temporary is a boon to the system of education. Imagine if the results of our learning, *i.e.* changes in behaviour might have been too temporary, then the strenuous efforts for making the students learn, remember and utilise the results of learning would have been too futile. Being temporary and transitory changes, all what was learnt by a child could have vanished in no time. Similarly the introduction of too permanent changes in one's behaviour through learning would have been a quite unpleasant experience as a student's learning to pronounce PUT as pat might become a life long mistake. The done could not be made undone and thus picking up of the bad habits on account of any learning might have ruined the future of ill-fated learners. In this way it is quite a welcome sign that changes introduced only through experience are termed as learning.

In this way, if we attempt to analyse the nature of changes introduced in our behaviour in reference to the factors responsible for such changes a proper definition of the term learning may be evolved in the following words.

Learning is a process of bringing relatively enduring or permanent changes in behaviour through experience or training.

Psychological Aspects

Reading and Education

Learning is very much helped and facilitated by the knowledge, principles theories and techniques of educational psychology. In other words, educational psychology may prove quite beneficial to the learners in the realisation of the learning objectives in the manner summarised below:

1. Educational psychology may help the learner in the task of knowing one's self. They may thus be acquainted with their abilities and capacities, interests and aptitudes, likings and dislikings, attitudes and dispositions, etc., related to the various aspects of their curricular courses and co-curricular means. Such knowledge of their strength and weaknesses may go a long way and adjust their level of aspiration and mode of working in getting desired success in their learning attempts.
2. The theories, principles used techniques related to motivation, ways of learning and remembering may help them well in their tasks of learning.
3. The knowledge of the processes and factors helpful in paying attention and remaining away from the forces of distraction

may help them in attending to their studies and learning processes as effectively as possible.

4. How much is it essential to remain adjusted to one's self and the environment? The knowledge and techniques helpful in seeking such harmony and enjoying better mental health can be better acquired through the applied aspect of educational psychology. It is no denying of the fact that those who remain adjusted and enjoy better mental health can be better learners and successful individuals in their lives.
5. The knowledge of the facts and principle related to group dynamics and group behaviour may help them to adjust and merge their behaviour according to the needs of the group learning situations-classroom and other cooperative ways of learning.
6. Through the study of mechanism of heredity and environment they may get acquainted with true roles of the hereditary and environmental forces in shaping and moulding their ways of learning and behaving, growth and development, etc. They must thus protect their self from being damaged with the rumours and incorrect information spread in the society in the name of perpetuation of caste, creed, colour and blood theories. As a result, a child born in the deprived section of the society may also acquire enough confidence to learn whatever he decides in the course of his life.
7. A students after learning the role of favourable and unfavourable factors, conditions situations and resources may be benefited to utilise or make full advantage of the better learning environment on one hand and on the other hand avoiding the situation or factors that may prove detrimental to his learning success.
8. The theory and mechanism related to remembering and forgetting may help the learner to learn retain, reproduce and thus utilise fully the fruits of learning as effectively as possible.
9. The knowledge of the mechanism of transfer of learning or training may provide them desired skill for getting proper

help from their past and related learning in their present learning assignment as well as utilise their present learning stock in almost all the possible ways in the learning or problem solving behaviour of the future.

10. The knowledge of educational psychology may also equip them with the facts and principles of behaviour modification and other therapeutic techniques. How to acquire desirable habits and proper ways of learning and how to break the bad habits and unlearn the improper ways and means of learning can thus be better acquired through the study and practices of educational psychology.
11. The knowledge of educational psychology acquaints the learner with the developmental stages of human life, the needs and characteristics of the learners at these specific stags of life. Accordingly the learner may direct and structure his path of learning and learning objectives according to the needs and characteristics of his developmental stage. It may on the long run help him to make his learning attempts and situations well with in tune of his developmental characteristics and thus be able to seek harmony in terms of his adjustment to self and the environment.
12. Educational psychology makes the learner realise the importance and facts related to the all-round growth and development of his personality in order to become successful in the realisation of the success in the processes and products of learning It makes him to strive for the harmonious and progressive growth and development of his abilities and capacities instead of one sided or lopsided development of his personality.

In this way it can be easily concluded that where knowledge and practices of educational psychology help the teacher in their tasks related to teaching and fulfilling their obligation as a teacher in all possible ways, the help rendered by it to the learners in their tasks of learning and shaping and moulding their lives in the desired ways is also worth appreciable.

There is no aspect of teaching-learning process that can remain untouched or unaffected by the positive results, impacts and influence of the knowledge and skill acquired by the teachers and students in the field of educational psychology. It definitely makes a learner a better learner and a teacher a better teacher and here lies the worthwhile function and contribution of the subject educational psychology in the field of education.

Importance of Reading

Education by all means, is an attempt to mould and shape the behaviour of the pupil. It aims to produce desirable changes in him for the all-round development of his personality. The essential knowledge and skill to do this job satisfactorily is supplied by Educational Psychology as Peel puts it in the following words:

> "Educational Psychology helps the teacher to understand the development of his pupils, the range and limits of their capacities, the processes by which they learn and their social relationships." (1956, p.8)

In this way, the work of the Educational Psychologists resembles with that of an Engineer, who is a technical expert. The Engineer supplies all the knowledge and skill essential for the accomplishment of the job satisfactorily... for example, construction of a bridge. In the same way Educational Psychologist, who is a technical expert in the field of Education, supplies all the information, principles and techniques essential for:

- Understanding the behaviour of the pupil in response to educational environment and
- Desired modification of his behaviour to bring an all-round development of his personality.

In this way, it is quite reasonable to call Educational Psychology as a science and technology of Education.

The Factors

The question which is, straightforwardly put often is What is the nature of Educational Psychology?

The answer of this question becomes almost clear when we try to examine the meaning and definitions discussed earlier. Its nature is scientific as it has been accepted that it is a science of Education. Its relations with Education and Educational Philosophy also throw light on its nature. We can summarise the nature of Educational Psychology in the following way:

1. Educational Psychology is an applied branch of the subject Psychology. By applying the principles and techniques of Psychology. It tries to study the behaviour and experiences of the pupils.
2. While Psychology deals with the behaviour of all individuals in all walks of life, Educational Psychology limits its dealing with the behaviour of the pupil (learner) in relation to educational environment.
3. It does not concern with 'what' and 'why' of Education, it gives the necessary knowledge and skill (technical guidance) for giving education to the pupils in a satisfactory way.
4. It is not a normative science as it is not concerned with the values of Education and does not concern itself with "what ought to be". It is an applied positive science.
5. Educational Psychology is not a perfect science. It has its own drawbacks. The human (as well as animal) behaviour is unpredictable. It is more variable and less reliable. Therefore, Educational Psychology, the applied behavioural science, cannot claim objectivity, exactness and validity as claimed by natural sciences or even applied sciences like medicine and Engineering, etc.
6. It employs scientific method and adopts scientific approach to study the behaviour of an individual in educational environment. Moreover, the controlling of the factors and prediction of the behaviour on generalised results gives Educational Psychology a complete scientific base. Therefore, it is proper to call its nature as scientific.

The Chances

What do you mean by scope of a subject?

When we are asked to point out the scope of a subject, we are supposed to answer the following questions:

1. What are limits of its field of operation?
2. What is to be included in its study or what subject-matter does it contain?

As pointed our earlier, Educational Psychology deals with the behaviour of the learner in educational situations (only). Therefore, it becomes imperative that Educational Psychology should limit itself within the four walls of the teaching-learning process and educational environment. It must try to solve the problems evolving in actual teaching-learning situations and help the individuals involved in this process. Let us judge what are the key factors in an educational process and list them one by one:

1. The learner (Pupil).
2. The learning experiences.
3. The learning process.
4. The learning situations or environment.
5. The teacher.

The subject-matter of Education Psychology, if it is at all necessary to draw its boundaries, revolves round these five pivots mentioned above.

The Learner: If we take the first pivot, the learner, we can find that Educational Psychology has the subject-matter knitted around the learner. With this section of its subject-matter it acquaints us with the need of knowing the learner and deals with the techniques of knowing him well. The topics like the following are included in this section: The innate abilities and capacities of the individuals, individual differences and their measurements, the overt, covert, conscious as well as unconscious behaviour of the learner, the characteristics of his growth and development at each stage beginning from childhood to adulthood.

***Learning Experiences*:** The second area is learning, experiences, Although Educational Psychology does not connect itself directly with the problem of what to teach or what learning experiences are to be provided for the learner yet it has the full responsibility of suggesting the techniques on acquiring the learning experiences. Once the task of Educational Philosophy to decide the aims and objectives of a piece of instruction at a particular stage is finished, the need of Educational Psychology is felt.

At this juncture, Educational Psychology helps in deciding what learning experiences are desirable, at what stage of the growth and development of the learner so that these experiences can be acquired with a greater ease and satisfaction. In this area, Educational Psychology has the subject-matter which deals with the knowledge and principles of Psychology which facilitates the selection of the desirable learning experiences for the learner.

The Learning Processes: After knowing the learner and deciding what learning experiences are to be provided, the emerging problem is to help the learner in acquiring these learning experiences, properly with ease and convenience.

Therefore, around this pivot, Educational Psychology deals with the nature of learning and how it takes place and contains the topics such as laws, principles and theories of learning, remembering and forgetting, perceiving, concept formation, thinking and reasoning process, problem, solving, transfer of training, ways and means of effective learning, etc.

Learning Situation or Environment: Around this pivot, Educational Psychology has the subject-matter dealing with the environmental factors and learning situations which come midway between the learner and the teacher. Topics like classroom climate and group dynamics, techniques and aids which facilitate, learning, evaluation, techniques and practices, guidance and counselling, etc., which help in the smooth functioning of the teaching-learning process come under the jurisdiction of this pivot.

The Teacher: The last, but not the least, is the teacher. He is a potent force in any scheme of teaching and learning and surely, Educational Psychology does not forget him. It emphasises the need of knowing the self for a teacher to play his role properly in the process of education It discusses his conflicts, motivation, anxiety, adjustment, level of aspiration, etc. It throws light on the essential personality traits, interests, aptitudes, the characteristics of effective teaching, etc., so as to inspire him for becoming a successful teacher.

By mentioning the areas around the above five pivots, the picture of the boundaries and limits of Educational Psychology cannot be taken as complete. In fact, sketching of such a full picture is quite a difficult task because of the fact that Educational Psychology is a developing and fast growing science. Like any other developing branch of science it multiplies itself every year. New ideas are coming into picture because of the result of new researches and experiments. The change is the law of nature and education being a dynamic subject is changing very fast The new problems in the process of education are coming with a faster rate and for their solution, Educational Psychology is trying harder with the result that new concepts, principles, and techniques are taking their birth in the sphere of Educational Psychology. Therefore, it is unwise to fix the hedge or boundary around the fertile ground of Educational psychology by defining its scope. It will not only hamper the progress of this developing subject but also prove an obstacle in the progress of Education.

Therefore, the boundaries of Educational Psychology must be left free for future expansion so as to facilitate the inclusion of all what is created in this field in future to solve the problems of Education and help the smoothening of teaching learning process.

The Work

Education Psychology, as defined earlier, is definitely that branch of psychology which is meant for helping the cause of teaching and learning. As science of education, it supplies all the information, principles and techniques which may help a teacher in his better teaching and a learner for his better learning. Let us see how does the knowledge of educational psychology help a teacher in his teaching and a learner in his learning. In other words, let us analyse and elaborate the functions served by educational psychology in the field of teaching and learning.

Functions of Educational Psychology with Regard to Teaching Education psychology with its broad coverage of the content material principles, theories, techniques and applied experiences first analyses the tasks of the teacher's teaching and then in its light tries to supply the knowledge and skills needed by the teacher. In brief, what is required by the teacher in respect to his classroom teaching and other activities needed for helping the students in their desirable behaviour modification and all round growth and development may be outlined as below:

To Know the Learner: Unless the teacher has some knowledge of the potentialities of the child, he cannot go ahead with his task. Educational Psychology equips the teacher for understanding the child in the following different ways:

1. His interests, attitudes, aptitudes and the other acquired or innate capacities and abilities, etc.
2. The stage of development linked with his social; emotional, intellectual, physical and aesthetic needs.
3. His level of aspiration.
4. His conscious and unconscious behaviour.
5. His motivational behaviour.
6. The aspect of his group behaviour.
7. The conflicts, desires and other aspects of his mental health.

To Select and Organise the Subject-matter or Learning Experiences: After knowing the child, when the stage is ready for educating the child, the following questions come in the way:

> What types of learning experiences or learning materials are to be provided?
>
> How should we organise or grade the materials or learning experiences?

To answer these types of questions, which belong to the area of curriculum construction, one needs the knowledge of the characteristics of the learner at each stage of his development, the nature and laws of learning, etc., which come under the domain of Educational Psychology.

To Suggest art and Techniques of Learning as well as Teaching: After deciding about the learner and the learning material the next problem is how to teach or learn is also solved with the help of Educational Psychology. Educational psychology explains the process of learning and suggests the means for effective and enduring learning. It reveals how to maintain interest in the learning process. In this way, it acquaints the teacher with the way of making the pupils learn and thus gives birth to the suitable methodology of teaching.

It also suggests that not a single method or technique is suitable for all kinds of learners in all circumstances. A teacher should select a proper device or method according to the learning situations he faces.

To Arrange Learning Situations or Environment: Midway between the learner and the teacher in the educational process are the learning situations or the environment. Much depends upon the appropriateness of this midway element.

The knowledge of Educational Psychology equips the teacher for taking care of the desirable learning situations and environment-where we should have individual learning or self-study and where the group learning or project work is suggested by Educational Psychology.

The knowledge of group dynamics and group behaviour gives the necessary art for teaching or learning in the group. In other words, the study of the impact of the learning environment (including equipment facilities and aid material, etc.) on the teaching learning process equips the teacher for taking care of the appropriate learning situations or environment.

To Acquaint him with the Mechanism of Heredity and Environment: The knowledge of the role played by heredity and environment in the process of growth and development of the child, is very essential for the teacher. He can weigh their relative importance and take a balanced decision for his work.

Helping in Maintaining Discipline: Knowledge of educational Psychology helps the teacher to have a creative type of discipline as it acquaints him with the nature of the child, his strength and weakness, his interests and aptitudes, etc., on the one hand, and with art and techniques of teaching and learning, on the other. Moreover, his knowledge of the needs drives, fatigue and motivational aspects of the learner and above all the knowledge of the behaviour pattern and personality characteristics of the children-all help him in the process of maintaining proper discipline.

Rendering Guidance Services: The knowledge of Educational Psychology helps the teacher in rendering guidance services to the pupils. He is the person who can know the child better, even more than their parents. With the knowledge of Educational Psychology at his command, he is in touch with the methods of behavioural assessment and appraisal.

He can better diagnose the abilities, interests and aptitudes of his pupils and consequently have an idea of the direction and speed of their development. In this way, with the help of Educational Psychology, the teacher can show the right direction to his pupils for their total development.

Helping in Evaluation and Assessment: While proceeding in the course of teaching-learning process, the need for evaluation is felt. After giving learning experiences to the child, the behavioural changes occurred in him are required to be examined and also in the beginning the potentialities are to be known.

In Educational Psychology, as applied behavioural science, evaluation, measurement and appraisal find its place, which make the teacher well-equipped in the task of evaluation with proper professional skill.

Solving Classroom Problems: There are innumerable problems like backwardness, truancy, bullying, cheating in the classroom situations which are to be faced by a teacher Educational Psychology helps the teacher on this front also. The study of the characteristics of the problem children, the dynamics of the group, behavioural characteristics and adjustment, etc. equip the teacher to solve the actual classroom problems.

Knowing about Himself: Knowledge of Educational Psychology helps the teacher to know about himself. His own behaviour pattern, personality characteristics, likes and dislikes, motivation, anxiety; conflicts, adjustment, etc., are all revealed to him. He also learns the psychology of being a teacher and acquaints himself with the traits of a successful teacher and characteristics of effective teaching. All this knowledge helps him in growing as a successful teacher.

By mentioning the above areas we cannot just say that it is all for which the knowledge of Educational Psychology is needed by a teacher:

> Teacher's needs and problems are too many and have so many aspects. Educational Psychology being a science and technology of education-helps the teacher in all the phases of teaching and learning whether informal or formal, curricular or co-curricular.
>
> It does not only equip him for the classroom instruction but also for the other duties assigned to him like-construction of time-table, organisation of co-curricular activities, to seek parental cooperation, etc.

Various Ideas

The subject, psychology like other natural sciences has two aspects-Pure and Applied. In its aspect of pure Psychology it formulates broad principles, brings out theories and suggests techniques for the study of human behaviour which finds the practical shape in its applied aspect, *i.e.* branches of Applied Psychology like Occupational Psychology, Clinical Psychology, Crime Psychology, Industrial Psychology, Educational Psychology, etc.

In its pictorial form these pure and applied aspects of the subject psychology alongwith their branches can be represented.

Therefore, Educational Psychology is nothing but one of the branches of Applied Psychology. It is an attempt to apply the knowledge of Psychology to the field of Education.

It consists of the application of the Psychological principles and techniques to human behaviour in Educational situations. In other words, Educational Psychology is a study of the experiences and behaviour of the learner in relation to educational environment.

From time to time Psychologists have tried to define Educational Psychology in their own ways. Some of these definitions are given below:

1. *Skinner Fefines it as:* "Educational Psychology is that branch of Psychology which deals with teaching and learning." (1958, p.1).
2. *Crow and Crow Puts it as:* "Educational Psychology describes and explains the learning experiences of an individual from birth through old age." (1973, p. 7)

   Both of these definitions emphasise that Educational Psychology is a Psychology of teaching and learning. Teaching and learning are the main processes of education and the pupil (learner) is a key figure in this process. Therefore, it is proper to define Educational Psychology as a study of the behaviour and experiences of the learner in response to educational environment.
3. There is one more definition of the term educational Psychology given by Peel which in my opinion, is the smallest and best of all the definitions suggested so far. It runs as: "Educational Psychology is the science of Education." (1956, p. 8)

Let us see the justification of calling Educational psychology as science of education by studying its relation with education.

Importance of Reading

Inspiration and Reading

According to Hull, the importance of motivation in process of learning is very great. Motivation does the work of a drive in organism. An organism cannot learn anything in the absence of motivation. It is motivation on account of which it performs some specified action. This motivation, on the one hand, forms a habit resulting from practice and, on the other hand, it is a source of practice in performance. When an organism lies inactive, it does lack practice, but there is an absence of motivation.

This motivation may be about food, freedom from some painful condition or about any other thing. As soon as motivation arises, the organism becomes active. In the presence of motivation, the actions of an organism are goal directed. When it gets a reward in acting in a particular way, it repeats the same action and, in this way, the specified response is confirmed by the reward in the form of motivation. On the other hand, the tendency of repeating the responses, which are not rewarded, is weakened. In this way, reward strengthens the relation between stimulus and a response in an organism. It is this reward which is called reinforcement. Hull has accepted reinforcements of two kinds-primary and secondary. Primary reinforcement means those stimuli which affect some motivation in a direct form. For example, for motivation of hunger, food does the work of reinforcement, and the action, which brings food to the organism, is repeated in the organism. The other kind of reinforcement is secondary, an example of which is watering of the mouth on seeing food.

Goal gradient or reinforcement-gradient is the central point of Hull's theory. His theory is, therefore, called reinforcement theory. The attainment of goal brings stability to the relation between stimulus and response. It reduces the tension of the organism which helps it in learning the specified response. For example, when a hungry rat is let loose in a puzzle-box, it learns to take the shorter route to food, because it brings a ready reward.

As has been said before, Hull, like Thorndike, accepts the importance of practice in learning. When an organism repeats the specified response to some stimulus again and again, a close relation is established between them. According to Hull, along with practice, reinforcement is also necessary here. In the absence of reinforcement, a mechanical practice alone is of no use. Needless to say that Hull's opinion here is different from Thorndike's mechanical theory of learning. Hull also agrees with other behaviourists that learning of all kinds can be explained on the basis of connecting response. Hull has presented 16 laws to explain the different aspects of learning, among which the laws of motivation and reinforcement are the chief laws and the other laws are derived by these two laws. Hull has expressed his theory with the help of the following formula:

S E R = f (H and D)

In this formula, capacity of response had been shown by the letter 'S', to determine practice by 'H' and motivation by 'D'. Middle reinforcement have special importance in the process of learning. Hull has accepted physiological and physical reinforcements in learning. He does not accept reinforcements of other kinds.

According to Hull, there are two main aspects of the transfer of learning, one of which is limited by stimulus and the other by response. The transfer limited by stimulus has been explained through generalisation, and the transfer limited by response. The transfer limited by stimulus has been explained through generalisation, and the transfer limited by response is explained through habit family hierarchy. When an organism fails in some situation due to some specified response, it tries some other response which previously brought success to it.

Influencing Factors: Psychologists have experimented widely on different subjects of learning and prescribed the different factors favourable to each of them individually. Different conditions are ideal for different subjects of learning, in the presence of which learning is quicker, more efficient and permanent and it is desirable to pay close attention to these conditions.

Generally speaking, learning may be accepted to be of three types:

1. Cognitive-Perceptual and Conceptual.
2. Motor.
3. Affective-Conative.

It will be advantageous to describe the ideal conditions for the three types' of learning individually.

Conceptual Learning: The cognitive, perceptual and conceptual type of learning is made effective by the following conditions:

Beginning the Work with Enthusiasm: The absence of enthusiasm is a detrimental factor because, while it prevails no perceptual or conceptual learning can be carried into effect. Learning is an active process and one which demands effort; the more enthusiastic a start, the more success is likely to attain the learning. Mere perception is inadequate for the understanding of a perceptual subject while personal application gives better results and this is the reason for the importance given to experiments in the study of psychology. The slow speed in learning is due, largely not to lack of intelligence but to the absence of enthusiasm.

Distribution of the Times of Study: It is better to learn a subject by introducing intervals in the times of study than to study uninterrupted for any length of time. The study of any subject should always be conducted on the interval pattern of time distribution. Spaced learning is better than unspaced learning.

Presence of Assisting Factors: The presence of assisting factors is of advantage in both perceptual and conceptual types of learning.

The assistant factors in conceptual learning are – dictionary, tables and graphs, preparing an outline, writing a precis, taking notes, etc. For perceptual learning the use of laboratory instruments in perception is desirable.

Whole or Part Learning: The approach to learning, whether as a whole or part, depends upon the capacity of the learner and quantity of the subject to be learnt. The whole method is good for intelligent learners and in shorter subjects, while the part method is used with advantage by the intellectually weaker learners and in large subjects. Suppose we have to memorise a poem. Now, if we read the whole poem at once, the relation between the various lines will become clear and assist in the learning of it. If, on the other hand, the poem is difficult and lengthy, it would be better to divide it into parts than to study it as a whole. A student used to the part method of study finds the whole method inflexible and cumbersome. As a matter of fact, as far as the matter of studying books is concerned, it is better if the student first reads the whole books and then studies the chapters individually.

Assistant Habits: These too are of some importance in learning. To succeed, the student should form the habits of consulting the dictionary, making a fixed time table for study, not working when exhausted, using sketches, illustrations and briefs, studying alone in the morning and evening, repeating the lesson, preparing according to plan and with regularity, minimising lip movement and reading silently and concentrating the mind, etc.

Other Assisting Conditions: Besides the conditions mentioned above, the following conditions also assist in study-absence of fatigue and boredom, presence of average brain, mental capacities and active attention, no nervous or emotional tension, absence of economic worries, absence of worry about personal and family problems.

Motor Learning: The above mentioned conditions are also applicable to motor learning as much as they are applicable to cognitive learning. Practice is of great importance in motor learning, because it is the only way of obtaining skill.

Affective Conative Learning: An important factor influencing learning is the knowledge for results. In fact, motor learning is seriously hampered in the absence of knowledge of results. In an experiment, ten female students were not given opportunity to have the knowledge of results. Due to this the curve of learning fell continuously. In the experiment the learners had knowledge of results upto 200 the effort. After that light was extinguished so that knowledge of results became impossible with the result that there was a steep fall in average scores. Knowledge of results creates a tendency to repeat successful activities. This improves performance and provides encouragement in learning.

The Resources: Feedback is a term drawn from mechanics or industrial production. In a mechanical or electrical system, it means regulating input by linking it to output. A governor on a steam engine or a thermostat in a home regulates output by reacting negatively to increasing out put. In neurology, feedback refers to the afferent impulses from preperceptive receptors that give rise to refers to motor movements. Feedback from such receptors is believed to be important in aiming, grasping and placing reaction. Thus it is a helpful factor in learning. More generally, feedback means any kind of return information from a source useful in regulating behaviour.

It has been found from experiments on learning method that the rate of learning increases with the strength of motivation. In one experiment, three groups of rats were taken. The first group was very hungry and very thirsty. The second was very hungry but only slightly thirsty and the third was very thirsty but only slightly hungry. In the first nine days of the experiment, the rats were rewarded with food. During this period it was seen that the first group of rats which were motivated both by hunger and thirst learned faster than the other two groups. This shows that two needs together have more motivating effect on learning than one need. In the last nine days of the experiment, only water was used as a reward for the rats. With this shift in reward, the first group was disturbed temporarily. At first, they showed an increase in the number of errors in learning, but at the end of experiment they were again better than the other two groups. Thus the shift in reward has little effect on the first group but it has a notable effect on the other two groups. The third group of rats, which were more thirsty and only slightly hungry improved their learning speed because water was given as a reward. On the other hand, rats of the second group which were more hungry and only slightly thirsty showed no improvement in learning because these animals had a greater need for food than water. Following two conclusions are drawn from this experiment,

1. Two needs together constitute a more effective condition for learning than one need.
2. Learning is faster if the motivating need is appropriately rewarded.

The Usefulness: The result of this experiment can be used very successfully with the children. A successful teacher increases the rate of learning of his students by giving various incentives. In one experiment with children, it was seen that the offering of a reward of a chocolate bar increased the learning by 52 per cent above the usual level. When a number of incentives like candy, a definite goal, rivalry and praise were presented, an increase of 65 per cent in learning was observed. In human activities it is seen that an increase in motivation leads to an increase of performance.

Motivation plays an important role in learning. It is the psychological factor in learning. It not only sets in motion the activity resulting in learning, but also sustains and directs it. It is the central factor in the effective management of the process of learning", (Kelly) because in the process of motivation, the learner's internal energies are directed towards the goal objects of his environment.

It Energises Behaviour: Motivation gives the child energy to learn. It channelises behaviour and also sustains. It initiates the tendency to act and learn for achievement. Through reward and punishment, the child can be initiated to learn for better achievement.

It Directs Behaviour: Motivation directs the behaviour towards specific goals. Through motivation child's behaviour can be directed towards learning and attaining good academic achievement.

Selection of Behaviour Pattern: Motivation helps to select the behaviour pattern. Through motivation a child can select such behaviour patterns that may facilitate learning and achievement.

Helps in Developing Interests: "Interest provides an initial of attracting the attention of pupils" (Horrock) and motivation helps in developing interests within the pupils for learning various school subjects as well as extra curricular activities.

Acquisition of Knowledge: Motivation helps in the acquisition of knowledge. Through adequate motivation teacher can initiate the pupils to attain more and more knowledge.

Adequate Motivation: Helps in developing good qualities and habits and initiates a child towards high ideals and morals. Through motivation a teacher can initiate the child learns good things and forms a good character.

Development of Social Qualities: Education aims at the all round development of an individual. Through motivation a teacher can initiate the pupils to take part in group activities and develop the feeling of cooperation and other social qualities.

Development of Sense of Discipline: Motivation also helps in developing a sense of discipline. Though adequate motivation a teacher can initiate the pupils to do good things and develop the sense of discipline within them.

Helps to Focus Attention: Motivation helps in focusing the attention. The teacher can initiate the students to focus their attention on curricular activities and learning, through motivation.

Changes Behaviour: Motivation helps in changing or moulding the behaviour. Through praise, reward or punishment, a teacher can mould and guide the pupils behaviour.

From the above discussion, it is clear that motivation occupies a very significant place in learning. It plays a very significant role in making teaching-learning effective. In short, it is the very heart of learning.

The Outcome: Uguroluand Walberg pointed out that adequate motivation not only sets in motion the activity which results in learning, but also sustains and directs it. Hence in order to make teaching-learning effective, it is very essential for a teacher to use effective methods of motivation. In the words of Kelly "Motivation is the central factor in effective management of the processing of learning. Some type of motivation must be present in learning".

In order to motivate the children to learn, the teacher should use the devices as follows –

Child-Centred Approach: Murstll said, "Motivation determines how well pupils learn and how long they keep on learning". Hence a teacher should follow a child-centred approach in motivating the child. He should keep in mind the child's abilities, interests and experiences, his physical and mental condition, etc. while teaching. Before starting his lesson he should also know whether the child is mentally prepared or not and teach accordingly.

Linking the New Knowledge with the Past: In order to make teaching-learning effective, the teacher should link the new knowledge or the experience to be given through the lessons with that of the past knowledge or experience gained from learning. By doing so the learning material becomes easy for the child to grasp and interesting. The child finds that the new learning material is related with the past one and takes interest in learning quickly.

Praise and Reproof: Praise and reproof are powerful devices of motivation. By using these devices the classroom atmosphere can be made appropriate for learning and students can be motivated to learn. They can be encouraged to take interest in the subject-matter. But which device will be more appropriate, depends on the aptitude and personality of the teacher and the student because more or less, the effectiveness of praise depends on the way of praising. Similarly the effectiveness of reproof depends on the way of reproving. Hence, a teacher should apply these devices only after careful analysis of child's nature.

Reward and Punishment: Unlike praise and reproof, effectiveness of reward and punishment depends on the way of rewarding or punishing. Generally three forms of rewards are used: material form, symbolic form and giving status. Reward has been found to be a positive kind of motivation whereby punishment is a negative kind of motivation since it is related with unpleasantness. Reward gives pleasure. It is well-established fact that we intend to do certain things again and again that are likely to give us pleasure. Punishment makes the personality dim and gives discouragement. As such reward is a more powerful device of motivation than punishment.

Effective Teaching Method: Use of effective teaching methods facilitates motivation and learning. Teaching method should be according to the interests and aptitude of students. It should be according to the mental state of the students. As such a teacher should use audio-visual means to explain the subject-matter to the students. Small children love stories and pictures. As such a teacher should arrange the subject-matter accordingly to draw students attention and interest and make teaching-learning effective.

Competition: Competition is a powerful device of motivation and success in performance. Hurlock carried on a study to know the effect of competition. He took 35 students from Class III, V and VIII and divided into two groups. He encouraged the students of one group for obtaining highest marks in arithmetic while the other group was left as it was. After a week's time, he took arithmetic test of both the groups and found that the group which was encouraged for the competition, record higher than the other group. Hence, through competition a teacher can encourage the students for successful performance.

Knowledge of Result: It is quite natural that whenever we do anything, we are curious to know the result. The knowledge of result gives us satisfaction and at the same time, it encourages us for better performance. Hence, a teacher should let the students know about their performance and also point out the drawback or errors in their performance. This helps them improve their performance in future and get better results. Woodworth pointed out, "Motivation comes from the immediate knowledge of results". Hence, a teacher should keep the records of the student's performance and let them know their achievements from time to time.

Factors of Language

If a child's birth has been normal, then he gradually gains command over language after passing through the different stages of linguistic development. This development is a process and its different stages can not be distinguished from each other. Neither is it necessary that each one of these stages should be distinctly apparent in the linguistic development of every child. Language ability does not develop and improve at the same rate in all children, and neither does it take the same time.

According to psychologists, a child speaks his first word when he is 13 or 14 months old. Language development, therefore, should be considered from his point. The period preceding this can be said to be a kind of preparation for the evolution of linguistic ability because during this period, the child indicates his requirements to others by making various audible sound. These sounds and signs, that he makes, play an important part in the development of his language ability.

By Communication: A child needs some means of communication by which he can communicate with the other people around him. Even during his infancy the child develops some signs and indications which help to transmit his needs to other people. Psychologists differ in their opinion about the first crying sound of the child at the moment of birth. Some consider it a desire to communicate while others think it is a reflex action. Nevertheless, all psychologists agree that the child develops some kind of sign language to communicate his needs. Even when the child is three weeks old, he uses different sounds and physical movements to indicate such physical conditions as hunger, cold, pain, wetness, etc. In this manner, one observes the following three kinds of signs in a child while he is preparing for language development.

Crying: This is the child's first sound and it does not have to be learnt for it is automatically produced by the vocal organs. Crying is uncontrolled and irregular. According to Leibnit and Start, the child cries during the first two weeks without any particular cause. Crying does not bring forth any tears, but the breathing becomes irregular, pulse rate increases, the fists are clenched and the body becomes red. Despite the fact that this crying is not motivated, the child normally questions down if it is picked up by the mother. After the third week this variety of crying grows less. Normally, crying in the first seven weeks indicates an excess of hunger, noise and light. According to Watson, the child cries because of hunger, exhaustion and fear. Buhler has indicated numerous causes of a child's crying-bright light, high pitched sound, physical discomfort, interruption of sleep, exhaustion, hunger, difficulty in movement caused by tight clothes, the taking away of toys, fear, etc. Many children are found to cry immediately before they are fed, and before they go to sleep. When a child is of three months, he cries when he wants to attract the attention of grown up people. A four month child cries when he is not allowed to play. A nine month child cries when he observes his mother going towards another child. Studies of the crying sound of children have indicated that they uttei the first sounds of vowels. If the parents pay too much attention when the child cries, then the child develops a habit of crying whenever he needs anything. It is better to attend to the child immediately he cries so that he should not have to cry for a long time in order to be attended to. Crying for long periods has a bad effect on the child's digestion, besides which it also causes nervous tension and loss of sleep. This creates a feeling of insecurity in the child, for he feels that he is being ignored by his parents. All these things have the effect of making future social adjustment difficult. Physical development also suffers.

Babbling: The stage of babbling begins in the third month and continues up to the eighth month. During this period the child's vocal organs develop. A child makes those sounds which give him pleasure and he repeats them because they add to his pleasure. If his parents indicate their delight at the sounds he is making then the child feels encouraged to go on repeating them. Most of the sounds are meaningless and should be treated as such. Older people, on the other hand, try to read some meaning into them and the way that the child is trying to say something. The child has to make an effort to produce such sounds. According to Jersild, these sounds later on die out and the child does not make them. In the beginning these sounds have some vocal quality, although the child learns to pronounce consonants only when he sprouts his front teeth. Some sounds become more definite than others because of repetition. Hurlock believes that the child continues to babble upto the age of twelve months. But it would be more accurate to say that the period of babbling depends upon the development of the child's speech organs and the encouragement he receives to speak. Babbling gives pleasure to the child and he is often seen babbling to himself. He grins and laugh when he hears the sounds proceeding from his own month. Compared to the normal child, a deaf one does not babble so much because he cannot hear the sound that he is himself making. It is in the process of babbling that the child learns gradually to control his vocal chords.

Gestures: The child uses different types of gestures and signs to express his meaning to others. He uses several parts of the body to make gestures. If he does not succeed in conveying his meaning through gestures he begins to weep. In infancy several types of gestures are spontaneously visible, as for example moving the head from side to side, smiling, stretching arms, weeping, throwing legs, etc. The parents follow the meanings conveyed by the child through these gestures. As the child learns to speak, the use of gestures becomes less and less, because they are not needed any more. But gestures are used even now due to imitation and sometimes to emphasise certain words.

After passing through different stages of language development, the child gradually begins to understand different words and their uses. At the age of 18 months, he can use ten or twelve simple words on an average. Some children can use as many as one hundred words at this age. In the next three or four month, the child's vocabulary increases very fast. At the age of 2 years, his vocabulary may include words in four figures and this goes on increasing till the age of 12 years when it reaches the limit of 10,000 words or more.

Different Ages: Some psychologists have described language development in different ages. This can be divided into the following three periods:

From 2 to 3 Years of Age: During this period the child begins to use words to form sentences. He uses pronouns though he cannot use 'I' and 'me' properly. At the end of this period, he begins to use plural and past tense. A child of three years can make complex and compound sentences.

Four to Five Years of Age: At the age of four, the child's ability to form a sentence is considerably improved and he begins to make use of the rules of grammar. He is very talkative at this age. He is interested in almost everything and asks questions without waiting for the answers. It appears that curiosity is not the only cause behind these questions, a reason in the exercise of the growing vocabulary. At the kindergarten age, the child achieves sufficient control over words; though he cannot understand their subtle meanings.

After Five Years: At this age most of the children go to school. They use language intelligently in talking with other persons. The school and the home play a very important role in language development at this stage. The child also learns to pronounce correctly.

Various Stages: The following are the four important stages in a child's language development from the point of view of various elements of language:

Comprehension: Comprehension means the ability to understand the meaning of the words uttered by others. According to the psychologists, the child's power of comprehension develops even before he begins to use words. The child can comprehend more words than he can speak. The ability of comprehension plays a more important role in learning any language than the ability to speak. Though it is not definite as to what part gestures and words play in comprehension, it can be said that they play a very important part in it. If gestures are used along with words in teaching the child, his learning is facilitated. According to Hurlock when gestures are used with a child of 18 months, he understands the meaning more properly as compared with mere use of words. The psychologists Gessel, Termann, Merrill, Cattle Garrison and Mcarthy have investigated into the child's ability of comprehension during different periods of age.

It has been found that an infant of four months moves his head while hearing human sound, and smiles at her mother. At the age of 6 to 8 months, he hears the words attentively and also tries to pronounce them. At the age of 12 months, the child can understand simple commands and instructions and also follow them. At the age of 5 to 6 years, the vocabulary of the child is so much developed that he can understand the talks of unknown persons. He can comprehend the meanings of stories told to him. He can understand similarity and distinction between words. It has been found by experiments that the child's power of comprehension can be immensely increased by means of radio and television.

Building a Vocabulary: The vocabulary of a child increases by hearing other's using different words. One can find general and particular words in a child's vocabulary. The general words are those which can be used in many situations, *e.g.*, sleeping, walking, good, bad, man, woman, etc. The particular words are those which are used in different situations at different ages. As a general rule the formal type of vocabulary is more developed than the later kind.

In the development of general vocabulary, the child first learns nouns and uses them in language. In these also he first learns words which are useful for him and which are easy to understand. On the other hand he seldom uses words which are difficult to pronounce and finds it difficult to learn them. Thus, the child learns pronouns in due course. He learns nouns at the stage of babbling, *e.g.*, daddy, grandfather, uncle, etc. The verbs are used after learning nouns.

In the beginning simple verbs such as come, go, get up, sit down, etc., are used. At the age of 18 months the child begins to use adjectives, such as cold, warm, good, bad, etc., and adverbs such as here, there, where, etc. According to Jersild in learning pronouns several types of 'T' are used and 'you' is used less often because the child is generally self-centred. According to the experiments of Young, Mcarthy and Garrison, the uses of pronouns and adverbs are very much found after first two years of age. At the nursery school, the child is found to use more pronouns, verbs and adjectives than nouns.

The growth of vocabulary is intimately connected with intelligence and motivation. These factors are not only conducive to the learning of the new words, but also in finding new meanings of words already learnt. In the first two years, the child's vocabulary grows slowly. It increases very fast after he enters the school, because their teachers teach new words and their uses. Vocabulary increases by contact with new things, persons and places, hearing a radio, watching television, and reading story books. The psychologists have found out that the range of words in the vocabulary of the school-going children is from 20 to 24 thousand in the first class, 50,000 in the VI standard and 88,000 in the High

School. Some psychologists including Smith, Mcarthy and Jersild have supported the conclusion of Crow and Crow that at the age of 12, the average vocabulary of a child is 10,000 words while in exceptional cases it may go upto 30,000 words or more. The increase of vocabulary helps the child's talking as well as his writing.

The progress of a child in education can be estimated by range of his vocabulary because he knows the world around him through words. In modern times the wide use of radio, television and films in the schools for the purposes of education has very much helped the increase of vocabulary. In the words of Garrison, "In an age of radio, television and films, rapid transportation and world relationships, the child needs to know many words and to be able to use them. Failure tends to result in impaired social adjustment."

The above discussion concerns with the development of general vocabulary. At the age of 3 the child begins to develop particular vocabulary. This includes words of different types, such as, words showing respect, etiquette, etc. As the child learns to behave with the elders, he learns such words. Secondly, as the child sees things of different colours, he knows the names of different colours. Again, at the age of 4 years the child learns numbers. At the age of 5 and 6 years, the child learns to distinguish between different seasons, days, months, etc. At the age of 4 or 5 years, he can distinguish between different coins. Just before adolescence, the children are seen talking in secret language, which is formed by different techniques.

Formation of Sentences: Upto the age of 1½ years, the infant generally uses only one word. He begins to construct incomplete sentences involving two or more words at the age of 2 years. At the age of 4 and 5 years he uses compound sentences. This ability of the sentence construction increases upto the age of 9 and 10 years, when the child can construct several types of sentences. The ability of constructing sentences increases with the cultural level of the child. According to Gessel, Garrison, Mcarthy and Jersild, a child of two and a half years uses complete sentences. The girls are generally more advanced than boys in sentence construction, because the speed of their intellectual development is more than that of boys.

Correct Pronunciation: According to Hurlock, the child learns to pronounce by imitation of others. If the others are pronouncing wrongly, the child also learns to pronounce wrongly hence pronunciation can be improved by demonstrating correct pronunciation to the child. In adolescence the pronunciations are more or less established and cannot be easily changed. The child's pronunciations improve after the age of 18 months and it is sufficiently improved at the age of 3. Besides age, one finds individual differences in pronunciation. While some children pronounce very correctly at an early age, others fails to do so, even at the advanced age. The main cause behind this distinction is the differences in the development of vocal organs, occasions of training and the amount of motivation. In the beginning the child's pitch of speaking is high, but upto the age of 3 years he learns to adjust it. The child should not be bluntly snubbed for speaking in the high pitch because this adversely affects the development of his vocal organs.

Learning Dispatch

The Definition

Sorenson: "Transfer refers to the transfer of knowledge, training and habits acquired in one situation to another."

Colsnik: "Transfer is the application of carry over of knowledge, skills, habits, attitudes or other responses from one situation in which things are initially acquired to some other situation."

Crow and Crow: "The carry-over of habits of thinking, feeling or working of knowledge or of skills, from one learning area to another usually is referred to as the transfer of training."

Encyclopaedia of Education: "The term learning would be applied to the special kind of transfer phenomena in which there is great similarity between training conditions and test conditions."

Various Kinds: Transfer of training is normally of the following two kinds:

Positive Transfer of Training: In this transfer, training of one kind has positive or beneficial influence upon learning of another kind and learning is assisted thereby. For example, in an experiment, one group was taught Latin while another group was not, members of either group having common interests and similar level of intelligence. Now both the groups were put in the same class and taught by one single teacher who endeavoured to teach them English. It was found that the group knowing Latin picked up the language and acquired proficiency in it much earlier than did the other group that was ignorant of Latin. The reason for this was that the training in Latin was positively transferred to the learning of English.

Negative Transfer of Training: In this the training acquired in one kind of learning has a negative influence upon learning in some other connection, or in other words, it obstructs this learning. For example, individuals interested in wrestling are often found to be weak in academic pursuits because wrestling deprives them of much of their energy and they have little left for any intellectual labour. In this way, wrestling proves to be obstructive to academic learning.

In certain cases, training or learning has no influence or effect at all, just as the learning of a Hindi poem has not the least effect on memorising facts of geography. In such contexts there is no transfer of training. In this way, transfer of training should involve at least some obvious influence or effect. If that effect is favourable, then it is positive but if it is disadvantageous it is negative.

According to Agencies: In the recent past, psychologists have made extensive tests and experiments concerned with the transfer of training and education, these efforts throwing considerable light on the subject under review. The major experiments in this connection have been conducted on sensory motor transfer concerning memory, reasoning and ideation, subjects in school, problem solving, etc.

Sensory Motor Transfer: Starch made experiments concerning sensory motor transfer with the help of mirror. In his experiment he examined the expediency that could be gained in drawing a star shaped figure with the left hand, while examining it through a mirror, it having been drawn under similar conditions with the right hand. In the experiment, the subject was asked to draw the figure with his left hand and the time taken therein was noted.

This practice was continued over a period of ten days. After this, the subject was asked to use the other hand, and this too was practised for the same period of time. In this it became apparent that in the second effort, the time taken was appreciably less, whereby it was deduced that the practice gained by the right hand was transferred to the left hand.

In this connection, it should be mentioned that experiments conducted by Evert, Munn and Bray have elaborated this transference in a different sense. They came to the conclusion that progress in the above experiment is not the outcome of any transference of training from the right to the left hand, but rather that this influence is the outcome of increase in the subject's self-confidence, improvement in his understanding of the problem, improvement of method, etc.

Webb experimented with the paths of a hide and seek and came to the conclusion that the practice of one sensory mother activity can be transferred to another sensory motor activity, although the extent of this transference depends upon similar elements in the two activities as well as upon their essential points of difference. In this experiment Webb tried to transfer the practice of one particular maze to the tackling of five other mazes.

To begin with, the man or animal was trained in tackling one particular maze and was then led to four other mazes, and the effect of previous training observed in the skill transferred to the latest tackling. After this round of activity had been completed, the subject was allowed to practise upon one maze and the influence of practices on other mazes, on this one maze activity was observed. It was observed that in either condition learning in one maze definitely helped in the learning of other mazes. In this experiment Webb found the extent of transference of learning varying from 20 to 77 per cent among various individuals.

Transference Concerning Memory: Among the experiments concerning transference in memory, those of W.G. Sleight are important. In his experiments he adopted the controlled group method, a group of female students being divided into four small groups. The first controlled group was not imparted any training.

Another group learnt a poem for twelve days for a period of one and half hour every day. The third group worked for a similar period for an equal number of hours but instead concentrated upon population and import-export tabulated figures. The fourth group of women spent the same period of time for twelve days in trying to learn historical, scientific and literary prose tracts read out to them. It was a kind of oral learning for them. These four groups were examined before and after the following elements being examined in the process:

1. Learning names and dates verbally.
2. Remembering non-sensical words verbally.
3. Remembering poetic piece, both read out by the teacher as well as read out individually.
4. Remembering prose tracts, both read out by the teacher as well as read out individually to one self.
5. Remembering the fundamental idea of a poetic piece verbally introduced.
6. Remembering the order of nine numerals seen once.

The above experiments concerning the transference of memory yielded the following facts:

1. Every group showed progress only in the matter practised upon.
2. Learning of one kind had sometimes a favourable and sometimes an adverse influence upon learning of another kind.
3. Learning poetry had beneficial influence upon the learning of tables, meaningless words and prose, whereas it had adverse influence upon the learning of the idea of a poetry piece or words.

Sleight came to the following conclusions:

1. Practice does not lead to any appreciable improvement in the general memory, and neither is there any evidence of working of a general memory.
2. Related and unrelated complex memory functioning came to light in very large numbers.

Although some other experimenters have discovered greater advantageous transfer of memory than Sleight has found, yet these tests do not prove that practice can help in the development of memory. The truth of the matter is that the functioning of memory is a complex process and the outcome of transfer depends upon the specific activity practised.

Transference of Perception: In an experiment conducted by Thorndike and Woodworth in 1901, it was observed that in estimating the area between 10 and 100 square centimetres, educated or trained individuals showed an improvement of 1/3 over the estimate of an area between 150 and 300 square centimetres. But another individual was given to practise upon estimating lines between half and one half inches long, and it was found that he showed no skill had been obtained when he was asked to estimate lengths between six and twelve inches

Transfer Concerning Reasoning: Educational psychologists have also made important experiments concerning transfer. W.H. Winch made a study of the transfer of school children's skill in solving arithmetical problems to the solution of other problems of reasoning. In this experiment, one definite group of students was put to practising the solution of arithmetical problems for ten weeks, while another group of equal strength was allowed to work according to the regular curriculum with the exception of arithmetical learning. Of the two groups, the one with training in mathematics or arithmetic showed 30 per cent results. On the basis of this and other similar experiments, it is believed that training in mathematics is transferred to other reasoning problems, and that much training helps in the solutions of rational problems.

Transference Concerning Ideation or Ideals: Using some of Aesop's fables as the basis of his tests, Barrel examined the extent to which they help in the development of ideals. In this test two experimental and controlled groups of children and adults were selected. Between the first and second tests, lessons were read out to the experimental groups for periods varying between 12 and 30 minutes and the group was trained in analysis, imagination and generalisation. Following examination, it was observed that the experimental group made better progress than the controlled group.

Transfer Concerning Problem Solving: Educational psychologists have also studied the question of transfer in the field of problem solving, although no district conclusions have been reached. In this connection. S.T. Gray made an experiment upon the transfer of code substitution. In this experiment the code substitution of two comparative groups was made the basis of tests. Following this, one of the two groups was taught a new code in which the logical connections were emphasised. The results of the test indicated that the group trained to observe rational relationships in its code performed its work some 20 per cent better than the other group.

Different Theories: The principle of transfer of training tool birth with the formal education system. According to this system, there are some subjects the study of which strengthens the faculties of the mind and which in turn help the study of other subjects. It was believed, for instance, that the study of Sanskrit, Latin and Mathematics disciplined the mind which then found it easier to grasp other subjects communicated to it. These notions of the formal education system were based upon faculty psychology which conceived of the mind as a conglomerate of various powers of faculties such as observation, memory, reasoning, decision, etc. Hence, it was essential that subjects should be chosen with a view to strengthening these faculties. The faculty of reasoning, for example, was believed to be strengthened by the study of law, philosophy and all such subjects that required the constant application of logical thinking.

Modern psychology does not give any credence to the faculty psychology. Hence, modern psychologists abandoned the above elucidation of the principle of transfer of training and replaced it with a multiplicity of explanations and principles. The following four theories are among the more important of them:

Thorndike's Theory of Identical Elements: According to Thorndike's opinion, identical elements are transferred from one situation to another situation, as for example, a knowledge of psychology helps in solving labour trouble and unrest.

Judd's Theory of Generalisation: According to this view, the recipient of one kind of training generalises the experience, knowledge and habits attained in it, and utilises this product in the new conditions created in the learning of another form of training. And, this transference is possible only if the recipient observes some similarity of elements between the two kinds of conditions.

Sandiford's Theory: According to Sandiford, there is no essential difference between the theories of Thorndike and Judd, as both have said the same thing, viz., that due to the similarity or identity of elements, training in one circumstance leads to its transfer in the other. According to Sandiford, this transfer depends upon the individual's intelligence as only the perceptive individual can observe an identity of elements in two circumstances and make generalisations. It is his view that the power of generalisation is indicative of the individual's intelligence. He conducted tests to substantiate this view that the intelligent student can assimilate facts that he has gleaned from the perusal of newspapers in his paper on the languages, whereas the unintelligent or backward student cannot utilise newspaper information in his language papers. Similarly, negative transfer of training will be equally powerful in the intelligent person's case. An intelligent person adept in English will have difficulty in learning the Hindi idiom because of his practice in the other language.

Skinners's View: According to Skinner, purely oral information cannot be utilised in transfer of learning so long as the person is incapable of using that in practical circumstances, and that the person's knowledge about using facts is not commensurate with or in proportion to his knowledge of the facts themselves. Secondly, if the individual carries a prejudicial attitude towards any learned fact, then this knowledge will not be of help in the gaining of other knowledge. Thirdly, a scientific interest helps us in the accumulation of knowledge, but it does not render any assistance in the transfer of knowledge. It becomes evident from these three points advanced by Skinner that only knowledge or scientific interest alone are not enough for transfer, it must also be used in practical conditions.

The Training: It is evident from the above description that contemporary psychologists are desirous of discovering the conditions that help in the transfer of training. Many experiments have also been performed concerning this phenomenon. The more important facts gleaned from this extensive experimentation are the following:

Subjects of Learning Differ in Respect of their Transference Value: Experiments upon the transference of subjects that are taught in school seem to indicate that these subjects have differing transfer values. As has been pointed out before, modern psychology does not believe that any one subject can serve to discipline the mind, yet there is no denying it that the transfer value of mathematics and science is very high. Then come the languages and social sciences. History and English have no transfer value. Cooking, stitching and dancing have a negative transfer value by which is meant that knowledge of them makes it difficult to learn other difficult subjects.

Transfer is Particular, not General: From the facts used in the preceding illustrations, it should not be concluded that the knowledge of language or science helps in the learning of every subject. It has further been pointed out that transfer takes place only if there is identity of circumstances or elements. Sanskrit may be of help in learning either Hindi or Bengali, as Sanskrit words are numerously used in these languages but a knowledge of Sanskrit can be of no conceivable use in learning Urdu or Persian. It is more probable that pronunciation may be adversely influenced by such knowledge.

Transfer Depends Much on the Learner's Intelligence and Innate Ability: It has been clearly stated earlier that transfer is considerably influenced by the learner's intelligence. Experiments indicated that the ability of the best one per cent students of high school as far as transference is concerned, is something like twenty per cent more than that of the worst one per cent students. Similarly, an individual can make use of his knowledge only through innate ability, and transfer is possible only if there is utilisation of knowledge.

For Achieving Transference it is Essential to Study Subjects that Admit of Transfer: If training in Sanskrit is to be transferred, then Hindi or Bengali should be taught, while proficiency in Latin can be utilised in the teaching of English.

Transfer Depends Upon the Use of Information: It has been mentioned more than once at previous stages that no knowledge or subject that has been grasped can be transferred unless it is first utilised in practice. Moral teaching in school can only be transferred to social education if the student makes use of it in his day-to-day life.

Transfer is Due to Similarity of Material and Methodology: It, too, has been frequently pointed out earlier that the transfer of training can only be achieved in the learning of that subject which has some affinity with the first in respect of matter as well as methodology. Arithmetic can be transferred to book-keeping.

From this description of transfer of training, it is apparent that it depends upon the learner's intelligence, innate ability, knowledge, practical ability, and use of acquired information in practice. Transfer takes place in particular subjects that have similar material and similar methodology, and in the teaching of such subjects. Transfer takes place in different quantities in differing subjects. There is no transfer in some while it is negative or obstructive in others.

Various Theories

Skinner: "Learning includes both acquisition and retention."

Pressy: "Learning represents experience that leads to a change or adjustment in performance and to the acquisition of new ways of behaving."

Gates: "Learning is modification of behaviour through experience."

Crow and Crow: "Learning involves the acquisition of habits, knowledge and attitudes."

J.P Guilford: "We may define the term very broadly by saying that learning is any change in behaviour, resulting from behaviour." In this definition, a distinction between change in behaviour, due to maturity and change in behaviour due to learning is unavoidable though both these activities occur simultaneously.

Garrett: "Learning is that activity by virtue of which we organise our responses with new habits." Thus, the element of organisation in learning is one of the importance of which cannot be over emphasised. Guilford too, has written that the meaning of learning is, inevitably, an organisation of behaviour. Thus, in learning to ride a cycle we have to organise the learning of turning the pedal, balancing the handle, etc., in order to be reasonably safe with the vehicle. It is another matter that a person does not learn this organisation at the outset and that he may take much longer time to learn to balance the handle than the time he may take to learn to turn the pedal. But his learning of the art of cycling will be completed only when he accomplishes this organisation.

R.S. Woodworth: The learning of a new acting is an addition to the person's store of experiences. Clarifying the statement further, Woodworth says that reinforcement too, is an indispensable element of the act of learning because this activity forms only successful responses and weeds out the unsuccessful responses.

He Wrote: "An activity may be called learning insofar as it develops the individual in any way, good or bad and makes his environment and experiences different from what it would otherwise have been."

Gardner Murphy: The persons, who stress external behaviour consider learning to be a change of behaviour while those who lay emphasis on internal changes are convinced that learning is change in the perspective of the individual. Combining these two view, Gardner Murphy wrote that, "From this point of view it would be legitimate to regard learning as a modification, both of behaviour and of the way of perceiving."

Hilgard: Many examples may be presented from every day life like, memorising a poem, working at the typewriter, manipulating knife and fork, etc. The following definition of learning given by Hilgard is an essence of all the foregoing definitions offered by other psychologists, "Learning is the process by which an activity originates or is changed through reacting to an encountered situation, provided that the characteristics of the change in activity cannot be explained on the basis of native response tendencies, maturity or temporary status of the organism." Despite the fact that this definition is unsatisfactory because of the shortcomings, it may serve its purpose for the time being:

1. Motor Learning.
2. Perceptual Learning.
3. Manual Skill Learning.
4. Conceptual Learning.
5. Appreciational Learning.
6. Associate Learning.
7. Attitudinal Learning.

One of the most important methods in learning is known as trial and error. It was Thorndike who for the first time declared that all learning is trial and error. Thorndike was interested in finding out how do the animals learn. He placed a hungry cat in a puzzle cage and put some food outside the cage. The cat was hungry and so it tried to come out of the cage. As the cat did not know the device, so it tried haphazardly, sometimes striking here and sometimes there.

Thus trying for a period of time it somehow pressed the button and came out of the cage. It was put in the cage and again it tried several times to come out of it and finally came out by pressing the button. When this was repeated several times, the cat learnt to come out of the cage by pressing the button. In this example, Thorndike found that the cat learnt the trick to open the cage by trial and error. Thorndike experimented on many other animals also and concluded that all learning is by trial and error.

The Connectionism: Learning is connecting says Thorndike. His theory is now known as S-R connectionistic theory. Psychologically, reinforcement in the effect of one process of mental excitation or activity in increasing the strength of second activity. Immediate rewards tend to reinforce.

Thorndike has developed a number of principles which explain his trial-and-learning theory. These explanatory principles are:

The learner is motivated for a certain kind of behaviour because he has a desire to get the reward and face the challenging situation.

A multiple and varied attack on the problem is made and a number of responses are made to the stimulating situation.

The unrewarding explorations are quickly eliminated and those responses that are followed by motive satisfaction are selected for continued use. A connection is established between stimulating situations and the resulting response R.

The connections are strengthened (reinforced) with repeated exercise of correct S-R connections when accompanied by both motive satisfaction and belongingness.

On meeting a similar situation having elements common with this one, the organism responds by analogy with a pattern of searching behaviour similar to that found successful in the particular problem.

The correct S-R connections could have been learnt more speedily, had the significant cues been more identifiable. The child in the present case could have learnt more easily, had he formed such a response readily available as seventh book from the left on the bottom shelf or had the book with candy hidden in it were marked distinctly.

Cause of Connectionism: According to Thorndike, Trial and Error creates following connections:

Set or Disposition: The set decides what the learner will do so as well as what will satisfy him.

Prepotency of Elements: The learner makes selective responses in a learning situation.

Response by Analogy: New situations are tackled on the basis of older ones or previous experiences.

Associated Shifting: Any response of which the learner is capable, gets associated or connected with the situation to which he is sensitive.

Various Theories: Thorndike's Connectionism is based on trial and error and a connection between stimulus and response. It has following implication for teaching:

1. Connection is helpful for mentally retailed children.
2. Learning is based on practice. Practice strengthens learning.
3. Trial and error enables the child to gain experience from the errors.
4. Connectionism is very useful in the teaching of mathematics, science and other social science subjects.

5. Trial and error enables the educant to find solution of his problems.
6. Trial and error enables the educant develop courage, patience, labour and similar qualities.
7. Connectionism helps the child to become optimistic and look forward for attaining success.
8. Connectionism is helpful in making children learn to read and write.
9. It is helpful in developing curiosity in children.
10. It helps in the formation of good habits in children.
11. It is helpful in developing the tendency to practice.

Conditioned Response is one of the important processes of learning. It was Pavlov, the famous Russian physiologist who for the first time experimented about the conditioned response in 1900. Pavlov operated upon a dog and removed its salivary system from the cheek in a set way so that the saliva can be gathered in a test tube and measured. The dog was made to stand before a window. In the experiment, the food was given to the dog through the window. Before giving the food the bell used to be rung. As soon as the bell was rung, saliva began to flow from the mouth of the dog, because the bell was taken as sign of food. As the bell is not the natural object for the response of the flow of salvia so the response is a conditioned one.

The salvia flowing from the mouth of the dog was collected in a glass pot which was gathered. As the saliva fell in the pot, there was pressure due to which the lever was pressed. Due to pressure on the lever the lines were drawn on the smoked screen. By these lines the experimenter could find out about the number of the drops of saliva and the regularity of its flow. From this experiment, Pavlov came to the conclusion that the response of the dog can be conditioned to a stimulus other than the natural one. In this form of learning, the individual or animal learns to behave towards an object other than the natural one, because of its connection with it. According to Pavlov, all learning is conditioned. This view was not admitted by the modern psychologist as soon as the other methods were found to be equally important in learning, e.g., the method of trial and error, the method of imagination, etc. Yet no one denies the importance of the conditioned response in learning in the animals as well as among human beings.

Controlling Factors

The Effect of the Motive: Motive has an important effect on the conditioned response. For the conditioning of the response, the stimulus must have the capacity to evoke the response. In Pavlov's experiment the dog was hungry, hence it associated the bell with the food.

Time Relation of the Two Stimuli: Another important factor controlling conditioning of response is the time relation of the two stimuli. The time relation between the two stimuli is important, since conditioning of response depends upon their being associated with each other. It is necessary that before the response subsides, the new stimulus must be preceived along with its natural sequence, that is to say that first their should be new stimulus and then the old one. In Pavlov's experiment, it was necessary to ring the bell before giving the food and food must be given after ringing the bell, before the response had subsided. If there is too much interval or lapse of time between the two stimuli, it shall be difficult for the animal to find out the relation between the two. Suppose a dog is given food after an hour of ringing the bell, it will not find out any relation between the two stimuli. The learner links only those stimuli which are closely related in time.

Repetition of the Stimuli: The third factor controlling conditioning of response is the repetition of the stimuli. In Pavlov's experiment, the dog was given food after the bell was rung several times. If the dog is given food always after ringing the bell, the saliva begins to flow from the mouth as soon as the bell is rung. The repetition of the stimuli is necessary in the beginning.

Absence of the Disturbing Stimuli: The fourth factor controlling conditioning of response is the absence of the disturbing stimuli. As the disturbing stimuli will increase, conditioning becomes difficult. In Pavlov's experiment, the room used was without windows and sound proof. If there is some other stimulus distinguishing between the two stimuli, the conditioning will be difficult because the learner will not be able to link the stimuli.

Benefits of Education

As a general rule, the higher the species of the animal, the more easily conditioning of response is achieved. Thus, conditioning should be the easiest in the case of human being. But man is a complex animal and hence the factors which distract his attention are larger in the number than in the case of other animals. However, in spite of these distracting elements in conditioning of responses, it certainly remains one of the most important methods of learning, especially in the case of children. In childhood many of the responses of the child are conditioned to particular objects and even when the individual becomes an adult, his conditioned response continues, *e.g.* if a man behaves wrongly with us, we develop a kind of fear, abhorrence or hatred with every person resembling that person.

It has been pointed out earlier that modern psychology does not uphold the view that all learning is conditioned, but no psychologist denies that conditioned response is an important method of learning both in the case of animals as well as among human beings. A person can find hundreds of examples of conditioning of response in his daily life, *e.g.*, if it is habitual with us to put our purse in our right pocket, our hand automatically goes to the right pocket or somewhere else. In this example, there is a clear conditioning of response which is a result of putting the purse in the right pocket and taking it out from that pocket so many times.

Thus, the activity of taking out the purse is, closely linked with the right pocket. In the case of tamed animals, the conditioning process is very much used to teach so many activities. The conditioning of response as it is established, can also be extinguished. In the establishment of the conditioning the stimuli has to be repeated, while in its extinction the stimuli has to be repeated, while in its extinction the stimuli is not repeated. Thus in the example of Pavlov's dog, if the dog's response has been conditioned by the ringing of the bell, it will be de-conditioned if food is not served in spite of the ringing of the bell or food is served without ringing the bell. Similar examples of de-conditioning process can be found in the case of human beings. Suppose a person is used to go out for a walk to a bridge with a certain friend, he will always remember his friend when he is absent. The sight of the bridge will make him recall his friend, because he always used to come with him to the bridge. Thus, the bridge and the presence of his friend have been linked. Now if the friend is absent and returns after a long time and the man has to go alone for a walk, he will forget his friend gradually and the sight of the bridge will no more awake the memory of him. In this example one finds de-conditioning of a certain response to a particular stimulus. Just as a response can be de-conditioned, it is also reconditioned. Conditioning, de-conditioning and reconditioning, are governed by the same fundamental principles.

The development of attitudes prejudices, conceptual meanings may be largely on the basis of conditioning and subsequent stimulus generalisations.

When a conditioned response has become established, the teacher can eliminate it if it is undesirable. For example, if a child has learnt to fear mathematics, the dislike which he has learnt through simple conditioning may be removed by encouraging him to make mathematical models and getting satisfaction out of this activity. This phenomenon is known as counter-conditioning.

Some school learning comes through simple conditioning and drill. Repetition and practice are justified on the basis of contiguity. It is important to lead the child to do what he is to learn. For example, in the elementary school the child is required to learn number combinations. Drill and repetition are adequate means for learning tables. The fundamental implication of theory of simple conditioning or contiguity is the principle of learning through making and doing.

Instrumental Conditioning: Classical conditioning is the theory of conditioning propounded by Pavlov. Operant conditioning is known by the work of Skinner. Skinners's system of operant conditioning is a descriptive behaviourism which seems to establish the laws of behaviour through the study of operant learning. An operant is an emitted response, in contrast to respondents, a class of behaviour studied by the technique of classical conditioning utilised by Pavlov B.F. Skinner, the American psychologist, pointed out, in contrast to the classical conditioning by Pavlov, that operants may be studied independently of the stimulus conditions that give rise to them. Indeed, in the usual case the stimulus may be unknown. The experimental arrangement for studying operant behaviour in the laboratory consists of what has come to be known as Skinner box. The Skinner box is an enclosure in which the animal is maintained free from distracting stimuli and in which he can receive a reinforcement upon emitting the proper operant. In the case of the rat, the operant is a bar press, and the reinforcement is a pallet of food. As many times as the rat presses the bar, a magazine will deliver a pallet and conditioning will proceed at a rapid rate. More recently the pigeon has come into extensive use in the Skinner box. In this case the operant is pecking at a dot, and the reinforcement is a measured bout of grain.

The fundamental law of operant conditioning is that if the occurrence of an operant is followed by a reinforcing stimulus, it will increase the rate of responding. The rate of responding is typically measured during a run to extinction, since the time consuming process of eating during the reinforcing series obscures the rate of responding. These reinforcers may be both positive and negative. Positive reinforcers are the stimuli such as food, water or sexual contact. These directly increase the probability of a response. On the other hand, negative reinforcers decrease the probability of a response, only when they are removed from the situation. Examples of negative reinforcers are electric shocks, bright lights, loud noises, etc.

The most important variable associated with reinforcement is the time schedule on which the reinforcing stimulus is delivered. Continuous reinforcement is the regular presentation of the reinforcement with each operant response. Intermittent reinforcement is irregular reinforcement delivered according to a predetermined time schedule. There are two important types of intermittent reinforcement, interval and fixed ratio. In interval reinforcement, the reinforcement is given at certain fixed intervals of time such as every two minutes, regardless of how frequently the animal responds. Under such conditions the periodic reinforcement and the shorter intervals yield the highest rates of responding. The animal is given reinforcement after a certain number of responses. For example, the pigeon might get a portion of grain only after pecking ten times. In ratio reinforcement very high rates of responding can be maintained with high ratios, provided these are approached gradually Reinforcement schedules may also be arranged as variable intervals or variable ratios under special research conditions. Secondary reinforcement occurs when a stimulus not originally a reinforcer becomes reinforcing through association with a reinforcing stimulus. For example, if a weak light is flashed each time the reinforcement is delivered upon the pressing of the bar by the animal, the light will come to have reinforcing qualities. It can be used to maintain bar pressing for long periods of time in the absence of any primary reinforcer.

Stimulus generalisation or induction can be studied by a process of having the reinforcer delivered upon presentation of a positive stimulus and not delivered upon presentation of a neutral or negative stimulus. For example, a tone of 256Hz may be followed by a delivery of food, while a tone of 100Hz will not be followed by a delivery of food. The animal will learn to press the bar only in response to the positive tone. The limits of discrimination may be studied by gradually reducing the separation between the stimuli.

The learning of complex skills can be studied by a process called shaping. In shaping, a series of acts is gradually brought under control of the reinforcement by reinforcing each separate act in turn.

Skinner's basic techniques of operant conditioning have been extended into the use of Jiuman teaching machines that operate on the principle of self reinforcing learning. By the use of reinforcement, human symbolic behaviour can be learnt according to the same principle that apply to more elementary forms of learning. Skinner and his associates have attempted to extend their method of operant conditioning into the field of behaviour therapy. In all his studies upon animals, Skinner used a box like structure in which the correct operation of a mechanism bring the animal a reward.

Learning by Insight: Insight is an important constituent in the solution of problems and is found in the higher class of animals and human beings. It is the best method among the methods of learning.

Meaning of Insight: According to Gestalt psychologists, a person can deduce the solution by insight if he perceives the situation as a whole. A German Gestalist, Kohler, prepared some simple problems with dogs, hens, monkeys and chimpanzees. In an experiment a hungry animal was released from the house while some food was placed behind the fence adjoining the wall. Both the dog and the hen trotted around in the vicinity of the wall but as soon as they found the way out, they made their exit and reached the food. This perception of the change in the meaning of the wall is insight. Before the insight the wall was an insuperable obstacle, but after insight it was no longer an obstacle but an object necessitating circumvention. The result of insight is the understanding of new relations, the discovery of new patterns and the formation of new organisations.

The most famous experiments conducted by Kohler in relation to insight were those that were carried out on chimpanzees. Some bananas were placed outside the cage of a chimp called Sultan, who was then given two sticks so constructed that they could be fitted together. Sultan tried to pull the bananas with the sticks, an effort which he kept up for an hour, but he got tired of the attempt and gave it up for playing. While playing, he brought the two ends together and suddenly he had an idea which resulted in his fitting the smaller stick in the hole of the bigger one. He then used the two together to draw the banana inward. The next day he took far less time to fit the two together. It is a peculiarity of insight that once the solution is learnt, it is not forgotten though its memory may become hazy with the passage of time.

Characteristics of Insight: The above experiments make it quite obvious that learning by insight has certain characteristics of its own. They are briefly as follows:

1. Insight is sudden.
2. Insight alters perception.
3. Old objects appear in new patterns and organisation by virtue of insight.
4. Insight is relative to the intellectual level. The higher species of animals including human beings have more insight than the members of lower species.

5. In insight, understanding is more useful than dexterity of hands.
6. In Woodworth's opinion, insight is sometimes hindsight and at others it is foresight. To quote him, "Foresight is seeing the way to the goal before taking it or preceiving the uselessness of a certain lead without trying it and hindsight is observing that a lead is good or bad after trying it. When the whole situation is clear and above board, there is a good chance for foresight, but when important characteristics of the situation have to be discovered by exploration and manipulation, hindsight is the best we can expect."
7. Previous experience is of assistance in insight, though its excess does not necessarily increase insight because organised perception too is an essential factor in learning.
8. Maturity also affects insight as evidenced by the smoother working of insight in older age that in adolescence.
9. If the pieces essential for the solution of the puzzle are present together when perceived, insight colies about earlier.
10. Some psychologists say that learning by insight is associative learning. Insight appears suddenly after the manipulation of thoughts or objects for a small, though significant length of time.
11. The insight gained in particular circumstances is of assistance in other circumstances. A verbal formula is generally extracted by people learning by insight and this formula is capable of facile application to other circumstances.

Bibliography

Addaval, S.B.: *Theory of Education,* NCERT, New Delhi, 1968.

Aggarwal, J.C.: *Development and Planning of Modern Education with Special Reference to India,* Vikas Publishing House, New Delhi, 1982.

——————: *National Policy on Education,* Arya Book Depot, New Delhi, 1979.

Andrew, W. Halping: *Administrative Theory in Education,* The MacMillan Company, New York, 1967,

Barrie, H.: *Theory and Practice of Education,* Pergamon Press, London, 1968.

Basu, A.: *Education and Political Development in India 1898-1920,* Oxford University Press, Delhi, 1970.

——————: *Growth of Education and School Management in India 1898-1920,* Oxford University Press, Delhi, 1970.

Bhatia, S.C.: *Education and Socio-Cultural Disadvantage,* Xerxes Publications, Delhi, 1982.

——————: *Education: Theory and Practice Disadvantage,* Xerxes Publications, Delhi, 1982.

Carlton, B.: *Foundations of School Management,* Englewood Cliffs, Prentice Hall, New Jersey, 1964.

Cattell, B.B.: *Educational Growth,* Houghton Mifflin Co., Boston, 1971.

Chauhan, S.S. *Principles and Techniques of Education,* Vikas Publishing House, New Delhi, 1982.

Cole, S. Brem: *Education and the Development of Nations,* Holt, Rinehart and Winston, New York, 1966.

Crow, A.: *An Introduction to Education Principles and Practices*, Eurasia Publishing House, New Delhi, 1962.

Denis, Lawton: *Education and Social Justice*, Sage Publications, London, 1977.

Diana, Pinto V.: *Education: Theory, Research and Practice*, Rand McNally College Publishing Company, Chicago, 1978.

Don, Adams: *Education and Modernisation in Asia*, Addison Wesley Publishing Company, London, 1970.

Dube, S.C.: *Educational Planning in India*, Allied Publishers, Bombay, 1965.

————: *Elementary Education in India: A Promise to Keep*, Allied Publishers, Bombay, 1975.

Erickson, E.E. Roeber E. C. and Smith G. E.: *Organisation and Administration of Guidance Services*, McGraw Hill, New York, 1955.

Frank, W.: *Education – Principles and Services*, Charles E. Merrill Books, New York, 1961.

Garret, A.: *Interviewing: Its Principles and Methods*, Family Service Association of America, New York, 1942.

Ghosh, S.C.: *Educational Strategies in Developing Countries*, Sterling Publishers, New Delhi, 1976.

Ginzberg, E.: *Towards a Theory of Occupational Choice*, Personnel and Guidance Journal, 1952.

Goel, S.C.: *Education and Economic Growth in India*, The MacMillan Company of India Ltd., Delhi, 1975.

————: *Education in India*, The MacMillan Company of India Ltd., Delhi, 1975.

Gore, M.S.: *Papers in the Sociology of Education in India*, NCERT, New Delhi, 1967.

Halping, W.: *Administrative Theory in Education*, MacMillan Company, New York, 1967.

Hanson, J. W. and Cole S. Brem Beck: *Education and the Development of Nations*, Holt, Rinehart and Winston, New York, 1966.

Haq, Ehsanul: *Education and Political Culture in India,* Sterling Publishers, New Delhi, 1981.

Jagannath, Mohanty: *Education for All,* Deep and Deep Pub., New Delhi, 1994.

Jeffries, Charles: *Illiteracy: A World Problem,* Pall Mall Press London, 1967.

John, V.: *Education for Tomorrow,* Penguin, London, 1966.

Jones, A.J.: *Principles of Education,* McGraw Hill, New York, 1963.

Joshi, R.N.: *Education – Elsewhere and Here,* Bharatiya Vidya Bhavan, Bombay, 1979.

Kamat, A.R.: *The Educational Situation and other Essays on Education,* People's Publishing House, New Delhi, 1973.

Kidd, J.R.: *Education for Perspective,* Indian Education Association, New Delhi, 1969.

Kochhar, S.K.: *Pivotal Issues in Indian Education,* Sterling, New Delhi, 1981.

Kripal, Prem: *A Decade of Education in India,* Indian Book Company, Delhi, 1968.

Lakshmana Swamy M.: *Education in India,* Asia Publishing House, Bombay, 1960.

Louis, Malassis: *The Rural World: Education and Development,* Croom Helm, London, 1976.

Moni, Mohan, Bose : *Female Education in India,* B. B. Gupta Publication, Kanpur, 1921.

Mukherji, S.N.: *Administration of Education in India,* Acharya Book Depot, Baroda, 1962.

Myrdal, Alva: *The Power of Education,* Lancer Books, New York, 1965.

Myrdal, Gunnar: *Asian Drama: An Inquiry into the Poverty of Nations,* Allen Lane, London, 1972.

——————: *School Management in India,* Abridged, Allen Lane, London, 1972.

Nair, P.R.: *Education: Population Growth and Socio-Economic Change,* Allied Publishers, New Delhi, 1981.

Narayan, G. Brij Raj Chauhan and T.R. Singh: *Scheduled Castes and Education,* Anu Publications, Meerat, 1975.

Niblett, W.R.: *Essential Education,* University of London, London, 1955.

Nural, Hasan S.: *Challenges in Education: Culture and Social Welfare,* Allied Publishers, Bombay, 1977.

Oldhan, J.N.: *Village Education in India,* Oxford University Press, London, 2000.

Pande, K.C.: *Panchayati Raj and Educational Administration,* Aalakli Publishers, Jaipur, 1976.

Prakash, G.: *After Colonialism: Imperial Histories and Post Colonial Displacements,* Princeton University Press, Princeton, 1995.

Prem, Kripal: *A Decade of Education in India,* Indian Book Company, Delhi, 1968.

Premi, M.K.: *Educational Planning in India,* Sterling Publishers, New Delhi, 1972.

Rajagopal, M.V.: *Kothari Commission on School Education,* Telugu Vidyardhi Prachuranalu, Machilipatnam, 1967.

Raju, V.B.: *Commentaries on the Constitution of India,* Eastern Book Company, Lucknow, 1973.

Rao, M.S.: *Sociology of Education in India,* NCERT, New Delhi, 1977.

Rao, V.K.R.V.: *Education and Human Resource Development,* Allied Publishers, Bombay, 1966.

Ratna, Revankar G.: *The Indian Constitution: A Case Study of Backward Classes,* Associate University Press, Canbury, New Jersey, 1941.

Riddle, W. and Fletcher, F.M.: *The Guidance Movement in India,* Personnel and Guidance Journal, 1962.

————————: *The Guidance Movement in India,* Personnel and Guidance Journal, New York, 1962.

Robert, H.: *Educational Policy and Practice,* Harper and Row, New York, 1962.

Roeber, E. C. Erickson E.E. and Smith G. E.: *Organisation and Administration of Guidance Services,* McGraw Hill, New York, 1955.

Rudolph and Rudolph: *Administration and Management in Schools,* Harvard University Press, Cambridge, 1972.

———: *Education and Politics in India Studies in Organisation, Society and Policy,* Harvard University Press, Cambridge, 1972.

———: *Education and Politics in India,* Harvard University Press, Cambridge, 1972.

Safaya, Raghunath: *Innovations and Latest Trends in Education,* The Associated Publishers, Ambala Cantt., 1976.

———: *Latest Trends in Education,* The Associated Publishers, Ambala Cantt., 1976.

Saini, S.K.: *Development of Education in India: Socio-Economic and Political Perspective,* Cosmo Publications, New Delhi, 1980.

Saran, Gunam: *Education and Social Change: A Study of Some Rural Communities in India,* The Minarva Associates, Calcutta, 1972.

Saraswat, R.K. and Gaur, J.S.: *Occupational Literature: An Annotated Biblography,* NCERT, New Delhi, 1978.

Saxena, Sateswari: *Education Planning in India: A Study in Approach and Methodology,* Sterling Publishers, New Delhi, 1974.

Sayalu, Y.B.: *Scheduled Caste Elite: A Study of Scheduled Caste Elite in Andhra Pradesh,* Booklinks Corporation, Hyderabad, 1978.

Shah, A.B.: *Education or Catastrophe?* Vikas Publishing House, New Delhi, 1976.

Sharma, G.S.: *Educational and Cultural Development of the Minorities – A Study in Social Effects of the Judicial Trends in India,* ICSSR, New Delhi, 1973.

Shipman, M.D.: *Education and Modernisation,* Faber and Faber London, 1971.

Shri, Prakash: *Educational System of India: An Econometric Study,* Concept Publishing Company, Delhi, 1977.

Shrimali, K.L.: *A Search for Values in Indian Education,* Vikas Publishers, Delhi, 1974.

Shukla, P.D.: *Towards the New Pattern of Education in India,* Sterling Publishers, New Delhi,1976.

Singhal, R.P. and Biswas Dutt Sunnittee: *The New Educational Pattern in India,* Vikas Publishing House, Delhi, 1916.

————: *The New Educational Pattern in India,* Vikas Publishing House, Delhi, 1916.

Singla M.M.: *The Constitution of India-Studies in Perspective,* The World Press, Calcutta, 1975.

————: *Management of School,* The World Press, Calcutta, 1975.

Siqueira, T.N.: *The Education of India: History and Problems,* Oxford University Press, London, 1952.

Smith, D. and Inkeles A.: *Becoming Modern,* Heinmann Educational Books, London, 1974.

Spearman, C.E.: *The Nature of Intelligence and Principles of Congnition,* Macmillan, London, 1923.

Sundaram, P.S. and A.B. Shah: *Education or Catastrophe?* Vikas Publishing House, New Delhi, 1976.

Sundaram, P.S.: *Education: Theory and Practice,* Vikas Publshing House, New Delhi, 1976.

Tiwari, D.D.: *Education at the Cross Roads,* Chugh Publications, Allahabad, 1975.

————: *Thoughts on Education,* Chugh Publications, Allahabad, 1972.

Tolber, E.L.: *Counselling for Career Development,* Houghton Miffin, Boston, 1974.

Ulrich, B.: *Development and Planning of Modern Education,* Vikas Publishing House, New Delhi, 1982.

Weitz, Henry.: *Practice of Education,* McGraw Hill, New York, 1964.

Zurich, D.: *Development of Education,* Allied Publishers, Bombay, 1978.

Index

❑❑❑